Joomla!® For Dummies

Cheat Sheet

DISCARD

Common Joomla Tasks

- ✔ **To navigate to the control panel:** Choose Site➪Control Panel.
- ✔ **To get a preview of the front end while logged into the back end:** Click the Preview link in the top-right corner of any page.
- ✔ **To take your site offline:** Choose Site➪Global Configuration to open the Global Configuration page, and select the Yes radio button in the Site Offline section.
- ✔ **To put your site back online:** Choose Site➪Global Configuration to open the Global Configuration page, and select the No radio button in the Site Offline section.
- ✔ **To switch templates:** Choose Extensions➪Template Manager to open Template Manager; select the radio button for the template you want to use; and click the Default button.
- ✔ **To direct Joomla to use search-engine-friendly URLs:** Choose Site➪Global Configuration to open the Global Configuration page, and select the Yes radio button in the Search Engine Friendly URLs section.

Joomla Managers

To Open This Manager . . .	. . . Choose This Command
Article Manager	Content➪Article Manager
Category Manager	Content➪Category Manager
Front Page Manager	Content➪Front Page Manager
Language Manager	Extensions➪Language Manager
Menu Manager	Menus➪Menu Manager
Module Manager	Extensions➪Module Manager
Plugin Manager	Extensions➪Plugin Manager
Section Manager	Content➪Section Manager
Template Manager	Extensions➪Template Manager
User Manager	Site➪User Manager

Create a New Article

1. **Click the Add a New Article icon in the control panel, or choose Content➪Article Manager to open Article Manager and then click the New button.**
2. **Enter the contents of the article in the article-editor window.**
3. **Click Apply to publish the new article or Save to publish the new article and close Article Editor.**

For Dummies: Bestselling Book Series for Beginners

Joomla!® For Dummies®

Cheat Sheet

Create a New Menu Item

1. **Choose Menus⇨Menu Manager to open Menu Manager.**

2. **Click the icon in the Menu Item(s) column of the menu to which you want to add a new menu item.**
   Menu Item Manager opens.

3. **Click the New button to open the New Menu Item tree page.**

4. **Click the layout of the article you want the menu item to point to.**
   The Edit New Menu Item page opens.

5. **Configure the menu item.**

6. **Click Apply to publish the menu item or Save to publish the menu item and close the Edit New Menu Item page.**

Install an Extension

1. **Download the extension's compressed file (see Chapter 12).**

2. **Choose Extensions⇨Install/Uninstall to open the Install/Uninstall page.**

3. **Click the Browse button to browse to and select the extension's compressed file on your computer.**

4. **Click the Upload File & Install button.**

Joomla Features

Feature	Function
Template	Sets the layout of individual pages.
Module	Usually appears around the periphery of a page. Consists of elements such as search boxes, newsflashes, and polls; can also include menus.
Component	Displays Web-page content (text and media), usually in the center of the browser page.
Plug-in	Code extension that augments Joomla. Examples include editors.

Joomla Modules

To specify what pages a module appears on:

1. **Choose Extensions⇨Module Manager to open Module Manager.**

2. **Click the module's name to open the Edit Module page.**

3. **In the Menu Selection list, select the pages on which you want the module to appear.**

4. **Click Save.**

To reposition a module on a page:

1. **Choose Extensions⇨Module Manager to open Module Manager.**

2. **Click the module's name to open the Edit Module page.**

3. **Choose the position of the module from the Position drop-down menu and the order of the module from the Order drop-down menu.**

4. **Click Save.**

For Dummies: Bestselling Book Series for Beginners

Joomla!®

FOR

DUMMIES®

Joomla!® FOR DUMMIES®

by Steven Holzner, PhD, and Nancy Conner, PhD

WILEY

Wiley Publishing, Inc.

Joomla!® For Dummies®

Published by
Wiley Publishing, Inc.
111 River Street
Hoboken, NJ 07030-5774

www.wiley.com

Copyright © 2009 by Wiley Publishing, Inc., Indianapolis, Indiana

Published by Wiley Publishing, Inc., Indianapolis, Indiana

Published simultaneously in Canada

For general information on our other products and services, please contact our Customer Care Department within the U.S. at 877-762-2974, outside the U.S. at 317-572-3993, or fax 317-572-4002.

For technical support, please visit www.wiley.com/techsupport.

Wiley also publishes its books in a variety of electronic formats. Some content that appears in print may not be available in electronic books.

Library of Congress Control Number: 2008942705

ISBN: 978-0-470-43287-7

Manufactured in the United States of America

10 9 8 7 6 5 4 3 2 1

WILEY

About the Authors

Steven Holzner is the award-winning author of more than 100 tech books, with more than 3 million copies sold in 18 languages. He's written ten *For Dummies* books and many computer-book bestsellers. He's written on nearly every Web topic (including JavaServer Pages, PHP, HTML, and XML), and he specializes in topics such as Web-site design. He earned his PhD at Cornell University, and he's been a faculty member at Cornell University and Massachusetts Institute of Technology. He used to design Web sites from scratch but uses Joomla! now.

Nancy Conner most recently wrote *Google Apps: The Missing Manual* (O'Reilly, 2008). Her ability to explain complex technical material in language that's clear, simple, and fun has made her a sought-after author. She's written on a wide variety of Web topics, including eBay, QuickBase, the Unified Modeling Language, and field-programmable gate arrays. Her first novel, a mystery, will be published in 2009.

Dedication

Steve: To Nancy (of course!)

Nancy: To Steve (naturally!)

Acknowledgments

We'd like to thank Kathy Simpson and Kyle Looper of Wiley for their tireless efforts on this book, as well as the Joomla community for its invaluable assistance in filling in many of the details.

Publisher's Acknowledgments

We're proud of this book; please send us your comments through our online registration form located at http://dummies.custhelp.com. For other comments, please contact our Customer Care Department within the U.S. at 877-762-2974, outside the U.S. at 317-572-3993, or fax 317-572-4002.

Some of the people who helped bring this book to market include the following:

Acquisitions and Editorial

Project Editor: Kathy Simpson

Acquisitions Editor: Kyle Looper

Copy Editor: Kathy Simpson

Technical Editor: Ed Ventura

Editorial Manager: Jodi Jensen

Editorial Assistant: Amanda Foxworth

Sr. Editorial Assistant: Cherie Case

Cartoons: Rich Tennant
(www.the5thwave.com)

Composition Services

Project Coordinator: Patrick Redmond

Layout and Graphics: Stacie Brooks, Reuben W. Davis, Melissa K. Jester, Christine Williams

Proofreader: Evelyn C. Gibson

Indexer: Becky Hornyak

Publishing and Editorial for Technology Dummies

Richard Swadley, Vice President and Executive Group Publisher

Andy Cummings, Vice President and Publisher

Mary Bednarek, Executive Acquisitions Director

Mary C. Corder, Editorial Director

Publishing for Consumer Dummies

Diane Graves Steele, Vice President and Publisher

Composition Services

Gerry Fahey, Vice President of Production Services

Debbie Stailey, Director of Composition Services

Contents at a Glance

Table of Contents

Introduction

*J*oomla (we're dropping the final exclamation point from *Joomla!* in the text of this book, following the convention in other books and making this book more readable) gives you total control of your Web site — the layout, the navigation menus, the text, everything. And this book gives you total control of Joomla.

Today, users are demanding more from Web sites. It's not enough to have static text on your Web site — not if you want a steady stream of visitors. You've got to update your pages continually, making your site fresh and keeping it new. You've got to have an attractively, professionally formatted site. You've got to have tons of extras: polls and e-mail signups and news-flashes and menus, and more.

Who can afford the time to maintain a site like that and write the content too?

Now *you* can. Content management systems (CMSes) like Joomla are coming to the rescue, letting people put together spectacular sites with very little work.

Want to publish a new article on your site? No problem. Want to let users rate your articles with a clickable bar of stars? Also no problem. Want to link your articles with a cool system of drop-down menus? No trouble. Want to let people log into your site to gain special privileges? No worries. Want to let users search every page on your site? Yep — no problem at all.

CMSes are all the rage on the Internet these days: They give you the complete framework of a Web site and allow you to manage it professionally with a few clicks. All you have to do is provide the content — such as text, images, and videos — that you want to display. Using a CMS is as easy as typing in a word processor (in fact, one way to think of CMSes is as word processors for the Web) but a lot more fun.

The CMS of choice these days is Joomla, which is what this book is all about. Joomla is free and dramatically powerful. Want a site that looks as though a Fortune 500 company is behind it? Coming right up in just a few minutes. You're going to find that Joomla is not only free but also remarkably trouble free.

In the old days, you had to build your own site from scratch using HTML. These days, Joomla takes care of all the details for you, allowing you to con-centrate on the content of your site instead of struggling with the details of how that content is presented.

Welcome to the new era.

How This Book Is Organized

Joomla is a big topic because Web-site possibilities are endless. Here are the various parts you're going to see coming up.

Part 1: Getting Started with Joomla

This part is where you get your start with Joomla. We give you an overview of Joomla as it's been put to work in Web sites both nationally and internationally.

You also see how to get Joomla (for free) and install it. This process can take a little doing, so Chapter 2 is devoted to the topic.

Finally, we show you how to jump right into Joomla, customizing the home page (called the *front page* on Joomla sites) by installing your own logo, adding text, modifying navigation menus, and more.

Part II: Joomla at Work

This part gives you the skills you need to put Joomla to work every day. We start this part with a chapter on those most basic Web-site skills: creating your own pages and customizing them with text and images, laying out their content as you want.

In this part, you also see how to work with menus, because menu items are very powerful in Joomla. Believe it or not, a Web page can't even exist on a Joomla site unless a menu item points to it — and menu items actually determine the layout of the Web pages they point to.

Part III: Working with Joomla Modules and Templates

Joomla comes packed with dozens of built-in modules that give you extraordinary power. These modules include search, polls, menus, newsflashes, and banners. This part is where you see how to use all the modules that come with Joomla.

Part III also looks at how to work with Joomla templates. Templates create the actual layout of your pages: what goes where, how modules are positioned, where the page content is displayed, what images and color schemes are used, and more. Although Joomla comes with only a few templates, thousands more are available on the Internet.

Part IV: Joomla in the Real World

This part takes you into the real world, dealing with real people. Joomla supports eight levels of users, and in this part, we show you how to manage them.

We also take a look at how to get users to come to your site through search engine optimization — the process of making your site friendly to search engines to get a high ranking. This topic is a big one in Joomla.

Finally, we discuss how to extend Joomla with extensions. Although the software is very powerful out of the box, thousands of extensions are just waiting to be installed — everything from games to complete shopping-cart systems, from site-map generators to multilingual content managers.

Part V: The Part of Tens

In Part V, we list ten top Joomla extensions, ten places to get Joomla help online, ten top sources of Joomla templates, and ten places to find Joomla tutorials.

Foolish Assumptions

We don't assume in this book that you have a lot of Web-site design experience. You don't need to know any HTML or Cascading Style Sheets (CSS) code to read and use this book.

We do assume that you have a Web site and that you can upload files to it, however. You're going to need that skill to create a Joomla site, so if you're unfamiliar with the process of uploading files to your Internet service provider, ask your provider's tech staff for help.

That's all you need, though. Joomla takes care of the rest.

Conventions Used in This Book

Some books have a dozen dizzying conventions that you need to know before you can even start. Not this one. All you need to know is that new terms are given in italics, _like this,_ the first time they're discussed.

Icons Used in This Book

You'll find a few icons in this book, and here's what they mean.

This icon marks an extra hint for more Joomla power.

This icon marks something you should remember to make sure you're getting the most out of Joomla.

This icon means that what follows is technical, insider stuff. You don't have to read it if you don't want to, but if you want to become a Joomla pro (and who doesn't?), take a look.

This icon warns you of things to be super-careful about!

What You're Not to Read

You don't have to read some elements if you don't want to — that is, Technical Stuff elements. Technical Stuff paragraphs give you a little more insight into what's going on, but you can skip reading them if you want to. Your guided tour of the world of Joomla won't suffer at all.

Where to Go from Here

You're all set now, ready to jump into Chapter 1. You don't have to start there, though; you can jump in anywhere you like. We wrote the book to allow you to do just that. But if you want to get the full Joomla story from the beginning, start with Chapter 1, which is where all the action starts.

Part I
Getting Started with Joomla

The 5th Wave   By Rich Tennant

HORNER BROS.
MAKERS OF PREMIUM
BELLS & WHISTLES

"As a web site designer I never thought I'd say this, but I don't think your site has enough bells and whistles."

In this part . . .

This part is where you begin putting Joomla to work. First, we give you an overview of Joomla as it's used today around the world. Then we show you how to get and install Joomla — or how to get other people to do the work for you (on pay sites)!

Finally, we dig into Joomla by helping you master the home page of any Joomla site — the *front page,* in Joomla lingo. You see how to add your own text to the front page, change the front page's logo, sling the menu items around, and more.

Chapter 1

Essential Joomla

● ●

● ●

*T*he head Web designer walks into your sumptuous office and says, "We landed the MegaSuperDuperCo account."

"That's good," you say.

"They want you to design their new Web site."

"That's good," you say.

"They want to use a CMS."

"That's bad," you say.

"What's the problem?" the head Web designer asks.

You shift uncomfortably. "Well, I have no idea what a CMS is."

The head Web designer laughs. "That's no problem. It's a content management system. You know — like Joomla."

"Like whomla?" you ask.

The head Web designer tosses a folder on your desk. "Take a look at these sample sites. Joomla provides an easy framework for managing the content of your Web site. You type in the content, and Joomla takes care of displaying it for you."

You pick up your cup of coffee as the head Web designer leaves and start leafing through the pages. Some of the Web sites are snazzy. Then you turn to your computer and start entering URLs. Welcome to Joomla!

What Joomla Can Do for You

As the head Web designer said, Joomla is a content management system (CMS), which means that after you set the site up, you (or your clients) are responsible only for entering text and figures. Joomla arranges the content, makes it searchable, displays it, and generally manages the Web site. You need little or no technical expertise to create and manage your own sites.

Setting up a cool site from scratch is not easy — especially if you want to keep that site updated. A person who runs a newspaper site with about 6,000 visitors a day once came to us utterly exhausted. It turned out that he was formatting his entire site from scratch, using HTML, which meant that he had to get up at five every morning to enter the news stories in HTML tables and format them for his Web site. He still had his day job (he wanted to quit, but the news site's advertising was just ramping up) and found that he was working a total 14 hours every day.

Joomla was the answer for him. Now all he has to do is copy and paste the stories into Joomla's Article Manager and click a few options. The stories are published — no fuss, no muss.

Sample Joomla Sites

A great way to get to know Joomla is to take a look at what it's capable of, which means taking a look at some Joomla-powered sites. The following sections introduce a few examples.

City of Longwood (Florida)

First, check out the City of Longwood Web site at www.longwoodfl.org (see Figure 1-1). The home page has a navigation bar of drop-down menus across the top and a menu of quick links on the right, some nice photos, a custom logo, and even a search box.

The site is well balanced, giving the impression of professionalism, and it's powered by Joomla, which is operating behind the scenes. You can't tell just by looking that the content of the page — the text, photos, and menus — is actually stored in a database. Joomla handles all the details.

Figure 1-1:
The official
city Web
site for
Longwood,
Florida.

NZMac.com

Another Joomla-powered site is NZMac.com, which caters to the New Zealand Macintosh community, at www.nzmac.com (see Figure 1-2).

This site is another good one, with a top menu bar, a login box, a Main Menu box, and even a Recent Topics box. This site is also powered by Joomla, even though it looks different from the City of Longwood site. This difference is one of the strengths of Joomla: It's easy to customize.

Royal Oak Public Library

Now take a look at www.ropl.org, the Royal Oak (Michigan) Public Library site (see Figure 1-3).

This site is another well-designed one, with plenty of fresh content. Joomla excels at keeping site content up to date and makes the process easy.

Jenerate and Everything Treo

Two other good examples are Jenerate.com at www.jenerate.com (see Figure 1-4) and Everything Treo at www.everythingtreo.com.

All these Web sites look professional, and they also look different. Yet they all use Joomla as their content management system. So just what is a CMS, and how does it work?

Figure 1-2: The New Zealand Macintosh community's Web site.

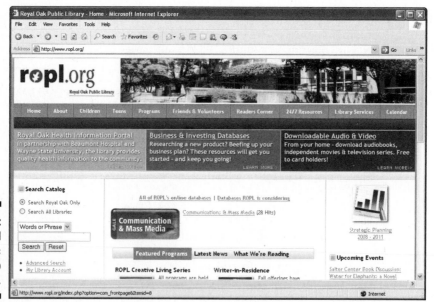

Figure 1-3: The Royal Oak Public Library Web site.

Figure 1-4:
The
Jenerate.
com Web
site.

All about Content Management Systems

When the Web was young, static Web pages were all that anyone needed.
These pages could be hand-entered in HTML for display in a browser, like this:

```
   _____
  |                     |
  | HTML |              |
  |      |              |
  |      |              |
  |      |              |
  |      |              |
  |      |              |
  |      |              |
  |      |              |
   _____
  |                     |
  }                     |
  }                     |
  V                     |
   _____
  |                     |
  | Browser |           |
  |         |           |
  |         |           |
  |         |           |
  |         |           |
  |         |           |
  |         |           |
  |         |           |
   _____
```

That kind of page served its purpose well for small sites. It gave people a Web presence and allowed them to display some images or maybe even add a little JavaScript to bring the page to life.

But as the Web grew and pages got larger and larger, people discovered an inherent problem: They had to mix the HTML that handled the visual presentation in a browser with the data that was displayed. This mix made Web pages hard to maintain and update, because site owners were working with both text data and HTML.

Good: Web pages with CSS

To handle this issue, Web designers created Cascading Style Sheets (CSS). CSS became primarily responsible for presenting the data in a Web page, although that page was still written in HTML, as follows:

```
  -----------------------   ----------------------------
 | HTML || CSS  |
 |  |||      |
 |  |||      |
 |  |||      |
 |  |||      |
 |  |||      |
 |  |||      |
  -----------------------   ----------------------------
 |  } |
 |  } |
 V  V
  -----------------------
 | Browser |
 |  |  |
 |  |  |
 |  |  |
 |  |  |
 |  |  |
 |  |  |
  -----------------------
```

Now the presentation details were separated from the formal HTML structure of a page — tags such as <html>, <head>, and <body>. But the actual content of the page was still wrapped up in the HTML; site owners had to format the content by putting in the HTML tags. In other words, the addition of CSS removed the presentation details from the rest of the Web page but hadn't yet separated the content from the HTML.

That situation was a problem for nontechnical people, who didn't want to have to fit their text into HTML tags. After all, when someone writes a book report, he doesn't have to worry about enclosing each paragraph in <p></p> elements, or styling text with <div> or <span> class elements. That's where CMSes came in.

Better: Dynamic Web pages via CMS

The whole idea of a CMS is to separate as much of the content as possible from the presentation details, which means that you don't have to embed HTML tags in the content you want to display. The CMS does all that for you. You just have to write your Web site's content, much as you would in a word processor. The CMS adds the CSS (from the Web-site templates you've decided on) and creates the actual HTML that goes to the browser, like this:

```
---------------------------   ------------------------
| Content || CSS |            |
| |||  from templates |       |
| |||   |
| |||   |
| |||   |
| |||   |
---------------------------   ------------------------
} |
} |
V V
-------------------------------
| CMS |
| generates the HTML |
| |
| |
| |
| |
-------------------------------
}
}
V
----------------------
| Browser |
| |
| |
| |
| |
| |
----------------------
```

In this scenario, you're responsible for only the content of your Web site; the CMS handles all the presentation details. That's the way things should be. Content should be king.

The upshot is that you end up writing what you want to say on your Web site and format it as you like, making text italic, large, small, or bold, just as you'd see in a word processor. The CMS takes what you write and displays it in a browser, using the Web-page templates you've selected and making hand-coded HTML and CSS obsolete.

Pretty cool, eh?

Reasons to Choose Joomla

The CMS of choice these days is Joomla. When we wrote this chapter in the summer of 2008, Wikipedia listed 86 free and open-source CMSes (http://en.wikipedia.org/wiki/List_of_content_management_systems), and Joomla was the most popular of them in terms of number of installations. A Google search on *content management system,* also done in the summer of 2008, returned Joomla first (following two generic Wikipedia articles), and a Google search on *Joomla* produced a mere 101 million hits — making this CMS more popular than *apples* (50.6 million hits) and *oranges* (20.1 million hits) put together.

Loyal users

What makes Joomla so popular? One reason is that it's free — but you can find dozens of free CMSes. Another reason is that it's been around for a long time — but dozens of other CMSes have been around for years as well.

No, the real reasons for Joomla's popularity are its reputation and loyal user base, both of which it has earned. All over the world, you'll find dedicated Joomla people who have created a very strong community. That community in turn has created thousands of items to extend Joomla — templates, components, modules, plug-ins, and so on — just waiting for you to use. This thriving community also specializes in providing help to novices.

Ease of use

Joomla is super-powerful, easy to use, and loaded with tons of extras (and even more tons of extras are available for download). Using Joomla makes creating a professional Web site nearly as easy as printing a word processing document.

Minimal learning curve

Although Joomla involves a learning curve, after you master a few basic skills, you're up and running. The technical expertise you need is minimal compared with the requirements of other CMSes.

Other advantages

Following are some other advantages of Joomla:

- Intuitive interface and management panel
- What-you-see-is-what-you-get (WYSIWYG) editing
- Rich formatting capabilities
- Thousands of downloadable page templates
- Full text searches
- Plug-ins for commercial sites, including complete shopping carts
- Search-engine optimization features (still rare in CMSes)
- Scheduled publishing

Where to Jump into Joomla

The main Joomla site is www.joomla.org (see Figure 1-5). This site is where you'll get your copy of Joomla; it's also your source for downloads and a great deal of help.

When you install Joomla, you get the default Web site shown in Figure 1-6, which is populated with all kinds of sample content.

Our job in this book is to help you understand and customize what you see in this figure so you can create stunning Web sites.

Figure 1-5:
The official
Joomla Web
site.

Figure 1-6:
The default
appearance
of a Joomla
site.

Chapter 2

Getting and Installing Joomla

· ·

In This Chapter

▶ Downloading and installing Joomla

▶ Putting Joomla on an ISP's server

▶ Putting Joomla on your own computer

▶ Getting acquainted with your site

· ·

This chapter is all about installing Joomla. You have two main ways to do this: on remote hosts like Internet service providers (ISPs) and on your local machine. We describe both methods in this chapter.

Installing Joomla on an ISP server requires some work with a File Transfer Protocol (FTP) client like FileZilla, CuteFTP, or even Internet Explorer. You have to upload the Joomla files to the ISP server, configure MySQL on that ISP, and then install Joomla. Not all Web hosts are capable of running Joomla; you also have to have PHP support, as described in this chapter.

Installing Joomla on your own computer is a good idea if you're going to be doing a lot of Joomla development; you can save a lot of time waiting for a Web server to respond over the Internet to everything you do. And fine-tuning your site is much easier if you have a local installation of Joomla as well as a remote one. In this chapter, you see how to set up a Joomla installation on your computer as well as remotely. Take your pick: online installation, offline installation, or both.

The first step in the process is getting Joomla itself.

Getting Joomla

You can get Joomla free at www.joomla.org. To get your copy of the program, click the Download Joomla button in the bottom-right corner of the home page.

Downloading the software

Joomla is distributed as a compressed file, and the name reflects the version number — something like `Joomla_1.5.6-Stable-Full_Package.zip`. The version number changes often to reflect small upgrades.

To work with the examples in this book, make sure to download Version 1.5 or later.

If you're downloading Joomla to a Windows machine, click the ZIP link on the download page. Your browser asks whether it should open or save the `.zip` file. Choose the Save option, and save the `.zip` file to your hard disk in a directory named something like `c:\joomla`.

If you're using an operating system other than Windows, click the Download Other Joomla 1.5.x Packages link; then select the appropriate `tar.bz2` or `tar.gz` file. (Your choice depends on your system.) When your browser asks whether it should save or open the file, choose the Save option, and save the compressed file to your hard disk.

The actual download is surprisingly small — just 6MB or less. A lot of functionality is packed into that small package, and to unleash it, you have to uncompress it.

Unzipping the software

Use your favorite uncompression utility, such as WinZip for Windows (`www.winzip.com/index.htm`), to extract all the files inside the compressed download. Joomla opens as a bunch of directories and files, as you see in Figure 2-1.

We're not going to describe in tedious detail what each directory contains, because Joomla handles the details for you. Besides, we rarely work with the directory structure directly in this book (and when we do, we tell you exactly which directory you need to work with).

Checking minimum requirements

You can install Joomla online (on an ISP server) or offline (on your own machine), but either way, you have to meet the minimum Joomla requirements so that you can actually run the program.

Online requirements

If you're installing Joomla on an ISP server, check out the minimum Joomla requirements listed in Table 2-1. You need support for the PHP scripting language MySQL (future versions of Joomla may support other database systems) and a Web server such as Apache.

You can check with your ISP to see whether it meets the minimum system requirements, but finding out can be difficult at times: ISPs often don't make public the version of their installed software. The easy way is to just go ahead and try to install Joomla; the second step of the installation process (see "Doing the preinstallation check," later in this chapter) tells you whether your host meets the minimum requirements.

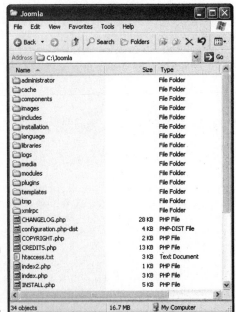

Figure 2-1:
Joomla
unzipped.

Table 2-1		Minimum Joomla Requirements		
Software	*Minimum Version*	*Recommended Version*	*Latest Options*	*Web Site*
PHP	4.3.10	5.2 +	5.x series	www.php.net
MySQL	3.23.x or later	4.1.x +	5.x series	http://dev. mysql.com/ downloads/ mysql/5.0.html
Apache	1.3 or later	2.x +	2.2 series	http://httpd. apache.org

Don't use PHP 4.3.9, PHP 4.4.2, or PHP 5.0.4; these versions have bugs that interfere with the installation of Joomla. A problem also occurred with Zend Optimizer Version 2.5.10 for PHP 4.4.x, so avoid it as well.

Offline requirements

You can install Joomla on Linux, Windows, and Mac OS X machines. Although the recommended Web-server software is Apache, you can also use Microsoft's Internet Information Services (IIS), which many Windows users already have installed in Windows XP and Vista. In this book, however, we stick with Apache.

Excellent — you've got your own copy of Joomla, you've met the requirements, and you're ready to install. The next step is finding a place to install the software. We start with installing on a host server; later in the chapter, we show you how to install Joomla on your own computer.

Installing Joomla on a Host Server

Most ISPs that give you access to PHP and MySQL can run Joomla.

In this section, we show you how to install Joomla on a Joomla-friendly ISP; in this case, we'll use Go Daddy (`www.godaddy.com`), which meets all the minimum Joomla requirements. We're not particularly recommending Go Daddy, but setting up an account with this host takes only about five minutes.

Make sure when you set up your account that it's a Linux account, not a Windows server account. Joomla doesn't run on Windows servers.

To be able to upload files, the best option is to get your own domain name, which you can do while signing up with your ISP. For this example, we chose the (not exactly inspired) domain `www.myjoomla123.com`.

After creating your account, log in with your username and password. If you're using Go Daddy, your next step is choosing My Hosting Account from the Hosting & Servers drop-down menu at the top of the page and then selecting your account in the My Account page.

Now it's time to upload the Joomla files you unzipped to your host's server.

Go Daddy will actually install Joomla for you. How's that for service? This offer has two small drawbacks, however. First, the host is usually a minor version behind the current one on the Joomla site. Second, and more annoyingly, Go Daddy installs the software in a directory named `Joomla`; by default, the directory has to be reflected in the URL, so you'll be left using a URL like www.*myterrificsite.com*/joomla for your main page instead of just www.*myterrificsite.com*. You can get around this problem with scripting and/or a more advanced Go Daddy account, but for purposes of this book, we show you how to do your own installation on the host server.

Uploading the Joomla files

Next, you've got to upload the Joomla files to your host. For this process, you use a File Transfer Protocol (FTP) application of the kind you use to upload ordinary HTML pages to a Web site.

Many FTP applications can upload files to a Web server. For the example in this section, we use FileZilla (www.uberdownloads.com/software/ftp-clients/filezilla.html).

To upload your Joomla files to the host server with FileZilla, follow these steps:

1. **Choose File⇨Site Manager to open the Site Manager page.**

2. **Click the New Site button.**

3. **In the resulting page, enter the site name.**

   For this example, type **myjoomla123.com**.

4. **Enter your FTP username and password; then click Connect.**

   You connect to your site (see Figure 2-2).

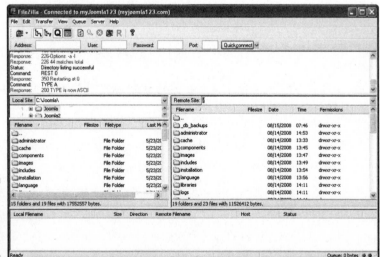

Figure 2-2: Connecting to your site via FTP.

 5. **In the left pane, select the directory that contains the Joomla files you've uncompressed, and in the right pane, make sure that the host server's root directory is selected.**

    The root directory is indicated by a forward slash (/).

 6. **Select all the Joomla directories and files in the left pane, and drag them to the right pane to upload them to your ISP's server.**

Uploading all these files takes some time, so grab a cup of coffee.

When you've uploaded all the Joomla files and directories, the next step is preparing MySQL.

Setting up MySQL

When you install Joomla, it expects MySQL to be ready for it to use, so in this section, you get MySQL ready for Joomla.

ISPs usually have only one MySQL installation that everybody shares, so you may need to set up a unique username and password to avoid interfering with anyone else on the host server. If you install Joomla on your own machine, you also install your own version of MySQL — a considerably easier process, as you see later in this chapter.

Creating the database

The first step in setting up MySQL for Joomla is creating the database. We show you how the process works for the Go Daddy account we used earlier in this chapter; adapt the process for your own ISP.

To create the database in Go Daddy, follow these steps:

 1. **On the home page, enter your username and password in the login boxes.**

 2. **Choose My Hosting Account from the Hosting & Servers drop-down menu at the top of the page.**

    The My Account page opens.

 3. **In the Hosting section, click the Manage Account link (see Figure 2-3).**

    The Hosting Control Center page opens.

 4. **Click the Databases bar to expose a MySQL icon (see Figure 2-4).**

 5. **Click the MySQL icon.**

    The database summary page opens (see Figure 2-5).

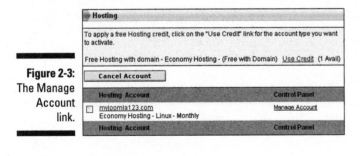

Figure 2-3:
The Manage
Account
link.

Figure 2-4:
MySQL icon.

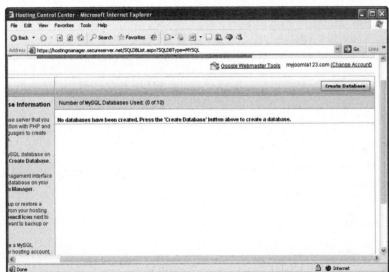

Figure 2-5:
Database
summary.

6. **Click the Create Database button.**

   The Create Database page opens.

7. **Enter a MySQL username.**

   For this example, we use JoomlaDB_Online, but you need to choose a
   different username to follow along, because MySQL usernames in Go
   Daddy must be unique.

8. **Enter and reconfirm the password you want to use for MySQL access,
   as shown in Figure 2-6.**

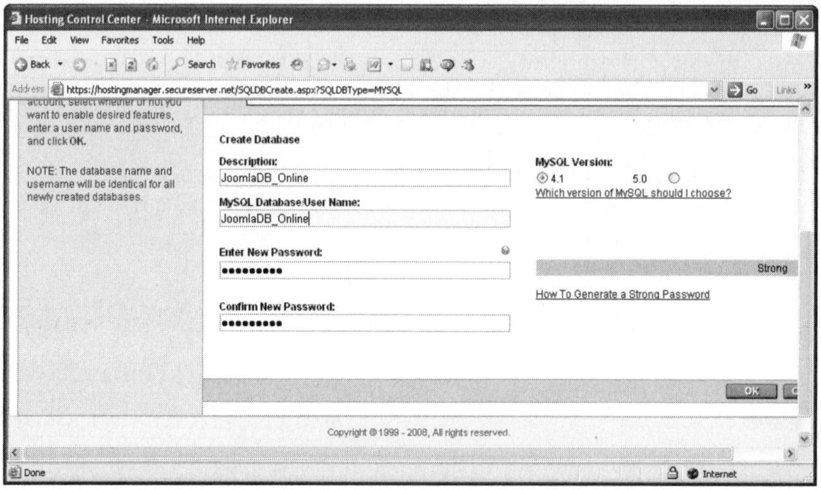

Figure 2-6:
Entering
MySQL user
information.

9. **Click OK.**

A new database summary page opens (see Figure 2-7).

Notice that the Status column reads *Pending Setup.* You have to wait until that column reads *Setup* to use the database; you can keep checking by refreshing the page in your browser. This process usually takes ten minutes or so, but on busy days it can take a couple of hours.

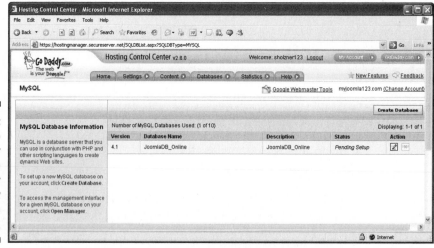

Figure 2-7:
The Go
Daddy
database
summary
with a new
database
pending.

Collecting database details

When your database is set up, you're almost done. You just need to get some details on the database to give Joomla when you install it. Again, we use the Go Daddy example in this section; adapt the procedure for your own ISP.

When your database is ready to use, click the pencil icon in the Action column (refer to Figure 2-7). The Database Information page opens (see Figure 2-8).

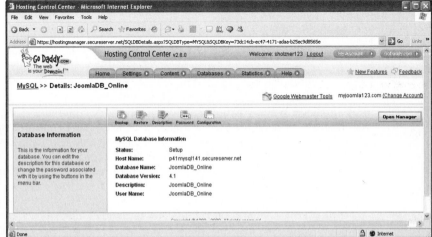

Figure 2-8:
Find infor-
mation
about the
new
database.

Record this information from the database information page:

- ✔ Status
- ✔ Host name
- ✔ Database name
- ✔ Database version
- ✔ Description
- ✔ User name

Note in particular the host name; you have to give it to Joomla when you install.

You've set the stage. Now it's time to install Joomla itself.

Installing the Joomla software

Installing Joomla involves seven steps:

1. Language selection

2. Preinstallation check

3. License acceptance

4. Database connection

5. FTP configuration

6. Main configuration

7. Finalizing

Here's how the process works: When you copy the Joomla files to the host server, you copy a file named index.php, written in the PHP online programming language. When you navigate to the directory containing index.php, that file runs, starting the installation. The primary job of the installation actually is to write a file named configuration.php that runs from then on, starting Joomla whenever you navigate to the directory where you installed the program. The configuration.php file stores the answers you give Joomla during the installation process.

You can find the official Joomla installation manual online at http://help.joomla.org/content/section/48/302/. But an even better set of installation instructions is at http://dev.joomla.org/content/view/2013/93/.

Selecting the language

The first of the seven steps is selecting a language. Follow these steps:

1. **Navigate to your site on the ISP's server (for the example in this chapter, www.myjoomla123.com).**

   You see the first Joomla installation page (see Figure 2-9).

   One of the big attractions of Joomla is that it's international, with many languages available. Surprisingly, however, only British English is available — not American English.

2. **Select the only English option: en-GB - English (United Kingdom).**

3. **Click the Next button.**

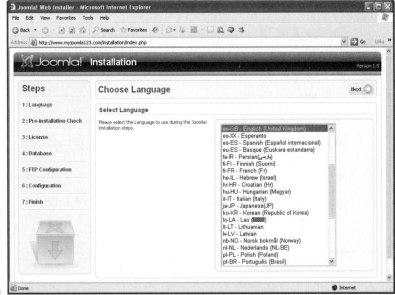

Figure 2-9:
The Choose
Language
page.

Doing the preinstallation check

Clicking Next in the Choose Language page navigates you to the next page,
Pre-Installation Check (see Figure 2-10).

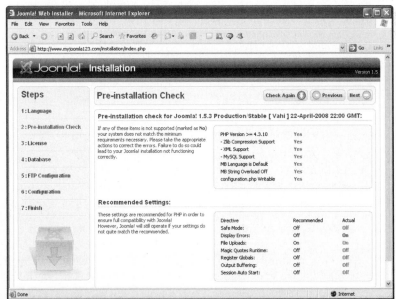

Figure 2-10:
The Pre-
Installation
Check page.

A Joomla installation involves a lot of technology — Web server, FTP, MySQL, PHP, and so on — and it would be a big pain to have to track down the correct settings of all those components from your ISP and check them against the minimum requirements in the Joomla documentation. No worries. Joomla looks up those items for you during the preinstallation check. Make sure that all items in the top pane on this page read Yes (if you don't see Yes, ask your ISP's tech staff about it):

- ✔ PHP Version >= 4.3.10
- ✔ Zlib Compression Support
- ✔ XML Support
- ✔ MySQL Support
- ✔ MB Language Is Default
- ✔ MB String Overload Off
- ✔ configuration.php Writable

It's particularly important to make sure that configuration.php is *writable,* meaning that the file can be created and written on your server to store your configuration when you start Joomla from now on. If not, you need to change the permission setting of the folder on the host server where you copied the Joomla files. An FTP application lets you change permissions; check with your ISP for the best setting.

This page also displays a list of recommended settings. If you're installing Joomla on an ISP's server, you don't have a heck of a lot of choice about these settings, because they're made by the ISP's tech staff. Following are the settings we recommend for the example in this chapter:

Setting	Actual	Recommended
Safe Mode	Off	Off
Display Errors	On	Off
File Uploads	On	On
Magic Quotes Runtime	Off	Off
Register Globals	Off	Off
Output Buffering	Off	Off
Session Auto Start	Off	Off

Everything agrees except the Display Errors setting for PHP, which most ISPs set to On.

If you want to change the settings in this page, you can click the Check Again button and make your changes, but we recommend starting the installation over again instead.

When you're satisfied with the preinstallation check, click the Next button.

Accepting the license

Clicking Next in the Pre-Installation Check page takes you to page 3 of the installation process: the License page.

Joomla uses the GNU general public license (a popular software license created by Free Software Foundation, Inc.), which gives you broad rights. You should at least scan the text of the document before clicking the Next button, which means that you accept the license.

Connecting to the database

Clicking Next in the License page brings up the Database Configuration page, shown filled out in Figure 2-11.

Figure 2-11:
The Database Configuration page.

This page is super-important, because Joomla doesn't store the pages in your site as actual pages at all — but as entries in a MySQL database. When you navigate to the page in question, Joomla extracts the content from the database and constructs its HTML page on the fly. You have to get the database connection right, because if you can't connect Joomla to MySQL, your site isn't going to run.

Here are the settings you have to make in this page, along with brief explanations:

- ✔ **Database Type:** probably MySQL
- ✔ **Host Name:** usually localhost or a name provided by the ISP
- ✔ **User Name:** the default MySQL username root, a name provided by the ISP, or a name you create while setting up your database server
- ✔ **Password:** the same password you use to access your database (may be preset by your ISP)
- ✔ **Database Name:** the name you used when you set up your database

If you followed along with the examples earlier in this chapter, you set all this information when you configured MySQL.

MySQL is notoriously finicky about usernames and passwords; case counts. Make sure that you pay attention to the difference between, say, *Steve* and *steve*.

When you finish, click Next. Joomla tests the connection to the database, and if everything works properly, it takes you to the next page.

Setting the FTP configuration

After a successful test of the database connection, Joomla displays the FTP Configuration page (shown filled out in Figure 2-12).

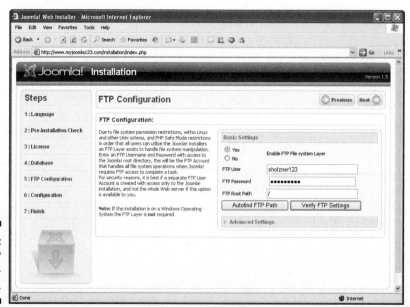

Figure 2-12:
The FTP Configuration page.

Configuring the database

The Advanced Settings section of the Database Configuration page contains a couple of radio buttons that you may want to look at if you're an expert:

✔ **Drop Existing Tables.** If you've already installed Joomla and want to reinstall it or upgrade to a newer version, select this option. It wipes the slate clean by clearing any Joomla data in the MySQL database under the username and password you'll be using.

✔ **Backup Old Tables.** Select this option if you have old Joomla data that you want to back up before installing Joomla again.

You don't need to configure the FTP server if you're installing in Windows. This page has mostly to do with Linux and other Unix hosts, because they can be a little finicky about file permissions. Later, if you have problems with uploading files to Joomla (such as image files or new templates), you can use the built-in FTP server (called the *FTP layer*) or your own FTP application to upload the files to the correct directories.

If you need to configure the built-in Joomla FTP server, follow these steps:

1. **Enter an FTP username and password.**

   This step creates the FTP account to handle all file-system tasks if Joomla needs FTP access.

2. **Enter the root path.**

   If your Joomla installation is in the main (root) directory of your site, simply enter a forward slash (/) in the FTP Root Path text box.

3. **Click the Verify FTP Settings button.**

   You should get a confirmation dialog box.

4. **Click OK to close the dialog box.**

5. **When you're done with the FTP Configuration page, click Next.**

Setting the main configuration

Clicking Next in the FTP Configuration page brings up the Main Configuration page, which lets you set information about your new Joomla site.

To enter the main configuration settings, follow these steps:

1. **Enter the name of your new Joomla site in the Site Name text box.**

This name will appear when you log in as an administrator. (For this example, we're using Joomla Super Jungle.)

2. **Enter an administrator e-mail address in the Your E-Mail text box.**

When you log into your new site, you'll be the *super administrator* (no cape or tights required). This fine-sounding title is as high as you can get in Joomla. The super administrator has maximum control of the site. (Just try not to let all that power go to your head.)

You can have several super administrators, but you can't delete a super administrator account.

Make sure that you enter a valid e-mail address, so that users of your site can contact you.

3. **Enter and then confirm the administrator password you want to use.**

Please remember this password. (You don't need to tattoo it on your forearm, but you may want to jot it down; you're going to need it throughout this book.)

As the super administrator, your username will be admin. You can change it later (which is a good security measure), but when you're logging in as the super administrator, use admin at least to start.

Joomla gives you the option of installing some sample data to see how the site works, and unless you're an experienced Joomla user, you should definitely do that.

4. **Select the Install Default Sample Data radio button; then click the Install Sample Data command button (see Figure 2-13).**

When you complete this step, the Install Sample Data button changes to the Sample Data Installed Successfully! button.

If you *don't* install the sample data, your Joomla installation starts off blank, and your home page is nearly empty. You may want to set things up this way later, when you're creating sites for clients, but if you're installing Joomla for the first time, load the sample data so that you can understand the structure of a Joomla site by playing around with the various management tools.

5. **Click Next.**

Later, you can also use the Main Configuration page to install a backup copy of the Joomla data from another Joomla installation, using a Joomla 1.5–compatible SQL script file, or you can migrate data from a previous version of Joomla. For details, check the Joomla! 1.5 Migration Guide at http://help.joomla.org/content/view/1933/294/.

Figure 2-13:
Settings in
the Main
Configura-
tion page.

Finishing the installation

Clicking Next in the Main Configuration page takes you to the Finish page
(see Figure 2-14).

You're all set — nearly. Note the message on the right side of the page, which
reminds you to remove the installation directory.

Pay attention to this message; you really *do* need to remove the installation
directory before you continue. Joomla requires this step for security reasons:
Details about your site are stored in the installation directory, and you don't
want those details hanging around.

To delete the Joomla installation directory, connect to your site in your FTP
program, and delete the directory there. (In FileZilla, for example, you right-
click the installation directory and choose Delete from the shortcut menu.)
As an alternative, you could rename the installation directory, but you have
no reason to keep it around.

After you delete the installation directory, you're ready to roll. You can click
the Site button to visit your new Joomla site or click the Admin button to
go to the administrator control panel. Skip to "Looking at Your New Joomla
Site," later in this chapter, which covers both options.

Figure 2-14:
The Finish
page.

Installing Joomla on Your Own Machine

To get your Joomla site out in the world, you've got to get it on the Internet, and that means using an ISP. But to develop Joomla sites and come up to speed on Joomla, installing the program on your own local machine often is much easier.

In this section, we show you how to do just that.

Installing Joomla locally is great if you're doing anything experimental, such as creating new templates or mucking around with the front page. You may have a dozen commercial sites that you've built, but rather than make changes publicly, you may want to get your changes running locally first. Also, response time is much faster when you don't have to upload new files and wait for browser refreshes all the time.

You have two ways to install Joomla on your local machine: the hard way and the easy way. We look at both methods — with special emphasis on the easy way, of course.

The hard way: Installing components

The hard way to get Joomla running on your local machine is to install the components you need, one by one, and get them running. Those components (and the URLs where you can get them) are

- **PHP** 4.3.10 or later (`www.php.net`)
- **MySQL** 3.23.x or later (`http://dev.mysql.com/downloads/mysql/5.0.html`)
- **Apache** 1.3 or later (`http://httpd.apache.org`)

Each of these components comes with its own installation manual; just follow the manual's directions. Unfortunately, however, you sometimes run into issues when you try to get all three components working together.

That's why we also cover the easy way to install the components you need to run Joomla: install XAMPP, which wraps all three components into a single installable package.

The easy way: Installing XAMPP

Most people (especially smart ones like you) find it easiest to install the Joomla environment as a single package via XAMPP. This package can be installed with minimal effort and in just a few minutes — so of course, we recommend this method.

When you install XAMPP, that package installs the Apache Web server, PHP, and MySQL for you all in one fell swoop — no fuss, no muss. XAMPP lays the full groundwork for Joomla; after you install XAMPP, all you've got to do is to unzip and install Joomla.

Currently, XAMPP supports these operating systems:

- Linux (tested for Ubuntu, SUSE, Red Hat, Mandriva [formerly Mandrake], and Debian)
- Windows 98, NT, 2000, 2003, XP, and Vista
- Solaris SPARC (developed and tested under Solaris 8)
- Mac OS X (still undergoing some development)

As a bonus, XAMPP contains more than just the three components you need for Joomla. The Windows version, for example, includes all the following: Apache, MySQL, PHP + PEAR, Perl, mod_php, mod_perl, mod_ssl, OpenSSL, phpMyAdmin, Webalizer, Mercury Mail Transport System for Win32 and NetWare Systems v3.32, Ming, JpGraph, FileZilla, mcrypt, eAccelerator, SQLite, and WEB-DAV + mod_auth_mysql. Whew!

You get XAMPP from the Apache Friends Web site at www.apachefriends.org/en/xampp.html. Just select the version you want — Linux, Windows, and so on — to go to a download page.

In the following sections, we take a brief look at installing XAMPP for Windows, Linux, and the Mac.

XAMPP for Windows

To install XAMPP in Windows, follow these steps:

1. **Download the executable installer file (such as xampp-win32-1.6.7-installer.exe).**

2. **Double-click the .exe file to open the XAMPP installer wizard (see Figure 2-15).**

Figure 2-15:
The XAMPP for Windows installer wizard.

3. **Click the Next button.**

4. **Follow the directions in the wizard to install XAMPP, which also installs Apache, PHP, and MySQL.**

Use the password you selected for MySQL (refer to "Creating the database," earlier in this chapter); the default installation gives you the username root.

Windows Vista users, take note: Because of missing or insufficient write permissions in the C:\program files directory in Vista, Apache Friends suggests that you install XAMPP in another directory, such as C:\xampp.

If your machine is already running Internet Information Services (IIS) — that is, you have a c:\inetpub directory and can bring up an IIS page when you navigate to http://localhost — you should disable IIS if you're going to install and run Apache on the same computer. By default, these servers use the same port and will conflict with each other. To disable IIS in Windows, open Control Panel, choose Administrative Tools⇨Services⇨IIS, right-click IIS in the Startup Type column (currently set to Automatic), choose Disabled from the shortcut menu, and then reboot your computer.

When the installation is complete, reboot your computer. The components of XAMPP run as Windows services. During installation, the wizard adds an icon for the XAMPP control panel to the bar at the bottom of the screen. Double-clicking that icon opens the control panel, shown in Figure 2-16.

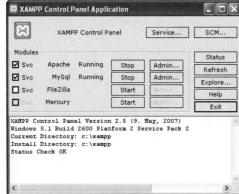

Figure 2-16:
The XAMPP control panel.

To test your new installation, open a browser and navigate to http://localhost. Click the Documentation link, and you should see something like Figure 2-17.

To test whether PHP is running, click the phpinfo( ) link on the left side of the main XAMPP page. This link runs a PHP function that displays a table of information about the PHP installation.

If you have problems installing XAMPP, check the XAMPP Frequently Asked Questions (FAQ) list at www.apachefriends.org/en/faq-xampp-windows.html/.

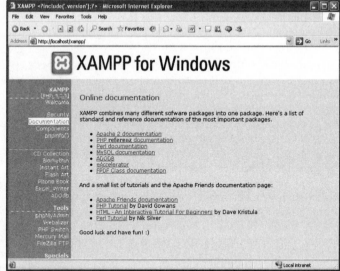

Figure 2-17:
The
XAMPP for
Windows
documenta-
tion page.

XAMPP for Linux

To install XAMPP in Linux, follow these steps:

1. **Download the .tar.gz installer file (such as xampp-linux-1.6.7.tar.gz).**

2. **Open a Linux shell.**

3. **Log in as the system administrator by entering the su command.**

4. **Extract the downloaded .tar.gz file to the /opt directory by entering this command:**

```
tar xvfz xampp-linux-1.6.7.tar.gz -C /opt
```

That's it. XAMPP is installed in a directory named /opt/lampp (LAMPP is the Linux version of XAMPP).

To start XAMPP, just enter this:

```
/opt/lampp/lampp start
```

You should get the following message:

```
Starting XAMPP 1.6.7...
LAMPP: Starting Apache...
LAMPP: Starting MySQL...
LAMPP started.
Ready. Apache and MySQL are running.
```

If you see this message, open a browser and navigate to `http://local host`; you should see the main XAMPP page.

If you have problems, check the XAMPP for Linux FAQ at `www.apache friends.org/en/faq-xampp-linux.html`.

XAMPP for the Mac

To install XAMPP on the Macintosh, follow these steps:

1. **Download the `.tar.gz` installer file (such as `xampp-macosx-0.7.3.tar.gz`).**

2. **Uncompress the compressed file to get a package, PKG, file, and double-click the PKG file.**

3. **Follow the installation wizard's steps.**

4. **Run the following command in Terminal (in an admin account):**

   `sudo su`

5. **Enter your password.**

6. **Enter the following command:**

   `tar xfvz xampp-macosx-0.7.3.tar.gz -C /`

That's all you need to do. To start XAMPP for Mac OS X in a Terminal window, enter this command:

```
sudo su
/Applications/xampp/xamppfiles/mampp start
```

You should see something like this:

```
Starting XAMPP for MacOS X 0.7.3...
XAMPP: Starting Apache with SSL (and PHP5)...
XAMPP: Starting MySQL...
XAMPP: Starting ProFTPD...
XAMPP for MacOS X started.
Ready. Apache and MySQL are running.
```

If that message looks OK, open a browser and navigate to `http://localhost`; you should see the XAMPP main page.

If problems pop up, check the XAMPP for Mac FAQ at `www.apachefriends.org/en/faq-xampp-macosx.html`.

XAMPP is still under development for the Mac, so the FAQ page may still be under construction.

Installing the Joomla program

Now that you've got XAMPP up and running, you have Apache, PHP, and MySQL. Cool. All you need to do now is install Joomla, and that process works the same way as installing Joomla on an ISP's server. Just follow these steps:

1. **Go to www.joomla.org, and click the Download button.**

2. **Download the compressed zip or .tar.gz file that's appropriate for your operating system.**

3. **Uncompress the Joomla files, using a program such as WinZip.**

   Your newly installed XAMPP directory contains a subdirectory named htdocs, which is where you put the files you want to access when you navigate to http://localhost in your browser.

   You can copy the uncompressed Joomla files directly to the XAMPP htdocs directory or to a subdirectory of htdocs. If you create a sub-directory of the htdocs directory named Joomla (that is, htdocs\joomla) and copy the uncompressed files to that subdirectory, Joomla will start when you navigate to http://localhost/joomla in your browser.

4. **Copy the uncompressed Joomla files to the htdocs directory, or create a subdirectory of htdocs and then copy the uncompressed files to that subdirectory.**

5. **Open your browser, and navigate to http://localhost or http://localhost/xxxx (where xxxx is the name of the subdirectory you created in Step 4).**

   The first Joomla installation page appears.

6. **Follow the directions in "Installing Joomla on a Host Server," earlier in this chapter, making these substitutions:**

   • Enter **localhost** as the MySQL server name.

   • Enter **root** as the MySQL username.

   • Enter the password you selected when you set up MySQL during XAMPP installation.

   • You can skip the FTP server setup page when you install on your own machine.

When the installation is complete, give Joomla a test drive. Click the Site button in the final installation page, or go to http://localhost (or http://localhost/xxxx, if you copied the Joomla files to a subdirectory of htdocs). You should see the Joomla front page.

Looking at Your New Joomla Site

Figure 2-18 shows your Joomla site as users will see it, displaying the sample data you installed earlier in this chapter. Congratulations — you've got your site up and running.

Figure 2-18:
Your Joomla
site.

The figure shows your new home page, called the *front page* in Joomla. In Chapter 3, we give you an in-depth look at it and show you how to modify it. But it bears a little examination now.

Ordering from the menus

You'll notice plenty of menus on the front page. Menus are much more important in Joomla than you may think. You can't publish content to your site without connecting it to a menu item — and the way you configure a menu determines the actual layout of the content when a user sees it. We describe the various menus in the following sections.

Top menu

The horizontal bar at the top of the page, which is called the *top menu* (also called the *pill menu* because of its shape) contains these general Joomla commands:

- About Joomla!
- Features
- News
- The Community

Main menu

The Main Menu pane on the left side of the page has these somewhat more important items:

- Home
- Joomla! Overview
- Joomla! License
- More about Joomla!
- FAQ
- The News
- Web Links
- News Feeds

Resources menu

The Resources menu contains links to several Joomla resources:

- Joomla! Home
- Joomla! Forums
- Joomla! Help
- OSM Home
- Administrator

Touring the modules

The front page is divided into sections, including Latest News, Popular, and Polls. Those sections are Joomla *modules,* which you start managing in Chapter 3. Working with each section as a discrete module makes front-page management a snap.

The actual content of the page, such as the Welcome to the Frontpage section, isn't a module; it's an article that's been published to the front page. In Chapter 3, you find out how to create articles and publish them to the front page.

The positions of the modules and other content in the front page — or any Joomla page, for that matter — is set by the Joomla template you're using for your site. You see in Chapter 9 how to work with different templates to change not only the color scheme of your site, but also the arrangement of its content.

Controlling the action

A link on the front page takes you straight to the administrator's control panel, which allows you to control the site behind the scenes. To see the control panel, click the Administrator link in the Resources menu or navigate to *yoursite*/administrator (such as www.myjoomla123.com/administrator).

Logging in as administrator

When you click the Administrator link, you see a page with the login section shown in Figure 2-19.

Joomla! Administration Login

Use a valid username and password to gain access to the Administrator Back-end.

Return to site Home Page

Username	admin
Password	••••••••
Language	Default

Login

Figure 2-19: Log in as the administrator of your site.

Enter the username **admin** and the password you entered in the Main Configuration page of the Joomla installation process; then click Login. Joomla displays the administrator control panel, which should look something like Figure 2-20.

Congratulations — now you're operating behind the scenes, and you've got the power to run things. Nice going, Joomla boss!

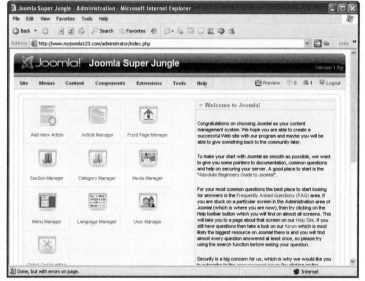

Figure 2-20:
The Joomla administrator control panel.

Meeting the managers

Take a look at the icons in the control panel. These icons represent Joomla managers, which you use to — surprise, surprise — manage your site. Even more managers are available from the Extensions drop-down menu at the top of the page. Chapter 3 describes them in more detail.

Working with and mastering these managers make up much of the book; you're going to get very familiar with all of them.

Chapter 3 digs farther into the front page, taking it apart piece by piece to show you what makes it tick.

Chapter 3

Mastering the Front Page

· ·

· ·

*Y*ou jump right into Joomla by seeing how to work with and modify what's going on in the front page. After all, the default front page that you're left with after a Joomla installation is nice, but as a dedicated Web designer, you know that your clients will want their sites totally customized.

To modify the front page, you need to know it, and you're going to start there, taking apart the front page to see what makes it tick.

Dissecting the Front Page

Take a look at the default Joomla front page in Figure 3-1 (with sample data installed).

A great deal of the information in a Joomla page is presented in *modules*. In Figure 3-1, you see the Latest News, Popular, Newsflash, and Polls modules. To handle these elements, you use Module Manager.

The figure also shows several menus. You control the items in them — and the names of the menus themselves — with Menu Manager. Menus are also presented in modules, so you can delete entire menus with Module Manager.

Site logo Main menu   Newsflash module

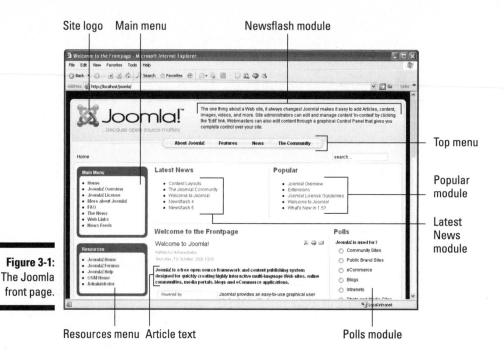

Top menu

Popular module

Latest News module

Figure 3-1:
The Joomla front page.

Resources menu Article text   Polls module

The central text of the page is an *article*. Articles aren't presented in modules; they're presented in what Joomla calls *components*. You manage articles with — you guessed it! — Article Manager.

So where are all these managers? They're available in the administrator control panel, which we discuss next.

Sitting in the Power Seat: The Administrator Control Panel

What you see in Figure 3-1 is the Joomla *front end,* which is available to non-administrators. This part of the site presents articles, menus, and modules for all to see.

To administer the site, you use the *back end,* where you find all the manager tools: Module Manager, Article Manager, and so on. The back end is well named; it's the part of the site that lets you work behind the scenes and pull the strings. To gain access to those tools, you have to be an administrator.

As an administrator, you can grant several levels of privileges to users of your site. Each level has different capabilities and different resources. A menu that appears to registered users (those who log in with their user-names and passwords) may not be visible to casual public Web surfers, for example. We discuss these privileges in the following sections.

Granting user privileges

Here are the front-end user levels, in ascending order of power:

- **Public:** casual Web surfers
- **Registered:** Web surfers who have registered with your site
- **Author:** users who can submit articles
- **Editor:** users who can submit and edit articles
- **Publisher:** users who can designate articles for publication to the site

Notice in particular the Author, Editor, and Publisher levels. Joomla emphasizes user interaction and contribution to your site (if you allow it, of course, by granting privileges in User Manager). Accordingly, users who have author privileges can submit new content to your site; editors can also submit content and edit other submissions; and publishers can mark content to be published to your site.

You may wonder how authors, editors, and publishers are allowed to submit, edit, and publish articles to your site if they don't have access to the administrative back end. The answer is that they can do what they do from the front end. When they log in, Joomla knows their privilege level. Authors, editors, and publishers see small icons on the page that link to article submission, editing, and publishing pages.

Actually publishing an article is still up to administrators, however. Publishers can mark an article for publication, but an administrator still has to approve it.

Granting administrator privileges

Joomla offers three administrator levels. You can grant these privileges in User Manager:

- **Manager:** users who have back-end privileges
- **Administrator:** users who have more back-end privileges than Managers do)
- **Super Administrator:** user who has the most back-end privileges

If you installed the site, you're the super administrator — and the super administrator is the ruler of everything.

Logging on as administrator

How do you log on as an administrator? You have several options:

✔ If Joomla is installed locally (on your own computer), navigate to `http://yoursite/administrator` (that's `http://localhost/administrator` or `http://localhost/xxxx/administrator` if you installed Joomla in the directory xxxx).

✔ If Joomla is installed remotely (on an ISP's server), navigate to `www.yoursite.com/administrator`.

✔ Pull up the default front page in your browser, and click the Administrator link in the Resources menu.

Whichever option you choose, you see a login page for administrators. Enter your username (that's **admin** for the super administrator of the default installation) and password; then click the Login button (see Figure 3-2).

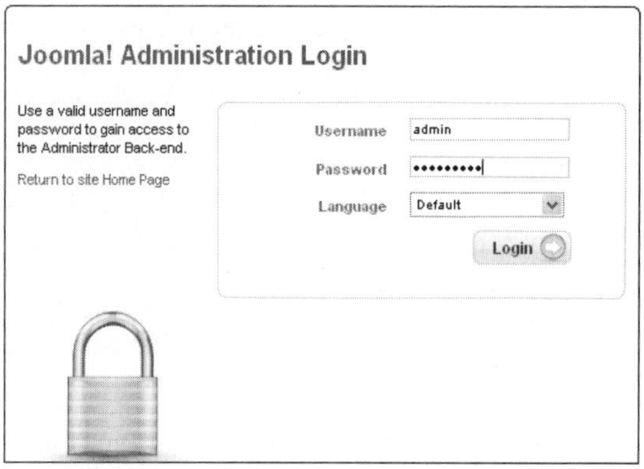

Figure 3-2:
Logging in as an administrator of your site.

Joomla! Administration Login

Use a valid username and password to gain access to the Administrator Back-end.

Return to site Home Page

Username	admin
Password	••••••••
Language	Default

Login

When you're logged in, you see the administrator control panel, displaying a set of manager icons. Cool — you're in.

Managing the managers

Figure 3-3 shows some of the managers that are available in the control panel.

The icons for these managers are displayed in the control panel by default:

✔ Add New Article

✔ Article Manager

✔ Front Page Manager

✔ Section Manager

✔ Category Manager

✔ Media Manager

✔ Menu Manager

✔ Language Manager

✔ User Manager

✔ Global Configuration

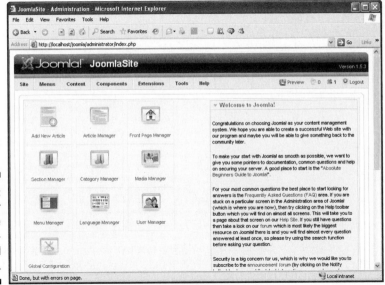

Figure 3-3:
Manager icons in the administrator control panel.

You can choose some additional managers from the Extensions drop-down menu at the top of the page:

✔ Module Manager

✔ Plugin Manager

✔ Template Manager

✔ Language Manager

Now that you're familiar with the control panel, you're ready to start putting some of this technology to work by creating an article to be displayed front and center on the front page.

Creating Articles

Creating any new article starts with clicking the Add New Article icon in the control panel. Joomla opens the article-editor page (see Figure 3-4).

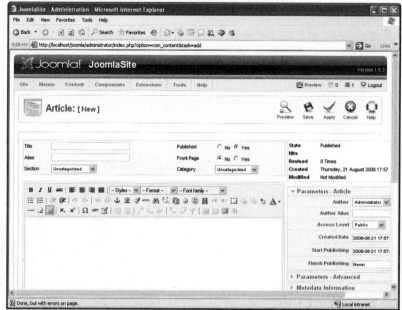

Figure 3-4:
Create new articles in this page.

This page is a WYSIWYG (what you see is what you get) editor, not an HTML editor. You enter straight text (and images) here; no knowledge of HTML is needed.

You can edit the raw HTML of an article in this page if you want, however; just click the HTML button in the article editor's toolbar.

Creating a new article

To create a new front-page article, follow these steps:

1. **Double-click the Add New Article icon in the administrator control panel.**

   The article-editor page opens.

2. **Type the article's title in the Title text box.**

   For this exercise, enter **Welcome to my site**.

3. **Leave the Section and Category drop-down menus set to Uncategorized.**

   You can manage your site's organization with Section Manager and Category Manager, both of which we discuss in detail later in the book. For now, though, leave this new article uncategorized.

4. **Enter the article text in the editor window, using the Bold and Italic buttons to add bold and italic formatting as desired.**

   For this exercise, enter the following text:

   Welcome to my site. Do you like it? This site uses Joomla! 1.5 for content management. Joomla! handles the details of the presentation and lets you focus on writing the content of the site. No complicated knowledge of HTML or style sheets is necessary. *Pretty nice site, eh?*

5. **To publish this article to the front page, select the Yes radio button in the Front Page section.**

6. **Click the Apply button.**

   Joomla displays a message that it has successfully saved the changes to your article (see Figure 3-5).

Figure 3-5:
Applying
changes
to a new
article.

7. **Preview your article in a new window by clicking the Preview link next to the Logout button in the top-right section of the page.**

8. **Click the Save button to close the article editor.**

The Apply button in the article editor causes Joomla to save the article; the Save button causes Joomla to save the article and close the article editor.

You can see the article on the front page when you navigate to your site (see Figure 3-6). Nice. You've published your first article.

But surely you don't want the default "Welcome to the Frontpage" title for the article. In the following section, we show you how to change it.

Figure 3-6:
The new article on the front page.

Tweaking article titles

Before you change anything on the front page (or anywhere in your Joomla site, for that matter), you have to do a little digging into how Joomla works. Knowing how articles are presented is very important. In Joomla, articles don't exist until they're requested, which is when their content is plucked from the database, formatted, and displayed.

Understanding article/menu links

Every article — including the one you just created — is linked to a menu item that makes it accessible, and that fact is of utmost importance in Joomla. In Joomla, menus have more power than you may be used to, because they're responsible for telling Joomla what to fetch from the database. Not only is the content of an article linked to a menu item, but also, that menu item specifies the layout in which the content is displayed.

That's a crucial fact in getting to know Joomla: Menu items specify both articles and the layout of those articles. Many content management systems are set up this way.

This fact is easier to remember if you bear in mind that an article doesn't even exist until the user clicks the menu item to which it's linked.

Changing an article's title

So what menu item points to front-page articles? The answer is Home, listed in the Main menu on the front page (refer to Figure 3-6). This menu item is responsible for the "Welcome to the Frontpage" title, so to change the title, you have to change the settings for that menu item.

To change the settings for the Home menu item, follow these steps:

1. **Go back to the control panel (choose Site⇨Control Panel in any back-end page).**

2. **Click the Menu Manager icon.**

   Menu Manager opens (see Figure 3-7).

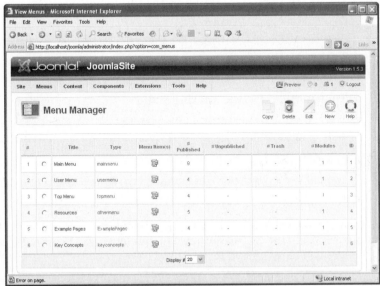

Figure 3-7: Menu Manager.

3. **In the Main Menu row, click the icon in the Menu Item(s) column.**

   Menu Item Manager opens (see Figure 3-8).

4. **Double-click the Home link.**

   Joomla displays the Home item's Menu Item page.

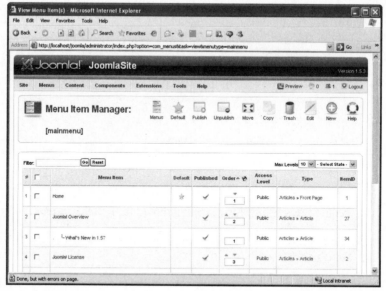

Figure 3-8:
Menu Item
Manager.

5. In the parameters pane on the right side of the page, click the Parameters - System bar to display the system parameters, as shown in Figure 3-9.

You see Welcome to the Frontpage in the Page Title text box, just waiting to be changed.

6. Change the title.

For this exercise, type **This is my site**.

If you wanted to remove the title instead, you would select the No radio button in the Show Page Title section of the system parameters.

7. Click the Apply or Save button.

Joomla saves your changes and displays a message to that effect.

8. Navigate to the front page of your site in a browser.

The title of the article has changed — in the example, from "Welcome to the Frontpage" to "This is my site," as shown in Figure 3-10. Cool!

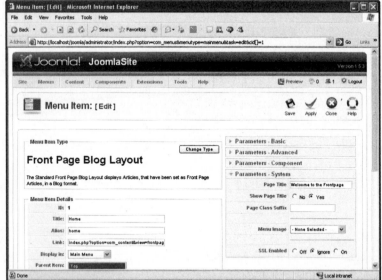

Figure 3-9:
System
parameters
in the Menu
Item page.

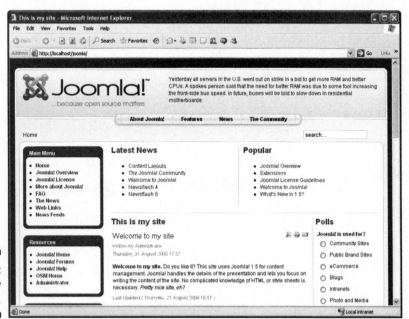

Figure 3-10:
The new
article title.

When Joomla times out

One annoying aspect of the back end in Joomla is that by default, it times out after 15 minutes of inactivity, and you have to log in again. That happens more often than you may think. You may find yourself keeping a back-end window open while you monitor other things on the site — and next thing you know, you're being asked to log in again.

You can change this timeout setting easily, however. To do that, follow these steps:

1. **Choose Site⇨Global Configuration in any back-end page to open the Global Configuration page.**

2. **Click the System tab at the top of the page.**

3. **In the Session Settings section, change the Session Lifetime setting.**

   You may want to change it to as much as 60 (minutes) if you're getting a lot of annoying timeouts.

4. **Click Apply; then click Save.**

Remodeling Modules

Most of the items around the edge of your front page are modules; even the login form is a module. You can manage all these elements with Module Manager (see Figure 3-11). To access this feature, choose Extensions⇨Module Manager in any back-end page.

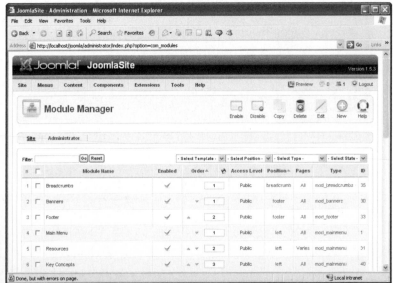

Figure 3-11: Module Manager.

When you're in article-editing mode, the drop-down menus are disabled. To get out of a page and enable the administrative drop-down menus, click Close.

Navigating Module Manager

First, note that Module Manager has two tabs at the top: Site and Administrator. In other words, Joomla has two sets of modules: one for the site as a whole (that is, the front end) and one for administrators (that is, the back end).

Also note that you see entries for three menus in Figure 3-11: Main Menu, Resources, and Key Concepts, all of which appear on the front page by default.

But don't you manage menus by using *Menu* Manager? Why do these menus appear in *Module* Manager?

Menus are actually modules, so when you want to work with a menu as a whole, you turn to Module Manager. When you want to work with only the content of a menu, you work with Menu Manager. That's another one of the things you just have to know about Joomla.

Now look at the Access Level column, which indicates the user level that can view specific modules. As you see in Figure 3-11, all the listed modules are visible to everyone — the Access Level column lists the Public user level.

Viewing modules

Now suppose that you want to remove the Latest News and Popular modules from the site. But when you click the Site tab and scroll up and down the list of modules, you don't see those modules. Where are they?

By default, Module Manager displays only 20 modules, which is why you don't see Latest News and Popular. To see all available modules, scroll to the bottom of the page and choose All from the Display drop-down menu.

Following are the 25 site modules available in the default Joomla installation:

✔ Breadcrumbs	✔ Banners
✔ Footer	✔ Main Menu
✔ Resources	✔ Key Concepts
✔ User Menu	✔ Example Pages
✔ Statistics	✔ Login Form
✔ Archive	✔ Sections

- ✔ Related Items
- ✔ Feed Display
- ✔ Who's Online
- ✔ Random Image
- ✔ Newsflash
- ✔ Popular
- ✔ Search

- ✔ Wrapper
- ✔ Polls
- ✔ Advertisement
- ✔ Syndication
- ✔ Latest News
- ✔ Top Menu

A few of these modules bear explanation. Breadcrumbs is the path to the current page (Home >>The Community, for example) that appears at the top of the screen. Wrapper is a wrapper for other Web sites that you can use to make those sites visible in Joomla. And Newsflash is the text at the top of a page, next to the logo.

Removing and deleting modules

To remove a module from view, click its green check mark in the Enabled column of Module Manager. For this exercise, click the green checks for Latest News and Popular. Each check you click changes to a red X, as you see (in glorious black and white) in Figure 3-12.

Figure 3-12: Removing modules.

You've removed the Latest News and Popular modules, but are they really gone? Yes indeed. Click the Preview link at the top of Module Manager to open a preview of your site in a new window. As you see in Figure 3-13, the page no longer displays those modules.

To delete a module — as opposed to just removing it from view — check its check box in Module Manager; then click the Delete button at the top of the page.

In the next section, you customize your site even more by working with menus.

Figure 3-13:
The updated front page.

Modifying Menus

You may have noticed that the Main Menu pane on the front page contains a Joomla! License menu item. That item is important for administrators, but you don't necessarily want to foist it on ordinary users.

So how do you modify a menu? If you said, "Menu Manager," you're right. Go to the control panel (by logging in to the back end or choosing Site⇨Control Panel in any back-end page), and open Menu Manager (see Figure 3-14).

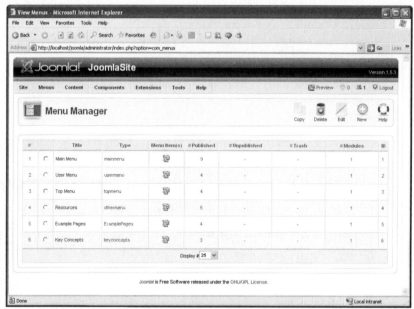

The default Joomla installation provides these menus:

✔ Main Menu

✔ User Menu

✔ Top Menu

✔ Resources

✔ Example Pages

✔ Key Concepts

Removing menus

Your task is to remove the Joomla! License menu item from the Main menu, so click the icon in the Menu Item(s) column of the Main Menu row to open Menu Item Manager (see Figure 3-15).

By default, you find these items in the Main menu:

✔ Home

✔ Joomla! Overview

- ✔ |_What's New in 1.5?
- ✔ Joomla! License
- ✔ More about Joomla!
- ✔ FAQ
- ✔ The News
- ✔ Web Links
- ✔ News Feeds

Figure 3-15:
Menu Item
Manager.

Notice that the What's New in 1.5? menu item is preceded by a vertical pipe and an underscore (|_). These characters mean that What's New in 1.5? is a submenu of the preceding item Joomla! Overview; when you click Joomla! Overview, it opens to show the submenu.

To remove (unpublish) a menu item, click the green check mark in its Published column, changing the check to a red X. For this exercise, click the check for Joomla! License. When you view the front page again, that menu item no longer appears in the Main menu, as you see in Figure 3-16. Nice.

In Chapter 4, you see how to create new menu items. For now, how about renaming a menu?

Figure 3-16:
Removing a
menu item.

Renaming menus

The Resources menu on the front page isn't really about general resources; it's about Joomla stuff. So you may want to rename it.

To change a menu name, you use Module Manager, not Menu Manager. (Menus are displayed in modules, remember?) Follow these steps:

1. **Choose Extensions⇨Module Manager in any back-end page.**

   Module Manager opens.

2. **Select the radio button for the module you want to rename.**

   For this exercise, select Resources.

   The selected module opens in Module Manager.

3. **In the Details pane, enter the new name in the Title text box.**

   For this exercise, type **Joomla! Stuff**.

4. **Click the Apply button.**

   Joomla! displays an Item Saved message (see Figure 3-17).

5. **Click Save to close Module Manager.**

6. **Preview the site.**

   The renamed menu (that is, module) appears, as you see in Figure 3-18.

You're mastering the front page, getting to know the differences between Menu Manager and Module Manager. Now meet a whole new feature: Article Manager.

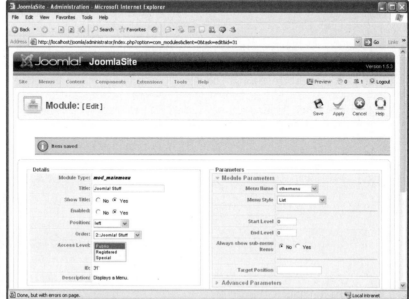

Figure 3-17:
Editing a module in Module Manager.

Figure 3-18:
A renamed module.

Strike That: Removing Articles

You cast your eye over the front page, noting in particular the article titled "We are Volunteers." Hmmm. You may be developing this page for a for-profit business, which may not want an article titled "We are Volunteers" on its front page.

Earlier in this chapter (in "Creating Articles"), we show you how to add a new article by using the Add New Article feature. Joomla doesn't have a Remove Old Article feature, though, so how do you remove an article?

You use Article Manager (see Figure 3-19) to work with existing articles. To open it, double-click its icon in the control panel or choose Content⇨Article Manager in any back-end page.

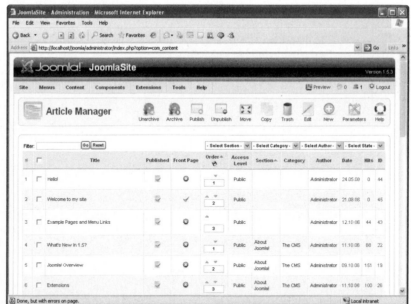

Figure 3-19:
Article
Manager.

Viewing articles

By default, Article Manager displays this information about articles:

✔ **Title:** The title of the article.

✔ **Published:** Indicates whether the article has been published.

✔ **Front Page:** Indicates whether the article is on the front page.

✔ **Order:** Indicates the location of the article on the page. You can move articles around by adjusting this setting.

✔ **Access Level:** Indicates who can see this article. Public means everyone, for example; Registered means only logged-in users.

✔ **Section:** The section of the article. (This setting is irrelevant for articles on the front page.)

✔ **Category:** The category of the article. (This setting is irrelevant for articles on the front page.)

✔ **Author:** The author of the article.

✔ **Date:** The date of the article.

✔ **Hits:** The number of hits the article has received.

✔ **ID:** The internal Joomla ID number for the article.

Note in particular the Published and Front Page columns, which indicate whether an article is published — that is, visible on your site — and whether it's on the front page.

Filtering articles

Many articles come with the default Joomla installation, but that number is nothing compared with the number of articles on a Joomla site that's been up for years. You may have to search through thousands of articles to find the one you want to manage in Article Manager. To zero in on the article you're interested in, you need to filter the results.

To filter the articles displayed in Article Manager, follow these steps:

1. **In the Filter text box in the top-left corner of the Article Manager window, enter a filter criterion (such as article title or article ID).**

   For this example, enter the title of the article you're looking for: **We are Volunteers**.

2. **Click the Go button next to the text box.**

   Joomla displays the filtered results (see Figure 3-20).

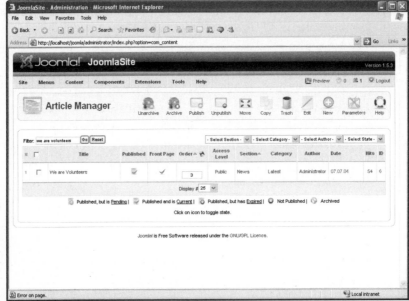

Bingo. You've found the article you want to work with.

Unpublishing articles

To unpublish an article, simply click the green check in its Published column. For this example, your task is to unpublish the "We are Volunteers" article, so click the icon in its Published column, changing it from a green check mark to a red X.

When you view the page in a browser, you no longer see the article. In Figure 3-21, in fact, an article titled "Stick to the Code!" has replaced the "We are Volunteers" article. (You can set the order of articles in Article Manager; see Chapter 4 for details.)

In the next section, you turn your attention to another front-page module: Polls.

Figure 3-21:
The updated front page after unpublishing an article.

Inquiring Minds Want to Know: Creating Polls

The poll in the default Joomla installation asks "Joomla! is used for?" and allows users to answer by selecting one of the following radio buttons:

- ✔ Community Sites
- ✔ Public Brand Sites
- ✔ eCommerce
- ✔ Blogs
- ✔ Intranets
- ✔ Photo and Media Sites
- ✔ All of the Above

The bottom of the Polls module provides two buttons: Vote and Results (which users can click to see how other people voted).

You may not want a Joomla poll. Instead, you may want a poll about how much money users plan to send you, including these options:

- ✔ Very little
- ✔ A little
- ✔ Not so much
- ✔ Pretty much
- ✔ A lot
- ✔ More than that
- ✔ None of the above

To change the poll, you need Poll Manager. (If you wanted to remove the poll, you could do that with Module Manager; refer to "Remodeling Modules," earlier in this chapter.)

Changing the default poll

Follow these steps to change the default poll:

1. **Choose Components⇨Polls in any back-end page.**

   The Poll Manager page opens (see Figure 3-22).

2. **Click the "Joomla! is used for?" title.**

   That poll opens (see Figure 3-23).

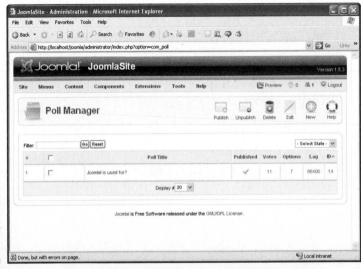

Figure 3-22:
Poll
Manager.

Figure 3-23:
Opening a
poll.

3. **In the Details pane, enter the new poll title in the Title text box.**

   For this exercise, type **How much money do you plan to give us?**

4. **In the Options pane's numbered text boxes, enter the poll answers.**

   For this exercise, make these entries:

   - Option 1: Very little
   - Option 2: A little
   - Option 3: Not so much
   - Option 4: Pretty much
   - Option 5: A lot
   - Option 6: More than that
   - Option 7: None of the above

5. **Click Apply; then click Save to close Poll Manager.**

6. **View the front page in a browser.**

   You see the new poll (see Figure 3-24). Not bad.

Figure 3-24:
A new poll.

Creating a new poll

Want to create an entirely new poll? You can do that too. Follow these steps:

1. **Choose Components⇨Polls to open Poll Manager.**

2. **Click the New button.**

   The New Poll page opens.

3. **In the Details pane, enter a title in the Title text box.**

4. **In the Options pane's numbered text boxes, enter your poll answers.**

5. **Click Apply; then click Save to close Poll Manager.**

6. **Choose Extensions⇨Module Manager.**

   Module Manager opens.

7. **Click the New button.**

   The New Module page opens.

8. **Select Poll, and click Next.**

9. **In the Module Parameters section, select the poll you want in the Poll list box.**

10. **Enter a title for the poll in the Title box.**

11. **Click Apply; then click Save to close Module Manager.**

12. **View your site in a browser.**

    You see the new poll.

Stop the Presses!: Changing the Newsflash

The *newsflash* is the text you see at the top of the main page. By default, it rotates various pieces about Joomla. You can put anything you want into your newsflash — information about your school, your neighborhood, anything. If you decide that a company like SuperDuperMegaCo wants its own newsflash, you can set about changing the default.

To change the default newsflash, follow these steps:

1. **Open the control panel, and double-click the Add New Article icon.**

   The article-editor page opens.

2. **In the text pane, enter your newsflash text.**

3. **In the Title text box, enter a title.**

   The title you enter won't be shown on the Web site. For this exercise, just type **Whatever you want.**

4. **Choose News from the Section drop-down menu.**

5. **In the Published section, select the Yes radio button.**

6. **Choose Newsflash from the Category drop-down menu.**

   At this point, your settings should resemble Figure 3-25.

7. **Click Save.**

   The article-editor page closes, and Article Manager opens.

8. **Choose News from the Section drop-down menu and Newsflash from the Category drop-down menu.**

9. **Deselect the newsflash articles you *don't* want to display (click their green check marks in the Published column to turn the checks to red X marks); then click the Unpublish button.**

   Normally, the newsflash module rotates through various newsflash articles each time the front page is displayed. If you don't want to display other newsflash articles, deselect them.

   Figure 3-26 shows all the newsflash articles deselected except the new one you created for this example ("Whatever you want").

Figure 3-25:
Creating a
newsflash
article.

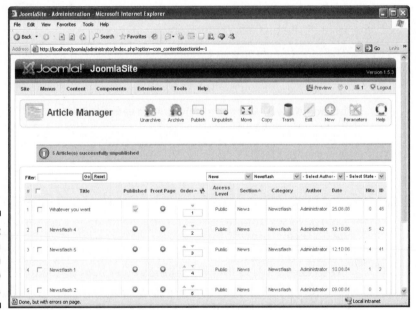

Figure 3-26:
Selecting a
newsflash
article to
display.

10. **Click the Unpublish button.**

11. **View the front page in a browser.**

    Joomla displays only the selected newsflash(es), as shown in Figure 3-27.

Figure 3-27:
An updated
newsflash
article.

To add more newsflash articles, double-click the Add New Article icon in the control panel, and repeat the procedure in this section. Joomla will rotate through all the selected newsflashes on your site.

Creating a New Logo for a New Look

By default, the logo on your new site is a Joomla logo. That logo isn't going to work for other kinds of sites, such as school or restaurant sites. How can you change it?

The current logo is stored with the current template, which by default is Milky Way. The actual logo is an image file named `mw_joomla_logo.png`, which is stored in the Joomla directory `templates/rhuk_milkyway/images`.

Are you wondering what .png files are? Portable Network Graphics files are the default format for template images in Joomla, and they're widely accepted by browsers. Long ago, after the GIF format started charging to create new images, people turned to PNG format images (JPG images aren't great on resolution), so Joomla uses PNG graphics images. If you're installing your own logo image, you can use your own JPG or GIF files, of course.

Changing the default logo

In this section, we show you a simple technique for changing the default logo. Follow these steps:

1. **Download or locate the `mw_joomla_logo.png` file.**

   If you installed Joomla on an ISP's server, connect to that server via your FTP program, and download the file; if you're working locally, just get the file from your hard disk.

2. **Open the file in a graphics program (see Figure 3-28).**

   Windows users may want to use Microsoft Paint, which is standard in Windows. (To launch it, choose Start➪Programs➪Accessories➪Paint.)

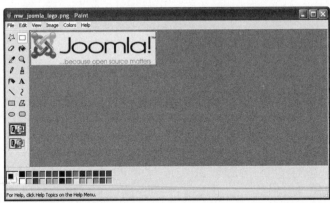

Figure 3-28: mw_ joomla_ logo. png in Microsoft Paint.

3. **Choose File➪Save As to display the Save As dialog box.**

4. **Choose a location (any directory on your hard disk) for the file from the Save In drop-down menu.**

5. **In the File Name text box, enter the new name you want to use.**

   For this exercise, type **superdupermegaco**.

   If you're using Paint, it automatically capitalizes the extension, for some reason, so you'll actually be saving a file named superdupermegaco.PNG.

6. **Make sure that the Save As Type drop-down menu is set to PNG format.**

7. **Click Save.**

8. **Open the renamed file in your graphics program.**

9. **Using the tools in your graphics program, change the logo the way you want it.**

   For this exercise, create a text logo that says SuperDuperMegaCo.

   If you're using Paint, for example, you could choose Edit⇨Select All; press the Del key to clear the image; click the Text tool; and then type the text you see in Figure 3-29.

Figure 3-29:
The new site logo.

10. **Save the new logo in the `templates/rhuk_milkyway/images` direc-tory, whether that's on your hard disk or on your ISP's server.**

Adding the new logo to the template

Now you're ready to tell Joomla to display the new logo `superduper megaco.png` (or `superdupermegaco.PNG`, if your graphic program is Paint). Follow these steps:

1. **Choose Extensions⇨Template Manager.**

   Template Manager opens.

2. **Select the default template, `rhuk_milkyway`, and click the Edit button.**

   The Edit Template page opens (see Figure 3-30).

   Many CSS (Cascading Style Sheets) files are connected with a template. For this exercise, you need to edit `template.css`.

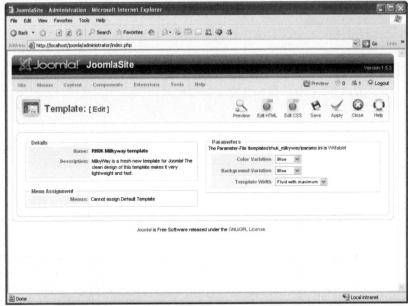

Figure 3-30:
The Edit
Template
page.

3. **Click the Edit CSS button.**

    The Template CSS Editor page opens (see Figure 3-31).

4. **Scroll down the page to select the radio button next to `template.css`.**

5. **Click the Edit button.**

    Joomla displays the Template Manager page for `template.css`.

6. **Scroll down to the section labeled div#logo, shown in Figure 3-32.**

7. **In the `background` line of the code, replace `mw_joomla_logo.png` with the name of your new image file, as shown in Figure 3-33.**

    For this exercise, type **superdupermegaco.png** or (for Paint users) **superdupermegaco.PNG**.

    Enter the name carefully; the code is case sensitive.

8. **Click the Save button to save your changes and close Template Manager.**

9. **View the front page of your site in a browser.**

    Your new logo is in place (see Figure 3-34).

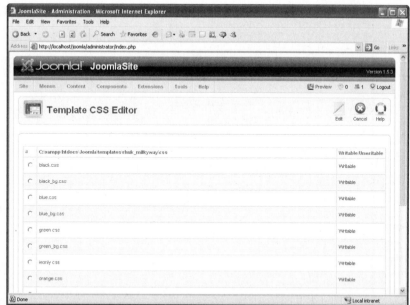

Figure 3-31:
The
Template
CSS Editor
page.

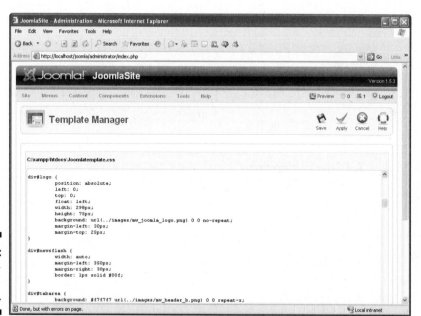

Figure 3-32:
The `tem-
plate.
css` page.

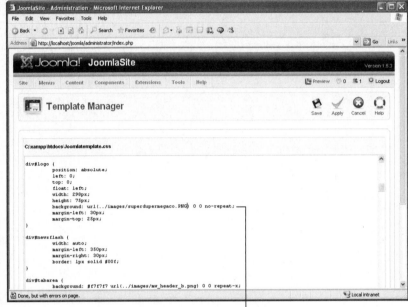

Figure 3-33:
Changing
the image
filename.

Background line

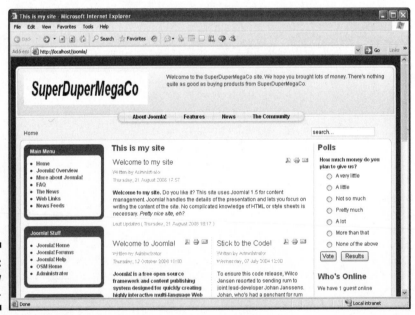

Figure 3-34:
The new
site logo.

Using a different-size logo

What if you're using a new logo that's a different size from the original? Take a look at the CSS entry for div#logo:

```
div#logo {
  position: absolute;
  left: 0;
  top: 0;
  float: left;
  width: 298px;
  height: 75px;
  background: url(../images/
    mw_joomla_logo.png) 0 0
    no-repeat;
```
```
  margin-left: 30px;
  margin-top: 25px;
  }
```

See the `width` and `height` parameters? Just change those values to the new logo's width and height.

If your new logo is exactly the same size as the current logo, an even easier method is to overwrite `mw_joomla_logo.png` with your new image (keeping the filename the same, because by default, Joomla looks for that file when it loads the logo).

Trying a New Template on for Size

Joomla templates are responsible for the overall look and layout of the modules and articles in your pages. Joomla makes a large number of templates available — many of them for free (take a look at www.joomla24.com, for example), as we discuss in Chapter 9.

Joomla comes with three default templates: Milky Way (which we discuss in "Creating a New Logo for a New Look," earlier in this chapter), Purity, and Beez (which is pronounced *bees*). You can switch easily between these two templates — and among as many other templates as you have — by using Template Manager.

In this section, we show you how to switch from the Milky Way template to the Beez template.

To switch to a new template, follow these steps:

1. **Choose Extensions⇨Template Manager.**

   Template Manager appears, open to the Site tab and displaying three templates: Milky Way (rhuk_milkyway), Purity (JA_Purity), and Beez (beez). The Default column of the active template contains a gold star.

TIP

If you want to see a preview of a template, let the mouse pointer rest on the template's name in Template Manager. A preview pops up at the pointer location.

2. **Select the radio button next to the name of the template you want to use.**

   For this exercise, select the Beez radio button.

3. **Click the Default button.**

   Joomla switches to the selected template.

4. **View your site in a browser.**

   You see your site with the new template applied (in Figure 3-35, the Beez template).

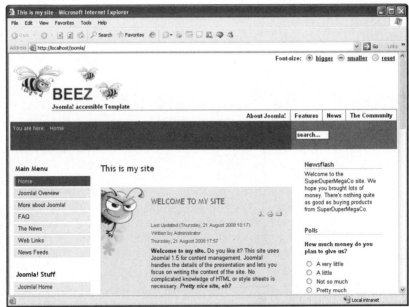

Figure 3-35: A new template applied in Joomla.

To revert to the Milky Way template, go back to Template Manager, select the Milky Way template's radio button, and then click the Default button.

REMEMBER

You may worry that installing a new template will make your site unusable. If that happens, how can you get back to the Milky Way template? Actually, that's not a worry; the Site and Administrator templates are different, so they have different tabs in Template Manager. (The default template in the Administrator tab is named Khepri.) So if a template messes up your site, you can always go back to Template Manager, which *won't* be messed up, and change the site back to a better template.

Part II
Joomla at Work

In this part . . .

This part really gets you into the thick of things. Here's where you acquire the everyday skills to make a Joomla site tick.

We start by showing you how to create and format new Web pages. Next, we show you how to create menu items that point to those new Web pages; in Joomla, you can't have Web pages without menu items that point to them. We finish the part with an in-depth treatment of the ins and outs of publishing Web pages on your site.

Chapter 4

Adding Web Pages to Your Site

*I*n Chapter 3, we show you how to create an uncategorized article and display it on the front page. Creating Web pages in addition to the front page is different. What you write for these pages isn't displayed on the front page but has to be reached through a link — that is, a menu item.

In this chapter, you find out how to create articles that don't appear on the front page. You start by creating an uncategorized article; then you create new sections and categories for a Web site. Finally, you see how to place an article in a particular section and category, and then add a link to it.

First, however, you need to understand how Web pages are organized in Joomla.

Organizing Web Sites

As sites get bigger, organizing them becomes more important. For that purpose, Joomla uses sections and categories.

It may be helpful to think of a section as a filing cabinet, a category as a file folder in that cabinet, and an article as an individual piece of paper in a folder.

You should make every effort to fit your articles into sections and categories. Your site may be fine with a few uncategorized articles for a while, but when it starts to grow, masses of uncategorized articles become very awkward.

Imagine that you run a law firm. When you're just starting out, keeping all the individual papers for all your cases on your desk may be fine, but as time goes by, you'd be buried in paper. You'd be much better off organizing everything in filing cabinets and folders. (Nancy does this with every piece of paper that comes her way, and things are always at her fingertips.)

Organizing your site in sections and categories is good practice not only from the back-end perspective, but also from the front-end perspective. You give your site users menus (sections) to help them navigate your site, and if you put articles in categories, you can display individual articles as menu items.

Seeing sections

Sections are the topmost divisions that you use to organize your Joomla site. Categories fall into sections.

Suppose that you have a client named SuperDuperMegaCo whose three product lines are ice cream, sandwiches, and ocean liners. People who navigate to the company's site to read about ocean liners probably aren't going to be interested in ice cream. So it makes sense to divide the Web pages on this site into three sections, one for each of the three product categories:

```
SuperDuperMegaCo
|
|_____ Ice Cream
|
|_____ Sandwiches
|
|_____ Ocean Liners
```

That way, site visitors can access pages that summarize each section.

Counting categories

Categories are essentially subdivisions of sections. In the SuperDuperMegaCo example, you could divide the Ice Cream section into three categories: Bars, Cartons, and Cones. Then you could divide the Sandwiches section into three categories: Subs, Wraps, and Triple Deckers. Finally, you could divide the Ocean Liners section into three categories: Yachts, Queen Mary Class, and Aircraft Carriers.

Sizing up the site

Next, you plan the organizational layout of the site.

In the example scenario, you would wind up with this section and category organization:

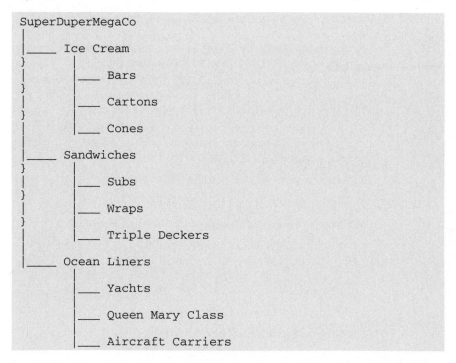

```
SuperDuperMegaCo
|
|____ Ice Cream
}        |
|        |____ Bars
}        |
|        |____ Cartons
}        |
|        |____ Cones
|
|____ Sandwiches
}        |
|        |____ Subs
}        |
|        |____ Wraps
}        |
|        |____ Triple Deckers
|
|____ Ocean Liners
         |
         |____ Yachts
         |
         |____ Queen Mary Class
         |
         |____ Aircraft Carriers
```

In addition, the client may want a few uncategorized pages on the site, such as its privacy policy.

How do you start building a site like this? First, we have you create an uncategorized page; then we show you how to organize pages in sections and categories.

Working with Uncategorized Articles

Uncategorized articles are free-floating on your site. Joomla thinks that you should have relatively few uncategorized articles — mostly loners that aren't related to other pages.

Many Joomla site developers don't have any uncategorized articles at all; they create sections and categories especially for loner pages. A privacy policy could go in a section called Notices and a category called Privacy, for example.

In this section, you create an uncategorized article — for this example, a policy page for the SuperDuperMegaCo Web site.

Creating an uncategorized article

To create an uncategorized article, follow these steps:

1. **Log in to Joomla by going to the administrator subdirectory of your site, which navigates you to the control panel.**

2. **Click the Add New Article icon.**

   The article-editor page opens.

   By default, new articles are uncategorized. The Section and Category drop-down menus both are set to Uncategorized, and you leave them that way for this exercise.

3. **Enter the article's title in the Title text box.**

   For this exercise, type **Privacy Policy**.

4. **Enter an alias for the article in the Alias text box.**

   An *alias* usually is a computer-friendly name for the article, often without spaces. Code scripts can use the alias to jump to the article page. You can leave the Alias box blank, however; Joomla will fill it in with the title you added, with hyphens replacing any spaces.

   For this exercise, type **privacy-policy**.

5. **In the text window, enter the article body.**

   For this exercise, use the following text:

   > Actually, we don't really have a firm privacy policy.

   > Does that mean we'll sell your email address to spammers?

   > Well, could be. . . .

   At this point, your changes should look like Figure 4-1.

6. **Click the Save button.**

   The article-editor page closes, and Article Manager opens, displaying the new article in the top row (see Figure 4-2).

   To display all articles, you may need to click the Reset button next to the Filter text box in the top-left corner of the page.

When you're done working with an article in the article-editor page, click Save or Apply — don't just close the page. Whenever you open an article in the editor page, Joomla checks that article out for you. If you just close the editor page without applying or saving your changes, you may see a padlock in the article's Published column in Article Manager from then on, which means that the article is still checked out. To check all articles back in, choose Tools⇨Global Checkin.

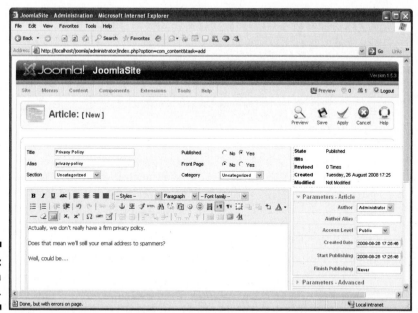

Figure 4-1:
Creating a
new article.

Figure 4-2:
A new
article in
Article
Manager.

Filtering uncategorized articles

As the number of articles on your site climbs, finding a particular uncategorized article will get harder and harder. You can always search for an article by title (if you remember the exact title) by entering it in Article Manager's Filter text box and then clicking Go. (Alternatively, you can enter the article's ID, although we're not sure why Joomla thinks you would remember an article's ID a year later.)

But the more articles you assign to sections and categories overall, the fewer articles you have to sift through to find the one uncategorized article you want. Easy organization is one of the primary reasons for categorizing most of your articles in the first place.

You've created a new article, but not a new Web page; you've just stored a new article in the database. How does a user get to your new article? And what does the new article look like? Those questions don't arise in Chapter 3, which shows you how to create articles for display on the front page, but they do come up here. To make an article accessible and to specify its actual layout, you need to link it to a menu item.

Linking Articles to Menu Items

Working with menu items in Joomla means working with Menu Manager. In fact, working with articles also means working with Menu Manager, which is where you set the layout of an article.

A menu item determines the layout of articles. That's one of the aspects of Joomla that you have to get used to. Web pages don't exist physically in Joomla — only articles in the database — until the article is accessed. Joomla takes advantage of this system by wrapping formatting options into menu items.

Creating the menu item

To create a new menu item to link to an article, follow these steps:

1. **Click the Menu Manager icon in the control panel or choose Menus⇨Menu Manager in any back-end page.**

   Menu Manager opens (see Figure 4-3).

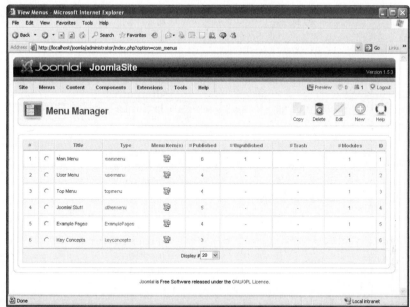

Figure 4-3:
Menu
Manager.

2. **Click the Menu Item(s) icon of the menu to which you want to add an item.**

   For this exercise, click the icon in the Menu Item(s) column in the Main Menu row.

   Menu Item Manager opens (see Figure 4-4).

3. **Click the New button.**

   The New Menu Item page opens, displaying a node tree.

4. **To create an *internal link* — one to an article on this Web site — click the Internal Link node to open it (see Figure 4-5), and then click Articles below it.**

5. **Below the Articles node, click Article; then click Article Layout below it (see Figure 4-6).**

   The Article Layout page opens (see Figure 4-7).

   Article Layout refers to the node you selected in Step 5; you don't actually select a layout in this page.

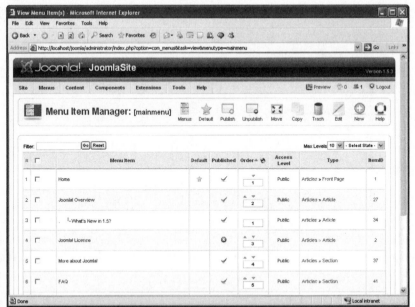

Figure 4-4:
Menu Item
Manager.

Figure 4-5:
Selecting an
internal link.

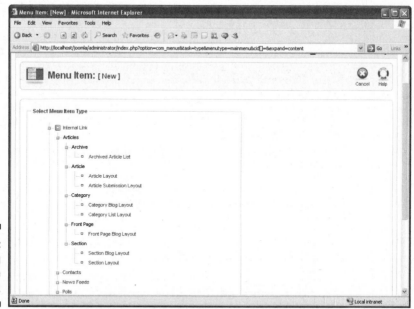

Figure 4-6:
Selecting
an article
layout.

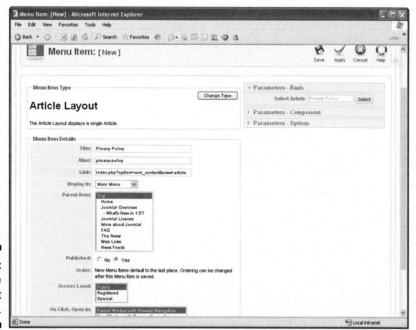

Figure 4-7:
The Article
Layout
page.

Setting the menu item's attributes

To set various attributes of the menu item you're creating, follow these steps:

1. **In the Title and Alias text boxes, enter the title and alias, respectively, of the new menu item.**

   For this exercise, type **Privacy Policy** as the menu item's title and **privacy-policy** as its alias.

2. **Make sure that the Display In drop-down menu is set to the correct menu.**

   In this example, Main Menu should be selected, because you clicked the Menu Item(s) icon in the Main Menu row to create the new menu item in the first place.

3. **Make a selection in the Parent Item list to specify whether the new menu item should be in a submenu.**

   You can make your new menu item a submenu item — that is, the child of a parent menu. If you leave Top selected, your new menu item will be a normal menu; if you select any other menu in this list, your new menu item becomes a child item of that menu (and the user can see it by clicking the parent menu item).

4. **In the Access Level list, set the access level of the new menu item.**

   You can choose among three levels:

   - **Public:** visible to everyone
   - **Registered:** visible to logged-in users
   - **Special:** visible to administrators

   For this exercise, accept the default setting (Public).

5. **In the On Click, Open In list, specify how Joomla should display the article when the user clicks your new menu item.**

   You have these choices:

   - Parent Window with Browser Navigation
   - New Window with Browser Navigation
   - New Window without Browser Navigation

   For this exercise, accept the default setting (Parent Window with Browser Navigation).

Linking the menu item to an article

The last step is linking the new menu item to a specific article. Follow these steps:

1. **Click the Select button in the Parameters - Basic section of the Article Layout page (refer to Figure 4-7).**

   The article-selection page opens on top of the Article Layout page, as shown in Figure 4-8.

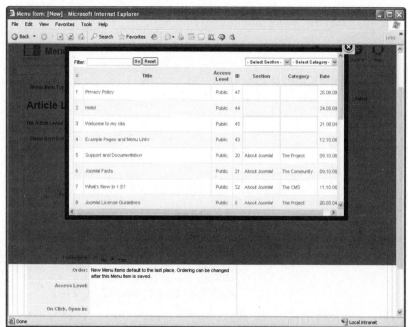

Figure 4-8:
The article-selection page.

Note the Section and Category drop-down menus in Figure 4-8. You can assign the new menu item to a section and category in this page, but leave the menus alone for this exercise, because the article is uncategorized.

2. **Select the Privacy Policy article.**

   The article-selection page closes.

3. **Click the Save button to close the Article Layout page.**

   You return to Menu Item Manager, which displays a message that the menu item was saved.

Testing the new menu item

But was your menu item really saved? Is it really active? Take a look at the front page now (refreshing it, if necessary) to check. As you see in Figure 4-9, the Main menu has a new item — Privacy Policy — at the bottom. Great!

Figure 4-9:
The front page with the new menu item.

Clicking the new Privacy Policy menu item opens the Privacy Policy page (created on the fly by Joomla), as you see in Figure 4-10.

What's an ad doing on your new page? That ad is the product of the Banners module, which displays banner ads. To remove those ads, unpublish the Banners module in Module Manager — that is, click the green check mark in its Enabled column to change it to a red X. (For more information on using Module Manager, refer to Chapter 3.)

Congratulations — you've added a new Web page to the SuperDuperMegaCo site. The head Web designer would be very proud. (Only 9,999 more pages to go!)

Now that you've created an uncategorized article, you're ready to create one that fits into a category for easier navigation by users. That's coming up next.

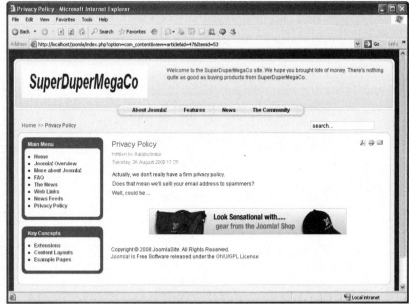

Figure 4-10:
The new
page.

Organizing with Sections

You can add new articles to existing Joomla sections and categories, of
course. All you need to do is select an existing section and category when
you create a new article. Joomla comes with three built-in sections:

- ✔ About Joomla
- ✔ News
- ✔ FAQs

But it doesn't come with the sections you need for the example
SuperDuperMegaCo site, which requires Ice Cream, Sandwiches, and Ocean
Liners sections. So how do you create them? This section shows you how.

Creating a new section

In Joomla, you create new sections with Section Manager. In this part of the
chapter, you use it to create a new section for the example Web site. Follow
these steps:

1. **Click the Section Manager icon in the control panel, or choose Content⇨Section Manager in any back-end page.**

   Section Manager opens (see Figure 4-11).

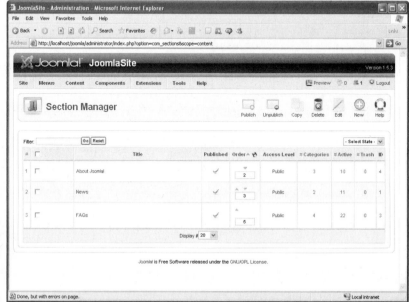

2. **Click the New button.**

   The New Section page opens. The Scope option is already set to content, meaning that the section will contain article content.

3. **Enter the new section's title in the Title text box.**

   For this exercise, type **Ice Cream**.

4. **Enter an alias in the Alias text box, if you want to use one.**

   For this exercise, type **ice-cream**.

5. **In the Published section, make sure that the Yes radio button is selected.**

   This option specifies whether the section is published — that is, visible to users.

6. **Select an option in the Access Level list — Public, Registered, or Special — to specify who can access the articles in the section.**

   For this exercise, select Public.

7. **If you want to give the section an image (see "Selecting a section image," later in this chapter), choose it from the Image drop-down menu.**

   For this exercise, choose `articles.jpg`.

8. **If you chose an image in Step 7, set its position by making a choice from the Image Position drop-down menu: Center, Left, or Right.**

   For this exercise, choose Left.

9. **In the Description window, enter a description of your new section.**

   For this exercise, type **This is SuperDuperMegaCo's Ice Cream Section.**

10. **Click the Save button.**

    The New Section page closes, and you return to Section Manager, which displays the new section (see Figure 4-12).

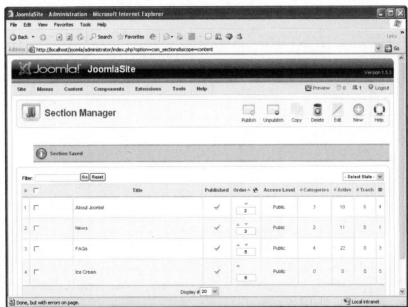

Figure 4-12:
A new section in Section Manager.

Selecting a section image

The default Joomla installation comes with several image files:

- ✔ articles.jpg
- ✔ clock.jpg

✔ ext_com.png

✔ ext_lang.png

✔ ext_mod.png

✔ ext_plugin.png

✔ joomla-dev_cycle.png

✔ key.jpg

✔ pastarchives.jpg

✔ powered_by.png

✔ taking_notes.jpg

✔ web_links.jpg

You can apply any of these images to a section in Section Manager. To pre-view an image, select it in the New Section page of Section Manager (refer to the preceding section), and Joomla displays it, as you see in Figure 4-13.

Figure 4-13:
Previewing
an image.

Organizing with Categories

The default Joomla installation comes with these nine categories (organized in these sections):

- ✔ The Project (section: About Joomla!)
- ✔ The CMS (section: About Joomla!)
- ✔ The Community (section: About Joomla!)
- ✔ General (section: FAQs)
- ✔ Current Users (section: FAQs)
- ✔ New to Joomla! (section: FAQs)
- ✔ Languages (section: FAQs)
- ✔ Latest (section: News)
- ✔ Newsflash (section: News)

Want to change the section a category is assigned to? Just click the category's name in Category Manager, choose the new section from the Section drop-down menu, and then click the Save button.

For the example site you're building, though, none of these categories will work. The Ice Cream section you just created needs three categories: Bars, Cartons, and Cones. In this section, you create a new category and assign articles to it.

Creating a new category

To create a new category, follow these steps:

1. **Click the Category Manager icon in the control panel, or choose Content⇨Category Manager in any back-end page.**

   Category Manager opens (see Figure 4-14).

2. **Click the New button.**

   The New Category page opens.

3. **Enter a title for the category in the Title text box.**

   For this exercise, type **Cartons.**

4. **Enter an alias in the Alias text box, if you want to use one.**

   For this exercise, type **cartons.**

5. **In the Published section, make sure that the Yes radio button is selected.**

6. **From the Section drop-down menu, choose the section you want this category to go in.**

   For this exercise, choose Ice Cream.

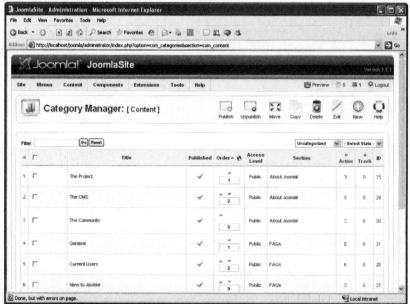

Figure 4-14:
Category
Manager.

7. Select an option in the Access Level list — Public, Registered, or Special — to specify who can access the articles in the section.

For this exercise, select Public.

8. If you want to give the category an image (refer to "Selecting a section image," earlier in this chapter), choose it from the Image drop-down menu.

For this exercise, choose `articles.jpg`.

9. If you chose an image in Step 8, set its position by making a choice from the Image Position drop-down menu: Center, Left, or Right.

For this exercise, choose Left.

10. In the Description window, enter a description of your new section.

For this exercise, type **This is SuperDuperMegaCo's Ice Cream Cartons category.**

At this point, your settings should look like Figure 4-15.

11. Click the Save button.

The New Category page closes, and you return to Category Manager, where you see the new category (line 8 in Figure 4-16).

Great — now you've added a new section (Ice Cream) and a new category (Cartons) to your site. Now how about adding some articles to that new section and category?

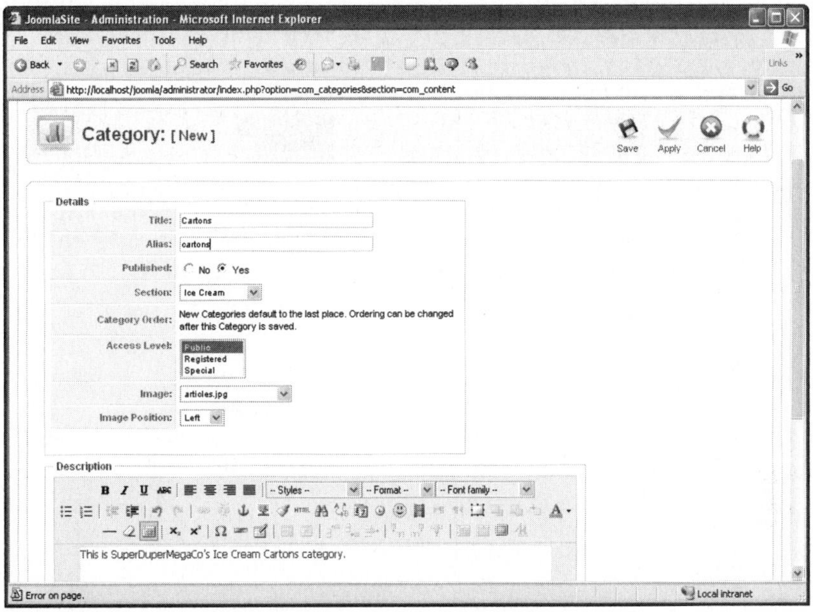

Figure 4-15:
Creating a
category.

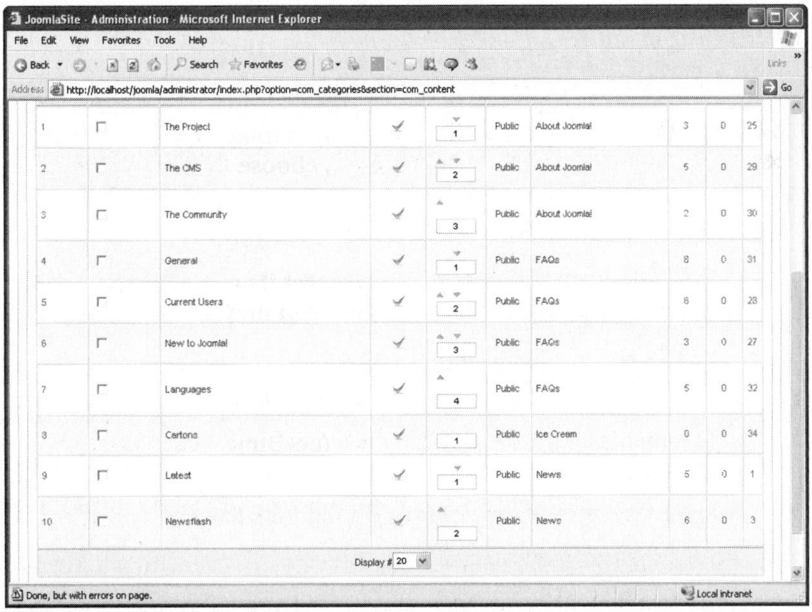

Figure 4-16:
A new
category in
Category
Manager.

Adding articles to a new category

In this section, you continue this process by creating new articles and adding them to the new category.

For your example site, you get an e-mail from SuperDuperMegaCo, indicating that the company offers the finest ice cream in three flavors: chocolate, vanilla, and sardine. You need to create new articles for each of these flavors and then add those articles to the Cartons category of the Ice Cream section. And you do just that in this section.

Adding one article

To add an article to a category, follow these steps:

1. **Click the Add New Article icon in the control panel.**

   The Add New Article page opens.

2. **Enter a title for the new article in the Title text box.**

   For this exercise, type **Chocolate Ice Cream.**

3. **Enter an alias for the new article in the Alias text box.**

   For this exercise, type **chocolate-ice-cream.**

4. **Choose Ice Cream from the Section drop-down menu.**

5. **Choose Cartons from the Category drop-down menu.**

6. **In the text window at the bottom of the page, enter a description.**

   At this point, your settings should look like Figure 4-17.

7. **Click the Save button.**

   The Add New Article page closes, and Article Manager opens, displaying the new article (line 37 in Figure 4-18).

Adding more articles

You can continue adding articles to a category by repeating the steps in the preceding section.

For the example Web site, repeat the procedure twice to add these articles:

- A Vanilla Ice Cream article in the Ice Cream section and the Cartons category
- A Sardine Ice Cream article in the Ice Cream section and the Cartons category

Now all three articles — Chocolate Ice Cream, Vanilla Ice Cream, and Sardine Ice Cream — appear in Article Manager, as you see in Figure 4-19.

Figure 4-17:
Creating a
new article.

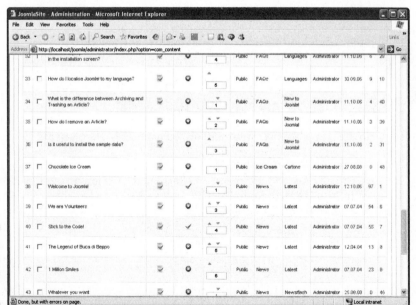

Figure 4-18:
A new arti-
cle in Article
Manager.

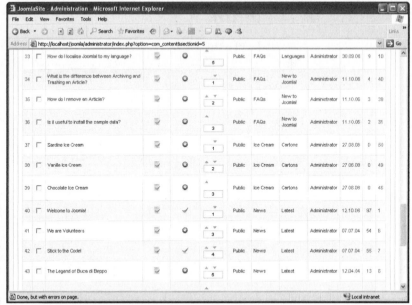

Figure 4-19:
Three new
articles
in Article
Manager.

As you may recall from "Linking Articles to Menu Items," earlier in this chapter, to make these three new articles visible on your site, you have to connect them to menu items. You do that in the following section.

Choosing a Menu Structure

Now it's time to link your categorized articles to menu items.

For the example site you're building, you need to make the Chocolate Ice Cream, Vanilla Ice Cream, and Sardine Ice Cream articles visible to users. You'll link them to the Main menu, because ice cream is one of SuperDuperMegaCo's main products.

You have three choices:

1. Add the three articles to the Main menu as three separate menu items.

2. Add an item to the Main menu that points to the Ice Cream section.

3. Add an item to the Main menu that points to the Cartons category.

You consider these choices.

Option 1: Adding three menu items

The first choice works like this:

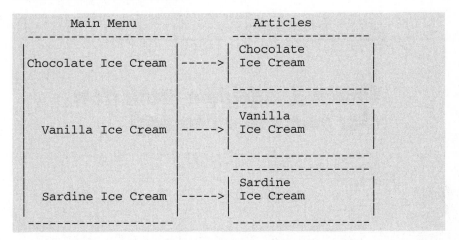

But this choice — add three new items to the Main menu, for chocolate ice cream, vanilla ice cream, and sardine ice cream — doesn't seem like such a good idea. As you added more articles, you'd need more menu items. And if SuperDuperMegaCo really *is* planning a site with 10,000 pages . . . well, that would be a lot of menu items.

Option 2: Adding a menu item that points to a section

The second choice works like this:

```
        Main Menu                Section        Articles
   ------------------          ----------     ----------------
  |                  |        |          |   |  Chocolate     |
  | Ice Cream Flavors|----->  | Chocolate|-->|  Ice Cream     |
  |                  |        |          |   |  ------------  |
  |                  |        |          |    ----------------
  |                  |        |          |   |  Vanilla       |
  |                  |        | Vanilla  |-->|  Ice Cream     |
  |                  |        |          |   |  ------------  |
  |                  |        |          |    ----------------
  |                  |        |          |   |  Sardine       |
  |                  |        | Sardine  |-->|  Ice Cream     |
  |                  |        |          |   |  ------------  |
   ------------------          ----------
```

This option — creating a menu item that points to the Ice Cream section — seems as though it might work. The problem is that such a menu item would take the user to a page that summarizes all the articles in the section, regardless of category. If you add the Bars and Cones categories to the Ice Cream section, not only are you going to have a lot of articles, but also, you may get the user mixed up. Which articles are for bars, which are for cones, and which are for cartons?

Option 3: Adding a menu item that points to a category

The third idea works like this (note that the example links to just a category, not a whole section):

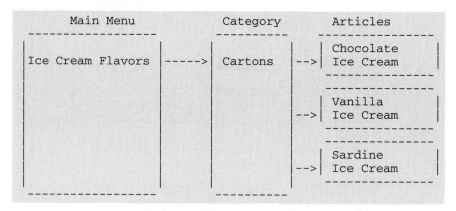

This plan — create a menu item for the Cartons category — seems to be the most workable. That way, all the flavors in that category will be summarized in a single page, and the user can choose among them. Ice cream bars and cones can have their own menu items, which will take the user to their own article summary pages.

In the following section, you put this plan to work.

Linking Categories to Menu Items

When you decide how you want to structure your menus to point to articles in specific categories, you're ready to do the actual linking.

For your example site, you want to create an Ice Cream Flavors item in the Main menu and link that item to the Cartons category. The link will display a summary of the three ice-cream-flavor articles, and users can select the one they want to read. The following sections show you how.

Creating the category menu item

To create a new menu item that points to a specific category on your site, follow these steps:

1. **Click the Menu Manager icon in the control panel or choose Menus⇨Menu Manager.**

   Menu Manager opens.

2. **Click the icon in the Menu Item(s) column of the Main Menu row.**

   Menu Item Manager opens.

3. **Click the New button.**

   Joomla displays the New Menu Item page.

4. **Expand the node tree by clicking Internal Link⇨Articles⇨Category (see Figure 4-20).**

Figure 4-20:
The expanded tree in the New Menu Item page.

5. **Below the Category node, click Category Blog Layout.**

   The Category Blog Layout page opens.

   This page doesn't actually create a blog. *Blog Layout* is Joomla's way of saying that each article will be summarized (the first sentence or two will be displayed) and that you can add a Read More link so that users can read the rest of the article. (See "Creating Read More Links," later in this chapter.)

6. **Enter a title for the new menu item in the Title text box.**

   For this exercise, type **Ice Cream Flavors.**

7. **Enter an alias for the new menu item in the Alias text box.**

   For this exercise, type **ice-cream-flavors.**

8. **On the right side of the page, click Parameters - Basic to expand that section, and choose Ice Cream/Cartons from the Category drop-down menu.**

   At this point, your choices should look like Figure 4-21.

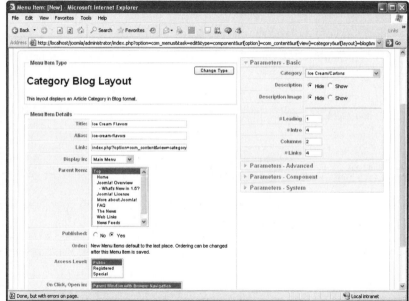

Figure 4-21: Creating a new category menu item.

9. **Click Save.**

   The Category Blog Layout page closes.

10. **View the front page in a browser or click the Preview link in any back-end page.**

    You see the new menu item — Ice Cream Flavors, in this example.

11. **Click the new menu item to display the new category page (see Figure 4-22).**

    If you scroll up and down the page, you can see all the articles: chocolate ice cream, vanilla ice cream, and even sardine ice cream. Looks good, right?

Figure 4-22:
A new cat-
egory page.

Creating Read More Links

What Joomla calls *blog layout* is really called that because it presents a summary of each article followed by a Read More link — not because you're actually writing a blog. In this section, you see how to add Read More links to a
category page, so that you don't have to display the entire text of each article
on the front page.

To add Read More links to a category page, follow these steps:

1. **Click the Article Manager icon in the control panel or choose
   Content➪Article Manager in any back-end page.**

   Article Manager opens.

2. **Open an article that you want to add a Read More link to.**

   For this exercise, open the Chocolate Ice Cream article in Article
   Manager.

3. **Scroll to the bottom of the page, where you find the Read More button.**

4. **Click the place in your article's text where you want that link to
   appear; then click the Read More button.**

   For this exercise, click after the second sentence.

   Joomla inserts a red dotted line (black in this book!), as you see in
   Figure 4-23.

Figure 4-23:
Inserting a
Read More
link.

5. **Repeat Steps 2–4 for any other articles to which you want to add links.**

   For this exercise, add links for the Vanilla Ice Cream and Sardine Ice Cream articles.

6. **View your front page again, and click the link to the category page for which you added Read More links.**

   For this exercise, click the Ice Cream Flavors link in the Main Menu pane.

   The category page opens, displaying your new Read More links (see Figure 4-24).

7. **Click a link to open the corresponding article in full (see Figure 4-25).**

That's great — but you may have noticed that Joomla got the order of your ice cream articles in the category page wrong. SuperDuperMegaCo wants this order:

✔ Chocolate

✔ Vanilla

✔ Sardine

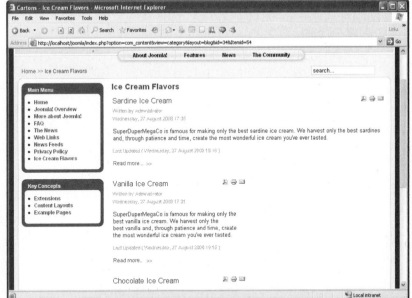

Figure 4-24:
A category page with Read More links.

Figure 4-25:
The full article.

But Joomla gave you this order:

✔ Sardine

✔ Vanilla

✔ Chocolate

This arrangement is in reverse because by default, the most recently created article goes at the top of the category. How can you fix the order? You see how in the following section.

Adjusting Article Order

How can you alter the position of articles? You use Article Manager (click the Article Manager icon in the control panel or choose Content➪Article Manager in any back-end page). As Figure 4-26 shows, however, Article Manager displays too many articles to work with conveniently.

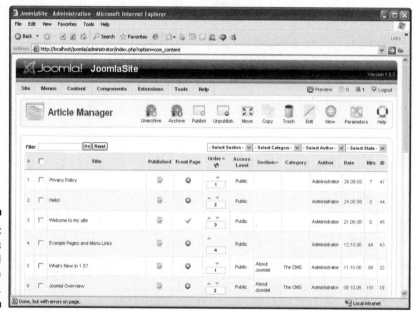

Figure 4-26:
Articles
displayed
in Article
Manager.

Now you see another advantage of dividing your articles into sections and categories: You can use those divisions to filter articles in Article Manager and work with just the ones you want.

Joomla currently has only two levels of organization: sections and categories. But plans are afoot to make the organizational levels infinite (presumably by numbering them) in future versions of Joomla.

Filtering articles

Chapter 3 also discusses filtering articles, but we give you a refresher in this section. To filter articles in Article Manager, choose the section and category you want to view from the Section and Category drop-down menus at the top of the page.

For this exercise, choose the Ice Cream section and Cartons category. Article Manager displays just those articles (see Figure 4-27).

Figure 4-27: Filtered articles in Article Manager.

Reordering articles in Article Manager

When you've filtered Article Manager to display just the articles you want to work with, you're ready to change their order. Follow these steps:

1. **In the Order column (refer to Figure 4-27), click the green up and down arrows to position articles where you want them, or enter ordinal numbers in the text boxes.**

For this exercise, enter **1** for Chocolate Ice Cream, **2** for Vanilla Ice Cream, and **3** for Sardine Ice Cream.

2. **Click the floppy-disk icon at the top of the Order column.**

Joomla displays the articles in the new order (see Figure 4-28).

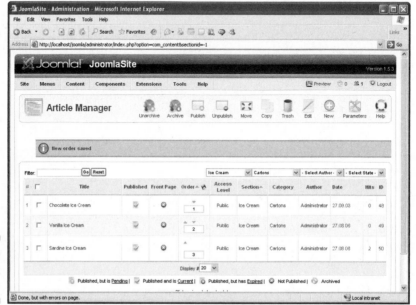

Figure 4-28: Reordered articles.

You did it, right? Actually, no. Changing the order of articles in Article Manager only changes the order of articles in Article Manager. If you look at the category page for the Cartons category, you see that the article order is unchanged.

To change the order in which articles appear in the category page, you need to use Menu Manager, as we show you in the following section. (For more information on Menu Manager, refer to "Creating the menu item," earlier in this chapter; also see Chapter 3.)

Reordering articles in the category page

To reorder articles in the category page, follow these steps:

1. **Click the Menu Manager icon in the control panel or choose Menus⇨Menu Manager in any back-end page.**

The Menu Manager opens.

2. **Click the icon in the Menu Item(s) column of the Main Menu row.**

   The Menu Item Manager opens.

3. **Click Ice Cream Flavors to open that menu item in an editor.**

4. **Click the Parameters - Advanced bar to open that section, as shown in Figure 4-29.**

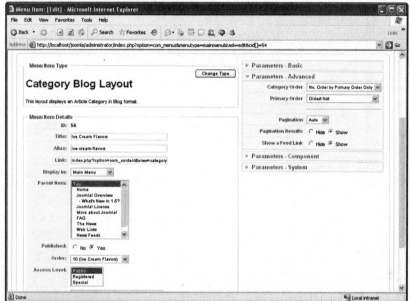

Figure 4-29:
The
Category
Blog Layout
page.

This page is where you set the order of articles as they appear in the category page.

5. **From the Primary Order drop-down menu, choose an option to specify the order in which you want orders to appear.**

   In your example site, your articles appear in chronological order (most recent first), and you want them to appear in reverse chronological order (oldest first). So for this exercise, choose Oldest First.

6. **Click the Apply button in the top-right corner of the page.**

7. **View the front page in a browser.**

8. **Click the link of the pertinent category page to view the new article order (see Figure 4-30).**

Figure 4-30:
Reordered
articles in
the category
page.

Success — the articles are now ordered the way you want them. But the menu items may not be quite right. We show you how to make them right in the following section.

Who's on First?: Setting Menu Item Position

As the preceding section shows, you can change the order of articles in Article Manager, but the layout of those articles doesn't actually change; you have to make that change in Menu Item Manager. Consequently, Menu Item Manager is more powerful than Article Manager when it comes to the actual layout of your articles.

Given that Menu Item Manager is the layout king, then, you shouldn't be surprised to discover that you can use it to set the order of menu items as well. This arrangement illuminates Joomla's inner workings: Joomla wraps up all the layout details in the pertinent menu items, not in the articles themselves.

Whereas adjusting the position of items in the Order column of Article Manager doesn't affect their layout on the page (layout is up to Menu Item Manager; refer to "Reordering articles in Article Manager," earlier in this chapter), changing the position of menu items in Menu Item Manager's Order column *does* change the position of a menu item on the page.

Reviewing the example site

In your example site, the order of menu items probably isn't what SuperDuperMegaCo wants. Currently, the items are in this order:

- Home
- Joomla! Overview
- More about Joomla!
- FAQ
- The News
- Web Links
- News Feeds
- Privacy Policy
- Ice Cream Flavors

But because ice cream is one of the client's major products, that item probably should appear near the top of the list, like this:

- Home
- Ice Cream Flavors
- Joomla! Overview
- More about Joomla!
- FAQ
- The News
- Web Links
- News Feeds
- Privacy Policy

So how do you move items around in a menu? Read on.

Changing the order of menu items

To change the order of the items in a menu, follow these steps:

1. **Click the Menu Manager icon in the control panel or choose Menus➪Menu Manager in any back-end page.**

   Menu Manager opens.

2. **Click the icon in the Menu Item(s) column of the Main Menu row.**

   Menu Item Manager opens.

   For your example site, the Ice Cream Flavors menu item is listed dead last in the Order column, as shown in Figure 4-31.

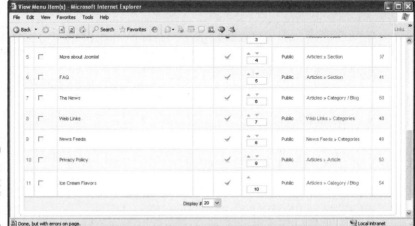

Figure 4-31: The current order of menu items.

3. **In the text box of the menu item's Order column, enter a new position number.**

   For this exercise, enter **2** for Ice Cream Flavor.

4. **Click the floppy-disk icon at the top of the Order column.**

   Joomla displays the menu items in the new order (see Figure 4-32).

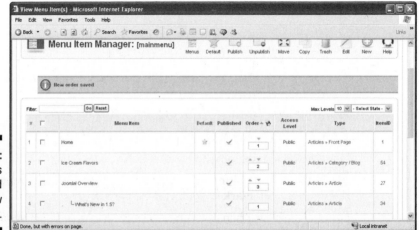

Figure 4-32: Menu items displayed in the new order.

5. **Click Save in the Menu Item Manager page to close it.**

6. **View the front page again.**

   You see the menu items displayed in the new order (see Figure 4-33).

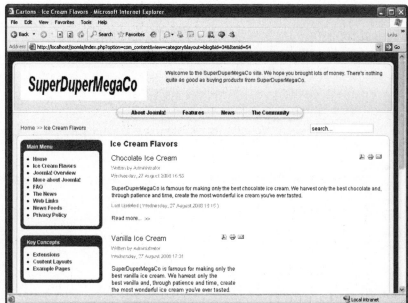

Figure 4-33: The new menu-item order.

Removing menu items

Another way to reorganize menus is to remove some menu items. You can either trash them or unpublish them. We show you both methods in this section.

Unpublishing items

To unpublish menu items, follow these steps:

1. **Click the Menu Manager icon in the control panel, or choose Menus⇨Menu Manager in any back-end page.**

   Menu Manager opens.

2. **Click the icon in the Menu Item(s) column of the Main Menu row.**

   Menu Item Manager opens.

3. **In the Published column of each menu item you want to remove, click the green check mark to change it to a red X.**

   For this exercise, change green checks to red X marks for the following menu items:

- Joomla! Overview

- What's New in 1.5?

- Joomla! License

- More about Joomla!

- FAQ

When you unpublish a menu item, it's unpublished immediately; you don't have to click the Save or Apply button.

4. View the front page again.

You see the new, leaner menu (see Figure 4-34).

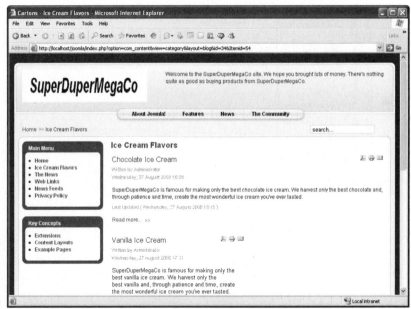

Figure 4-34: A trimmer menu.

Trashing items

Besides unpublishing items in Joomla, you can delete them by trashing them. So should you unpublish or trash unused items?

Trashing an item (and deleting it by emptying the trash) is forever, so we favor unpublishing items, because you can easily publish them again. As time goes on, however, the performance of your site can degrade significantly if you have too many unpublished items, which Joomla still has to manage behind the scenes.

If you have items (menu items, articles, and so on) that you *know* you'll never use again, you should trash them. Here's how:

1. **Complete Steps 1 and 2 of "Removing menu items" to open Menu Item Manager.**

2. **Check the check box at the beginning of the item's row.**

3. **Click the trash icon in the top-right corner of the page.**

   You've just moved the item to the trash, however. To delete it, you have to use Trash Manager.

4. **Choose Menus⇨Menu Trash to trash a menu item.**

   or

   Choose Content⇨Article Trash to trash an article.

   The appropriate Trash Manager opens.

5. **For each item you want to delete, check the check box at the beginning of its row.**

6. **Click the Delete icon in the top-right corner.**

   Trash Manager deletes the item forever.

7. **Choose File⇨Control Panel to go back to the control panel.**

Chapter 5

Building Navigation into Your Site with Menus

Menus in Joomla are central to everything — more so than people not in the know can imagine. You can't view a Web page in Joomla that doesn't have a menu item pointing to it, and when you create a menu item, you select the layout of the Web page to which it points.

Joomla packs a lot into menus, and this chapter is theirs.

All about Joomla Menus

Because Web pages don't exist in Joomla until the data in is accessed through menu items, Joomla wraps all the presentation details of Web pages into menu items. Templates (see Chapter 9) may be responsible for what goes where in a page, using a mix of HTML and CSS, but the menu item determines what template Joomla uses to lay out the resulting Web page.

When you create a menu item, you specify the layout that Joomla will use to display the linked-to Web page, and you can choose among a large number of options. You can create standard Web pages (stand-alone articles), category pages (which show an overview of all the articles in that category), and section pages (which show an overview of all the articles in that section).

You can publish to the front page of your site or to external sites. You can also link to specific types of modules: polls, search boxes, wrappers (which present external pages in Joomla pages; see Chapter 8), and so on.

All these layout options give you a rich tool set — richer than in other content management systems. The previous chapters show you how to work with menu items, because you can't get anywhere in Joomla without them, but this chapter is where menus really shine.

To make menu creation easier to understand, we use a single example throughout this chapter, but feel free to substitute your own site structure and text.

Under and Over: Creating Submenu Items

Because it's impossible to display Web pages in Joomla without a menu item pointing to that page, Chapters 3 and 4 show you the basics of working with menus. In this chapter, however, you discover more in-depth menu power.

We start by showing you how to create *submenu* items: menu items that appear below other menu items.

As an example, this section works with a Web site that has an Ice Cream section and a Bars category, with the following articles in that category:

```
Bars
    |
    |____   SuperDuperMega Bar
    |
    |____   Tutti Fruity Bar
    |
    |____   Broccoli Bar
```

(Yes, we know that it's usually spelled *tutti frutti.*)

You can use three submenus to display these articles.

Creating the section and category pages

First, you need to create the section and category pages. (If you completed the exercises in Chapter 4, you may already have them on your computer; apply these directions to your own situation.) Follow these steps:

1. **Click the Section Manager icon in the control panel or choose Content⇨Section Manager in any back-end page to open Section Manager.**

2. **Click the New button to open the New Section page.**

3. **Enter the new section's title in the Title text box.**

   For this exercise, type **Ice Cream**.

4. **Click the Save button.**

5. **Click the Category Manager icon in the control panel or choose Content⇨Category Manager in any back-end page to open Category Manager.**

6. **Click the New button to open the New Category page.**

7. **Enter a title for the new category in the Title text box.**

   For this exercise, type **Bars**.

8. **From the Section drop-down menu, choose the section in which you want to place the new category.**

   For this exercise, choose Ice Cream.

9. **In the Description text box at the bottom of the page, enter a description.**

   At this point, your settings may resemble Figure 5-1.

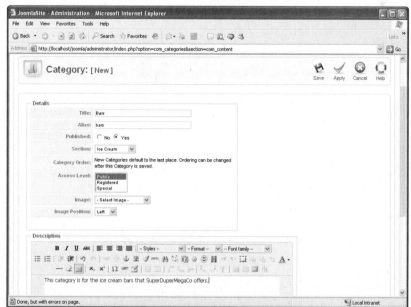

Figure 5-1:
Creating a
category.

10. **Click the Save button.**

    You return to Category Manager, which displays the new category. (If you completed the exercises in Chapter 4, you may also see a Cartons category.)

Creating target Web pages

Next, you need to create an article for each submenu item: the target Web page to which that submenu item points. Follow these steps:

1. **Click the Add New Article icon in the control panel, or choose Content⇨Article Manager in any back-end page to open Article Manager and then click the New button.**

    The article-editor page opens.

2. **Enter a title for the article in the Title text box.**

    For this exercise, type **SuperDuperMega Bar**.

3. **Choose the appropriate section from the Section drop-down menu and the category from the Category drop-down menu.**

    For this exercise, choose Ice Cream as the section and Bars as the category.

4. **In the text box at the bottom of the page, enter the article text.**

    At this point, your settings may resemble Figure 5-2.

5. **Click the Save button.**

    Article Manager opens, listing the new article.

6. **Repeat Steps 1–5 to add as many articles as you want.**

    For this exercise, create two more articles: Tutti Fruity Bar and Broccoli Bar. Assign both of them to the Ice Cream section and the Bars category. When you finish, your Article Manager page should resemble Figure 5-3.

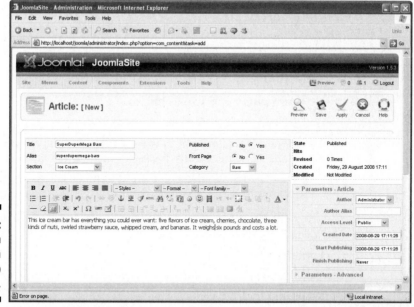

Figure 5-2:
Creating an
article for a
target Web
page.

Figure 5-3:
Three
articles for
three target
Web pages.

Creating the parent menu item

After you have the articles for the submenu items, you need to create a parent menu item (refer to Chapter 4) for the submenu items. Follow these steps:

1. **Create a new dummy article to link to.**

   For this exercise, title the article Ice Cream Bars.

2. **Click the Menu Manager icon in the control panel or choose Menus⇨Menu Manager in any back-end page to open Menu Manager.**

3. **In the row of the menu where you want to place the parent menu, click the icon in the Menu Item(s) column.**

   For this exercise, select Main Menu.

   The Menu Item Manager page opens.

4. **Click the New button.**

   The New Menu Item page opens, displaying a node tree.

5. **Click Internal Link⇨Articles⇨Article⇨Article Layout to open the Article Layout page.**

6. **Enter a title for the new menu item in the Title text box.**

   For this exercise, type **Ice Cream Bars**.

7. **In the Parameters - Basic pane, click the Select button to browse to and select the article that you want to link to the menu item.**

   For this exercise, select the Ice Cream Bars article.

8. **Click the Save button.**

   You return to Menu Item Manager.

9. **If you want to change the order in which the menu items appear, enter new ordinal numbers in the Order columns of the menu items; then click the floppy-disk icon at the top of the column.**

   For this exercise, type **3** in the Order column of the Ice Cream Bars menu item.

10. **Click the Preview link to view your site.**

    Joomla displays the updated menu, which may resemble the one shown in Figure 5-4.

Figure 5-4:
The new
parent menu
item on the
Web site.

Main Menu
- Home
- Ice Cream Flavors
- Ice Cream Bars
- The News
- Web Links
- News Feeds
- Privacy Policy

Creating the submenu Items

To add the submenu items, follow these steps:

1. **Click the Menu Manager icon in the control panel or choose Menus⇨Menu Manager in any back-end page to open Menu Manager.**

2. **In the row of the menu that you want to use as the parent menu, click the icon in the Menu Item(s) column.**

   For this exercise, select Main Menu.

   The Menu Item Manager page opens, displaying a node tree.

3. **Click Internal Link⇨Articles⇨Article⇨Article Layout to open the Article Layout page.**

4. **Enter a title for the submenu item in the Title text box.**

   For this exercise, type **SuperDuperMega Bar**.

5. **In the Parent Item list, select the new submenu item's parent menu.**

   For this exercise, select Ice Cream Bars (refer to "Creating the parent menu item," earlier in this chapter).

6. **In the Parameters - Basic pane, click the Select button to browse to and select the article that you want to link to the submenu item.**

   For this exercise, select the SuperDuperMegaBar article (refer to "Creating target Web pages," earlier in this chapter). At this point, your settings should resemble Figure 5-5.

7. **Click the Save button.**

8. **Repeat Steps 2–7 to create as many submenu items as you want.**

   For this exercise, create two more submenu items: Tutti Fruity Bar and Broccoli Bar.

9. **Click the Preview link to view your site.**

   Joomla displays the new submenu items, which may resemble Figure 5-6.

Clicking any of those new submenu items takes you directly to the page to which the item is linked.

Because the menu item to which an article is linked determines how Joomla displays that article, you turn your attention next to layout options. Chapter 4 presents article layout and blog layout. The other major layout type is list, which we cover in the following section.

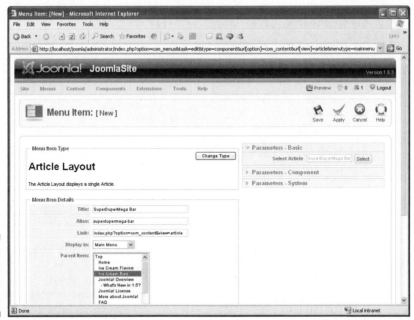

Figure 5-5:
Creating a
submenu
item.

Figure 5-6:
The new
parent and
submenu
menu items.

Click Me: Working with List Layout

List layout is like blog layout in that you use it to display an overview of
Joomla articles. Instead of displaying introductory text for articles, however,
list layout shows a simple list of links to articles.

For the example in this section, you create a Cones category in the Ice Cream
section and apply list layout to the articles in that category:

```
Cones
        |
        |____  SuperDuperMega Cone
        |
        |____  Sprinkles Cone
        |
        |____  Gravy Cone
```

Creating the category

To start, create the new category, as follows:

1. **Click the Category Manager icon in the control panel or choose Content⇨Category Manager in any back-end page to open Category Manager.**

2. **Click the New button to open the New Category page.**

3. **Enter a title for the new category in the Title text box.**

   For this exercise, type **Cones.**

4. **Choose a section from the Section drop-down menu.**

   For this exercise, choose Ice Cream.

5. **In the Description text box at the bottom of the page, enter a description of the new category.**

6. **Click the Save button.**

   You return to Category Manager.

Creating the articles

Next, you need to create the articles for the new category. Follow these steps:

1. **Click the Add New Article icon in the control panel, or choose Content⇨Article Manager in any back-end page to open Article Manager and then click the New button.**

   The article-editor page opens.

2. **Enter a title for the article in the Title text box.**

   For this exercise, type **SuperDuperMega Cone.**

3. **Choose the appropriate section from the Section drop-down menu and the category from the Category drop-down menu.**

   For this exercise, choose the Ice Cream section and the Cones category.

4. **In the text box at the bottom of the page, enter the text for the article.**

5. **Click the Save button.**

   You return to Article Manager.

6. **Repeat Steps 1–5 to add as many articles as you want.**

   For this exercise, add two more articles: Sprinkles Cone and Gravy Cone. Assign both articles to the Ice Cream section and the Cones category.

Creating the menu item

To create the menu item to which you'll link the new articles, follow these steps:

1. **Click the Menu Manager icon in the control panel or choose Menus⇨Menu Manager in any back-end page to open Menu Manager.**

2. **In the row of the menu to which you want to add the new item, click the icon in the Menu Item(s) column.**

   For this exercise, select Main Menu.

   The Menu Item Manager page opens, displaying a node tree.

3. **Click Internal Links⇨Articles⇨Category⇨Category List Layout to open the Category List Layout page.**

4. **Enter the title of the new menu item in the Title text box.**

   For this exercise, type **Ice Cream Cones**.

5. **Enter an alias for the menu item in the Alias text box.**

   For this exercise, type **ice-cream-cones**.

6. **From the Display In drop-down menu, choose the parent menu for the new menu item.**

   For this exercise, choose Main Menu.

7. **In the Parent Item list, select the parent menu's level.**

   For this exercise, because you're using the Main menu, select Top.

8. **In the Published section, select the Yes radio button.**

9. **In the Access Level list, select Public.**

10. **In the On Click, Open In list, select Parent Window with Browser Navigation.**

11. **In the Parameters - Basic pane, choose the category from the Category drop-down menu.**

For this exercise, choose Ice Cream/Cones. At this point, your settings may resemble Figure 5-7.

12. **Click the Save button.**

You return to Menu Manager, which displays the new menu item.

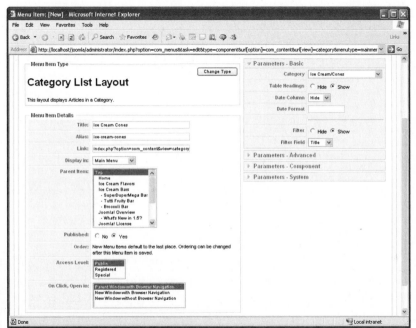

Figure 5-7: Creating a menu item.

Changing the order of menu items

You can see the new menu item in Menu Manager, but it's been added to the bottom of the list of menu items — and, therefore, will appear last in its parent menu. You can change that arrangement by entering new ordinal numbers in the menu items' Order columns and then clicking the floppy-disk icon at the top of the column.

For this exercise, type **4** in the Ice Cream Cones menu item's Order column, and click the floppy-disk icon at the top of the column to save the new order. Now you've got the menu items in the order you want (see Figure 5-8).

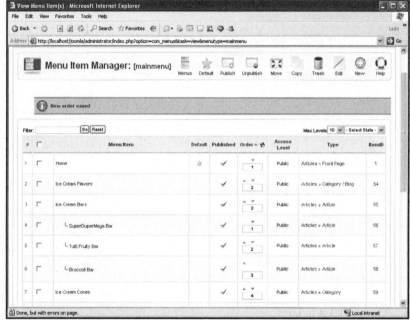

Figure 5-8:
Menu
Manager
displaying
menu items
in a new
order.

Viewing the list layout

To see what your site looks like at this point, click the Preview link at the top of any back-end page to open a preview of your site in a new browser window). You should see the new menu item you added. Now click that menu item, and you should see the articles that you linked to it displayed in list layout. Figure 5-9 shows an example. The article titles in the list are links, and you can click them to open the associated articles.

Changing article order in list layout

If the articles don't appear in the order you had in mind, you can rearrange them. Do you use Category Manager? Nope. Article Manager? Nope. You use Menu Item Manager.

In Joomla, the layout of a page is determined by the menu item that links to that page (and the template used in that page).

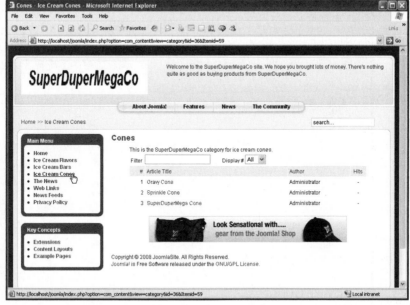

Figure 5-9:
A new menu item displaying articles in list layout.

To rearrange the order of articles in list layout, follow these steps:

1. **Click the Menu Manager icon in the control panel or choose Menus⇨Menu Manager in any back-end page to open Menu Manager.**

2. **In the row of the menu to which you want to add the new item, click the icon in the Menu Item(s) column.**

   For this exercise, select Main Menu.

   The Menu Item Manager page opens, displaying a node tree.

3. **Click the name of the menu to open the Edit Menu Item page.**

   For this exercise, click Ice Cream Cones.

4. **Click the Parameters - Advanced bar to open that pane.**

5. **Choose a new order from the Primary Order drop-down menu.**

   For this exercise, choose Oldest First. At this point, your settings may resemble Figure 5-10.

6. **Click the Save or Apply button.**

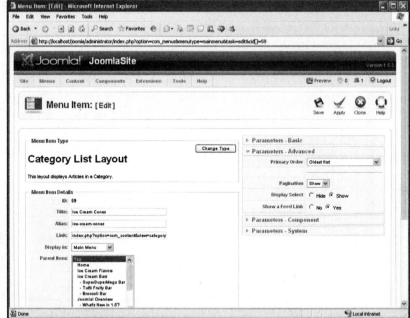

Figure 5-10:
Changing
article order
in list layout.

Now you've mastered list layout.

The following sections give you an in-depth look at the options available for the three most common types of menu-item layouts: standard article layout, blog layout, and list layout. Together, those three layout types make up the majority of menu-item layouts in Joomla sites, and you have to know what's available to use them effectively.

Choice, Choices: Taking Advantage of Your Menu Options

Joomla offers a long list of options for different types of layouts, including those shown in Figure 5-11.

We haven't got space in this book to examine all these options, so we give you a brief overview and then show you how to use a few selected options.

Typically, four parameters panes are available when you set the layout connected with a menu item: Basic, Advanced, Component, and System. We discuss these panes in the following sections.

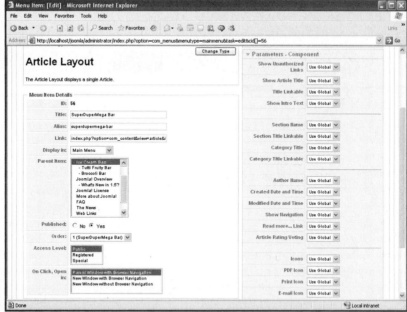

Figure 5-11:
Article
layout
options.

Basic parameters

The top parameters pane in menu-item layout pages is always Parameters - Basic, which offers a limited number of options. Typically, this pane is where you select the article you want to link to or the section or category in which you want to display a page. Here are typical options in the Parameters - Basic pane:

- **Select Article:** The article to link to
- **Category** and **Section:** The category and section to create a layout page for
- **Description:** A section or category description (show or hide)
- **Description Image:** An image for a section or category (show or hide)

Advanced parameters

Advanced parameters are available for category or section layouts, not standard article layouts. Here are the kinds of items you're likely to see in the Parameters - Advanced pane:

- **Category** or **Section Order:** The order of the articles in a section or category layout. You can sort by primary order (see the following item), alphabetically by title, or reverse-alphabetically by title.

- **Primary Order:** The order of the articles in a section or category layout. Your options include oldest or newest article first, alphabetically by title or author, and most or least hits.

- **Pagination:** Whether to display pagination (show or hide).

- **Show a Feed Link:** Whether to display an RSS link (show or hide).

Component parameters

The items in the Parameters - Component pane are the same in most types of layouts: article, category, section, and so on. Here are the parameters you're likely to see:

- **Show Unauthorized Links:** Whether to display unauthorized links (show or hide) — that is, links that the user doesn't have sufficient privileges to view

- **Show Article Title:** Whether to display article titles (show or hide)

- **Title Linkable:** Whether the title should be a link

- **Show Intro Text:** Whether to display introductory text for each article (show or hide)

- **Section Name:** Whether to display the section name (show or hide)

- **Section Title Linkable:** Whether the section name should be a link to the section

- **Category Title:** Whether to display the category title (show or hide)

- **Category Title Linkable:** Whether the section name should be a link to the category

- **Author Name:** Whether to display the author name (show or hide)

- **Created Date and Time:** Whether to display the creation date and time (show or hide)

- **Modified Date and Time:** Whether to display the date and time of the last modification (show or hide)

- **Show Navigation:** Whether to display navigation links between articles (show or hide)

- **Read More:** Whether to display a Read More link for each article (show or hide)

- **Article Rating/Voting:** Whether users are allowed to rate articles

✔ **Icon options:** Whether to display Print, PDF, and E-Mail icons (show or hide)

✔ **Hits:** Whether to track hits

System parameters

You usually have a Parameters - System pane for all layout types. Here's what you find in this pane:

✔ **Page Title:** The title of the page

✔ **Show Page Title:** Whether to display the page title (show or hide)

✔ **Menu Image:** An image for the menu

✔ **SSL Enabled:** Whether the menu will appear in a secure connection using SSL (Secure Socket Layer)

Setting Some Powerful Menu Options

You have plenty of options when it comes to configuring your menu items in Joomla. In the following sections, you put a few of these options to work. Mastering these options is crucial to creating a professional-looking site.

Turning article titles into links

When you use category list layout, all the article titles in a category are links automatically, but they're not when you use category blog layout. You can change that situation via the settings in the Parameters - Component pane. Follow these steps:

1. **Open the menu item that links to the article you want to change by clicking that menu item in Menu Item Manager.**

   For this exercise, open the category blog layout page for the Ice Cream Flavors menu item.

2. **In the Parameters - Component pane, choose Yes from the Title Linkable drop-down menu (see Figure 5-12).**

3. **Click the Apply button (to apply your change) or the Save button (to apply your change and close the Menu Item Editor page).**

   Joomla now displays linked article titles in category blog layout. Figure 5-13 shows an example.

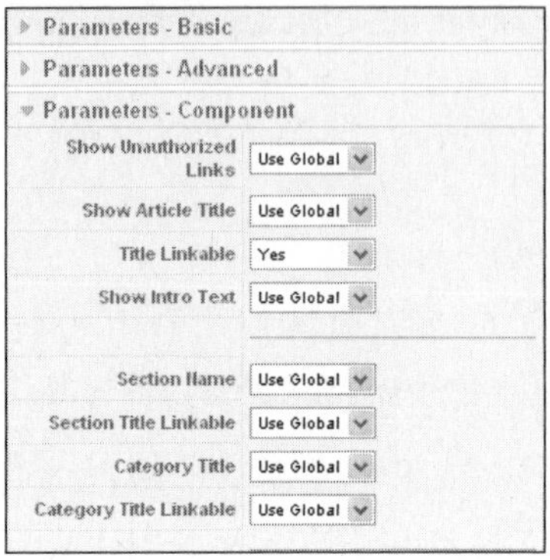

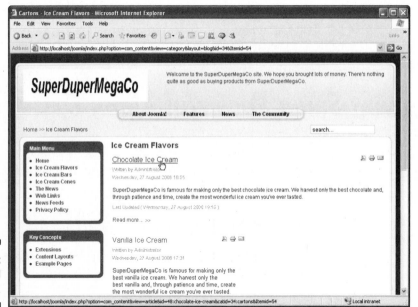

Figure 5-12:
Setting link
options for
articles.

Figure 5-13:
Linked
article titles.

We recommend that you always set your article titles as links when you use category blog layout, because users expect titles to be links.

Showing article ratings

How about letting users rate an article? To do that, follow these steps:

1. **Open the menu item that points to the article you want to let users rate by clicking that item in Menu Item Manager.**

2. **In the Article Layout page, click the Parameters - Component bar to open that pane.**

3. **Choose Show from the Article Rating/Voting drop-down menu (see Figure 5-14).**

4. **Click the Apply or Save button.**

5. **Click the Preview link in any back-end page to view your site.**

   Users can now rate the article via a series of radio buttons, from Poor to Best (see Figure 5-15).

Figure 5-14: Showing article ratings.

Figure 5-15: An article's ratings.

Setting menu access

Suppose that you want to allow only logged-in users to access a certain article. To do that, follow these steps:

1. **Open the pertinent menu item in the Menu Item Editor by clicking that item in Menu Item Manager.**

2. **Make a selection in the Access Level list.**

   For this exercise, select Registered (logged-in users only).

3. **Click the Save button.**

   Now any user who isn't logged in can't see the article.

Opening articles in new windows

Perhaps you want a new browser window to open when a user clicks a certain menu item. To set up that behavior, follow these steps:

1. **Open the pertinent menu item by clicking that item in Menu Item Manager.**

2. **In the On Click, Open In list, select New Window with Browser Navigation (see Figure 5-16).**

3. **Click the Apply or Save button.**

   Now when the user clicks the menu item, a list of articles in that category opens in a new window. When the user clicks the name of an individual article, however, the article appears in that same window.

If you want to open a new browser window without an address bar, toolbars, or menu bar, select New Window without Browser Navigation in Step 2.

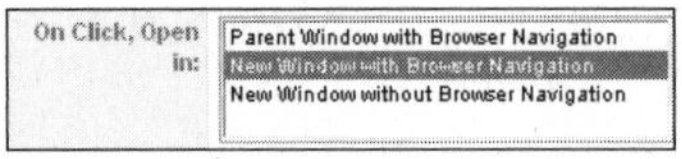

Figure 5-16:
Setting
a new
browser
window to
open.

On Click, Open in:	Parent Window with Browser Navigation
	New Window with Browser Navigation
	New Window without Browser Navigation

Hiding author names

You may want to clean up your Joomla site's pages a little. One place to start is the *Written by Administrator* line that appears at the top of every article by default. You can hide this author name, or any other author name, in individual articles linked to a menu item or in all articles on the site. We show you both methods in the following sections.

By menu item

To hide an author's name in one or more articles linked to a menu item, follow these steps:

1. **Open the pertinent menu item by clicking that menu item in Menu Item Manager.**

2. **Click the Parameters - Component bar to open that pane.**

3. **Choose Hide from the Author Name drop-down menu (see Figure 5-17).**

4. **Click the Apply or Save button.**

5. **Click the Preview link in any back-end page to view your site.**

   The author name no longer appears in any articles linked to that menu item.

Figure 5-17:
Hiding an
author
name.

Across the site

You can also remove author names from *all* articles on your site by resetting the global article parameters. Follow these steps:

1. **Choose Content⇨Article Manager in any back-end page to open Article Manager.**

2. **Click the Parameters button.**

   A pop-up window appears, displaying global article settings (see Figure 5-18).

   This window is where you set the global article parameters used by default in menu item layouts.

3. **In the Author Name section, click the No radio button.**

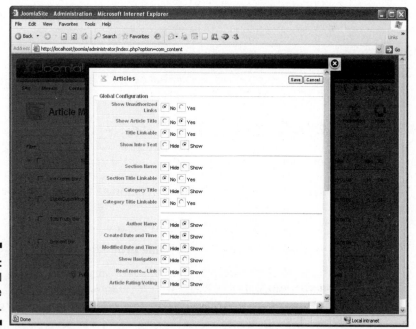

Figure 5-18:
Global
article
settings.

4. **Click the Save button to close the pop-up window and return to Article Manager.**

5. **Click the Preview link to view your site.**

   Author names no longer appear on articles.

Showing article-to-article links

You can display navigation links from article to article in a category or section, if you like. In a menu item's Parameters - Component pane (which you reach by clicking the item in Menu Item Manager and then clicking the Parameters - Component bar on the right side of the Menu Item Editor page), simply choose Show from the Show Navigation drop-down menu, and click the Apply button.

Now users can navigate the articles in a category by using Prev and Next links (see Figure 5-19).

 Speaking of navigation, links like Home >> Ice Cream Cones >> Sprinkle Cones are called *breadcrumbs*. Breadcrumbs appear by default; you can turn them off in Module Manager. For details, see Chapter 7.

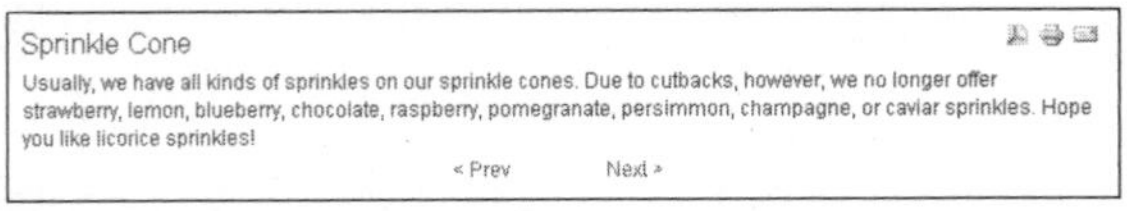

Figure 5-19:
Navigation
links
enabled.

Sprinkle Cone

Usually, we have all kinds of sprinkles on our sprinkle cones. Due to cutbacks, however, we no longer offer strawberry, lemon, blueberry, chocolate, raspberry, pomegranate, persimmon, champagne, or caviar sprinkles! Hope you like licorice sprinkles!

< Prev   Next >

Setting Default Menu Items

Some menu items are activated by default in Joomla, such as the Home item in the Main menu, because it points to the front page. You can determine what menu item is the default by looking at the menu's Default column in Menu Item Manager. Home is the default item in the Main menu when you install Joomla — but you can change that.

To set a new default menu item, follow these steps:

1. **Click the Menu Manager icon in the control panel or choose Menus⇨Menu Manager to open Menu Manager.**

2. **Click the icon in the Menu Item(s) column of the menu you want to change.**

   Menu Item Manager opens.

3. **Check the check box of the menu item that you want to make the default.**

4. **Click the Default button.**

   The Menu Item Manager page updates, and you see a gold star (black and white in this book) in the menu's Default column (see Figure 5-20).

To restore your site, repeat this procedure to make the original default item the default again.

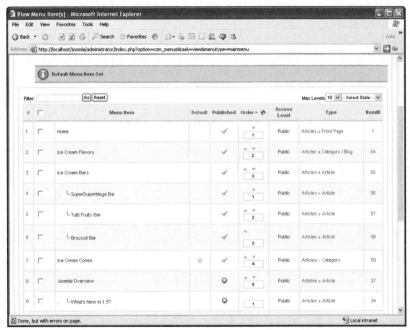

Figure 5-20:
Setting a
new default
menu item.

Creating Menu Separators

As our last topic for this chapter, in this section we show you how to create menu separators. A *menu separator* is an inactive menu item that you use to group or offset other menu items. You create separators with the Separator menu item type.

To create a menu separator by changing a menu item's type, follow these steps:

1. **Open a menu item in the Edit Menu Item page by clicking the menu item in Menu Item Manager.**

2. **Click the Change Type button.**

The Change Menu Item page opens, displaying a list of possible types (see Figure 5-21).

3. Select the Separator type.

The Separator page for the selected menu item opens,

4. In the Title text box, enter the character(s) you want to display as the separator.

For this exercise, enter a hyphen (-).

5. Click the Apply button.

6. Click the Preview link in any back-end page to view your site.

You see the new separator in the menu (see Figure 5-22).

You can also create menu separators from scratch, of course. Just select the Separator menu type when you create a new menu item.

Figure 5-21:
The Change
Menu Item
page.

Figure 5-22:
The new
menu
separator at
work.

Chapter 6

Mastering Web Page Creation

* *

In This Chapter

▶ Setting article options

▶ Working with the editor

▶ Formatting and embellishing articles

▶ Using tables and columns

▶ Adding a table of contents

▶ Scheduling publishing (and unpublishing)

▶ Making your site interactive with user roles

▶ Counting page hits

▶ Taking down the site

* *

There's a terrific amount of Web-page power in Joomla, and this chapter takes a look at it in depth. You can set up articles so that Joomla starts publishing them at a later date automatically — or even stops publishing them automatically at a later date. You can insert images in articles, track page hits, set up article columns, and create automatic tables of contents. You can even allow some users to edit articles from the front end (not the back end), although you get the chance to approve or disapprove their edits before they get published.

That's the kind of stuff that's coming up in this chapter. We introduce writing Web-page content in Chapter 4, but this chapter is where this topic really takes off. To start this chapter, you get control of the article-creation process, seeing what options are available and putting those options to work.

Working with Article Options

Take a look at Figure 6-1: an uncategorized privacy policy open in the Joomla article editor. (To open the article editor, click the Article Manager icon in the control panel, or choose Content⇨Article Manager in any back-end page.)

Figure 6-1:
An article
open in the
article
editor.

You're going to see this page a lot as you work with Joomla, so it really pays to know what's going on in it. The following sections give you an overview of the options in the article editor; then you put some of these options to work.

Article options

These options appear in the top-right corner of the article-editor page:

- ✔ **Article ID:** Joomla's internal ID for the article. (You can search for articles by ID or title.)
- ✔ **State:** The article's state (published or unpublished).
- ✔ **Hits:** The number of times the article has been viewed.
- ✔ **Revised:** The number of times the article has been revised.
- ✔ **Created:** The article's creation date.
- ✔ **Modified:** Setting indicating whether the article has been modified and the date it was modified.

Below this list of options are the parameters you can set for the article, which we describe in the following sections.

Parameters - Article options

The Parameters - Article section, directly below the options we list in the preceding section, contains these items:

- ✔ **Author:** The username of the article's author.

- ✔ **Author Alias:** An alias for the author, should you want to use one. If you list an alias, it appears on the Web page instead of the author's username.

- ✔ **Access Level:** The access level that users must have to see this article. Here are the options:

    - **Public:** Everybody

    - **Registered:** Logged-in users

    - **Special:** Administrators

- ✔ **Created Date:** The date the article was created.

- ✔ **Start Publishing:** The date and time you want to start publishing the article.

- ✔ **Finish Publishing:** The date and time you want Joomla to stop publishing the article, if any.

Parameters - Advanced options

Here are the advanced parameters in the Parameters - Advanced section of the article editor. For most options, your choices are Use Global (that is, use the setting in the Global Configuration page, which you access by choosing Site⇨Global Configuration), Yes/Show, and No/Hide.

- ✔ **Show Title:** Indicates whether you want to show the article title

- ✔ **Title Linkable:** Indicates whether the article title, if visible, should be a link to the full article

- ✔ **Intro Text:** Indicates whether introductory text for the article should be visible

- ✔ **Section Name:** Indicates whether the section name of the article should be visible

- ✔ **Section Title Linkable:** If the section title is visible, indicates whether you want it to be a link to the section

- ✔ **Category Title:** Indicates whether the category name of the article should be visible

- ✔ **Category Title Linkable:** If the category title is visible, indicates whether you want it to be a link to the category

- ✔ **Article Rating:** Indicates whether users can rate the article (see Chapter 5)

- ✔ **Author Name:** Indicates whether the article author's name is visible

- ✔ **Created Date and Time:** Indicates whether you want the date and time the article was created to be visible

- ✔ **Modified Date and Time:** Indicates whether you want the date and time the article was modified to be visible

- ✔ **PDF Icon:** Indicates whether you want to display a PDF icon to allow users to download the article in PDF format

- ✔ **Print Icon:** Indicates whether you want to display a print icon for the article

- ✔ **E-Mail Icon:** Indicates whether want to display an email icon to let users e-mail the article to others

- ✔ **Content Language:** Specifies the language the article is written in

- ✔ **Key Reference:** Allows you to enter a text key that allows users to find the article

- ✔ **Alternative Read More:** Allows you to enter additional text in the Read More link

Metadata options

You can also enter metadata information about the article, to be stored in `<meta>` HTML tags. Search engines like Google use metadata to categorize your article. Here are the items in the Metadata Information section of the article-editor page:

- ✔ **Description:** The article's human-language description

- ✔ **Keywords:** The list of comma-separated keywords you want your page to be indexed under (the terms users should be able to search on)

- ✔ **Robots:** Keywords targeted to search-engine robots

- ✔ **Author:** The author's name

Getting to Know Your Editor

The actual mechanics of creating an article occur in the editor section in the bottom-left corner of the article editor (refer to Figure 6-1). For detailed information on creating an article, see Chapter 4. The editor that comes built into Joomla — TinyMCE — wasn't actually created by the Joomla developers. Currently, Joomla uses Version 2 of this powerful, JavaScript-based editor.

TinyMCE is a WYSIWYG (what you see is what you get) editor with three toolbars. It provides these features (among many others):

- Supports colored text and backgrounds
- Supports insertion of images, HTML, links, horizontal rules, emoticons, and more
- Allows table creation and manipulation
- Supports layers
- Provides total CSS support

If you're working in Windows, you can also use XStandard Lite — a Joomla plug-in. To enable XStandard Lite, choose Extensions⇨Plugin Manager to open Plugin Manager; disable TinyMCE by clicking the green check mark in its Enabled column, changing it to a red X; then enable XStandard Lite by clicking the icon in its Enabled column, changing that icon from a red X to a green check mark.

After you create an article in any editor, you have to create a menu item that points to it, using Menu Item Manager. And if you want to juggle the positions or appearance of menus in Joomla, you can do that with Module Manager (which you access by choosing Extensions⇨Module Manager). For details, see Chapter 7.

Dressing Up Your Articles with Emoticons and Images

Emoticons and images are two staples of modern Web pages, and Joomla lets you work with both. Embedding them in your articles is a snap; just use the following instructions.

Smile!: Adding emoticons

Emoticons are small colored icons depicting happy or sad faces. They add a touch of emotion to your text — something that might not come through otherwise.

Suppose that your site has a privacy policy containing this text:

Actually, we don't really have a firm privacy policy.

Does that mean we'll sell your email address to spammers?

Well, could be. . . .

That looks a little menacing, you decide. How about adding a smiley face at the end? To do that, click to position the insertion point at the end of the text and then click the Emoticons button in the middle toolbar of the TinyMCE editor to open the Insert Emotion dialog box (see Figure 6-2).

Click the emoticon you want to use to insert it into the text (see Figure 6-3).

Figure 6-2: TinyMCE's emoticons.

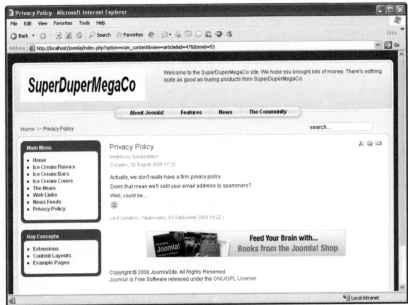

Figure 6-3: An added emoticon.

Adding images

Web pages often show whole images. Can you insert images into articles? Sure you can.

Say, for example, that you want an image to illustrate the timeliness of an article. After looking around, you decide on the perfect one: an image of a clock (see Figure 6-4). This image, `clock.jpg`, is preinstalled with Joomla.

Figure 6-4:
A clock
image.

Images that can be inserted into articles are stored in the Joomla `images/stories` directory, or a subdirectory of that directory.

To insert an image into an article, follow these steps:

1. **Open the article in which you want to insert the image (choose Content⇨Article Manager and then click the article's name to open it in the article editor).**

2. **Click the Image button below the text window.**

   The image-insertion dialog box opens (see Figure 6-5).

3. **Select the image you want to use.**

   If you don't see the image you want, click the Browse button in the Upload section of the image-insertion dialog box to find an image on your local computer; then click the Start Upload button to upload the image.

4. **In the article editor, click the place in the text where you want to insert the image.**

5. **Click the Insert button in the image-insertion dialog box.**

   Joomla inserts the image into the article (see Figure 6-6).

Figure 6-5:
Selecting
an image.

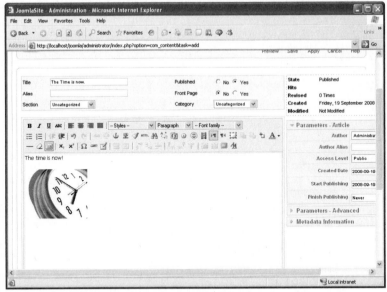

Figure 6-6:
The image
in the
article.

Just as you can insert images into articles, you can insert multimedia. To do so, click the Insert or Edit Media button in the TinyMCE editor's middle toolbar. The types of multimedia you can insert are Adobe Flash, QuickTime, Adobe Shockwave, Windows Media, and Real Media.

Now you can insert images into articles — and, therefore, into Web pages. What else can you do?

Formatting Articles with HTML Tags

You can add some pizzazz to an article by adding HTML tags while you work with it in the article-editor page. To insert HTML tags with the TinyMCE editor, follow these steps:

1. **With the article you want to format open in the article editor, click the Edit HTML Source button in the middle toolbar.**

   The HTML Source Editor window opens, displaying the text of your article enclosed in paragraph tags (`<p>`/`</p>`).

2. **To enter a heading, type** `<h1>`*heading*`</h1>`**, where** *heading* **is the heading text.**

   If you want to use the raffle example, you might type **`<h1>RAFFLE!</h1>`** (see Figure 6-7).

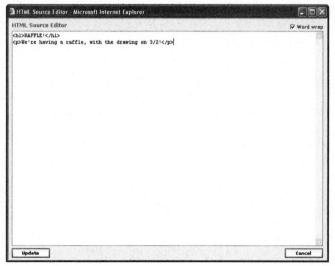

Figure 6-7:
Entering
HTML
heading
tags.

3. Click the Update button.

You see the result in the text window (see Figure 6-8).

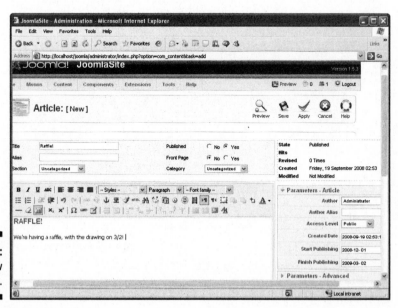

Figure 6-8:
A new
heading.

Actually, the HTML editor in the TinyMCE editor isn't really worth that much. You could have made the same change by typing the heading text in the text window, selecting it, and then choosing Heading 1 from the Format drop-down menu.

If you insert HTML tags that TinyMCE deems to be nonstandard, such as a `<marquee>` tag to create a scrolling marquee in Internet Explorer, TinyMCE removes that tag (not the enclosed text). The same goes for JavaScript. If you try to insert an HTML `<form>` tag for a control like a button in your article, TinyMCE strips the `<form>` tag out of the article.

Working with Tables and Columns

If you've got data that you want to organize visually in your Web pages, what better constructions could you use than tables? Tables are neat and lay out your data in a concise form.

Suppose that you're creating a school site, and you want to list the top honor-roll students in an article. How about creating a table that lists them like this?

Student	Rank
Fred	1
Ethyl	2
Lucy	3
Ricky	4
Ralph	5

Creating a table in an article

To place a table in an article, follow these steps:

1. **With the article open in the article editor, click Insert New Table.**

   The Insert/Modify Table dialog box opens.

2. **In the General tab, set the options you want to use.**

   Figure 6-9 shows an example.

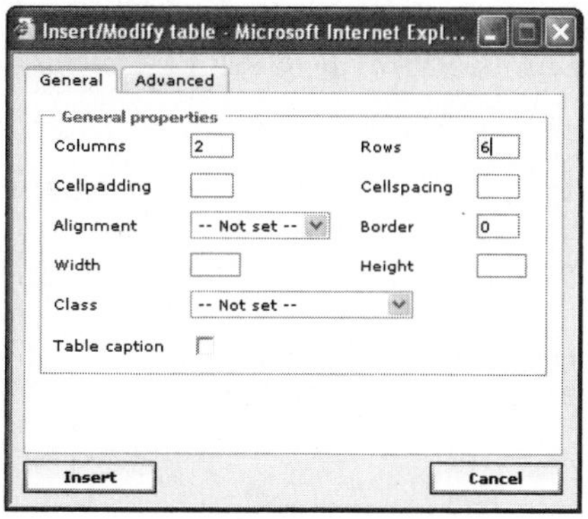

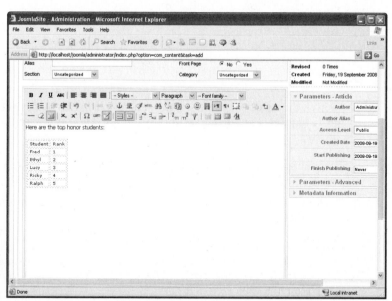

Figure 6-9:
Setting table
options.

3. **Click the Insert button.**

   A blank table grid appears in your article.

4. **Type the table text in the table cells (see Figure 6-10).**

Figure 6-10:
Adding
table text.

Formatting a table

That's good so far, but now you want to apply some formatting — to make the column heads to stand out, maybe, and to add a border. To format a table, follow these steps:

1. **Select the top row of the new table, and click the Table Row Properties button in the bottom toolbar of the TinyMCE editor.**

   The Table Row Properties dialog box opens.

2. **From the Row in Table Part drop-down menu, choose Table Head (see Figure 6-11); then click the Update button.**

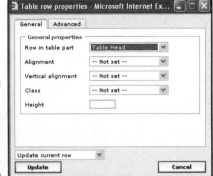

Figure 6-11:
The Table
Row
Properties
dialog box.

Joomla converts the headers in the top row of your table to actual table headers (that is, the `<th>` tag will be used for the headers, not the `<td>` tag).

3. **To give the table a visible border, click inside the table and then click the Table Cell Properties button in the bottom toolbar of the editor.**

   The Table Cell Properties dialog box opens.

   By default, all table borders are white, so they won't show up on a Web page that has a white background. But you can change that setting.

4. **Click the Border Color box, and choose a new color from the pop-up color palette.**

   You may want to choose black (hex code #000000).

5. **To apply the new color to the border of all cells, choose Update All Cells in Table from the drop-down menu in the bottom-left corner of the dialog box (see Figure 6-12).**

6. **Click the Update button.**

The appearance of the table in the article editor doesn't match what the final table will look like on your site. To see what the table will actually look like, click the Preview link in the top-right corner of the article-editor page (see Figure 6-13).

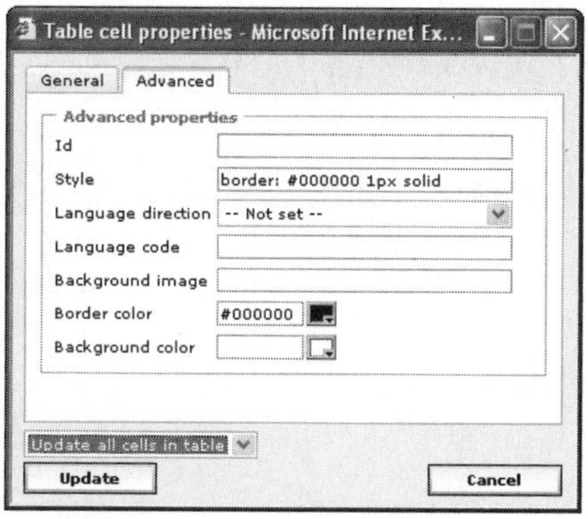

Figure 6-12:
Applying a border color.

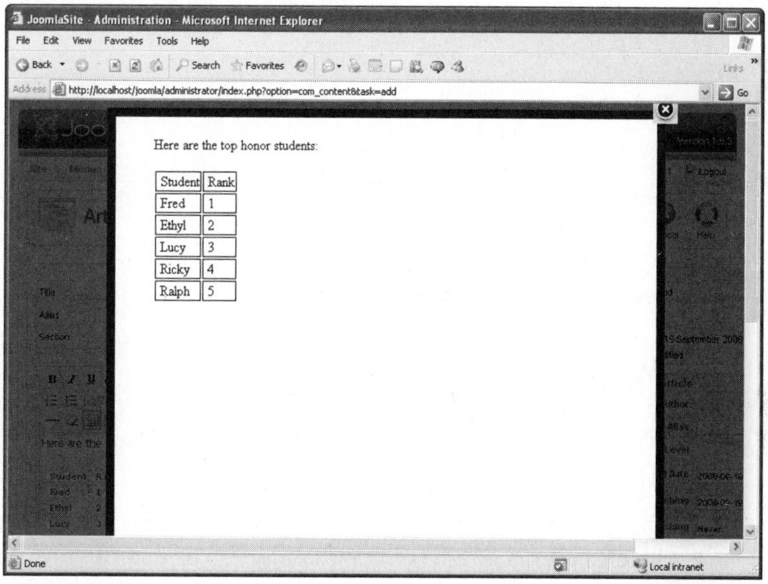

Figure 6-13:
Previewing the new table.

Changing an article's columns

Want to change the number of columns that an article's content is divided into? You may think you'd do that with Article Manager or the article editor, but the number of columns is a layout issue, so you set it in Menu Item Manager. (To open Menu Item Manager, choose Menus➪Menu Manager in any back-end page; then click the icon in the Menu Item(s) column of the menu whose items you want to edit.)

To change the number of columns, enter a new value in the Columns text box of the Parameters - Basic section. Figure 6-14, for example, is set to display two columns. You can format articles in as many columns as you like.

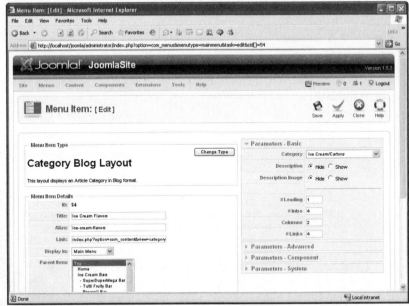

Figure 6-14:
Setting the
number of
columns in
an article.

Creating a Table of Contents

Joomla lets you break your articles up by adding a table of contents, which is particularly good for longer articles. If you have an article that's 30 pages long, for example, you don't want to make your users wait while the whole thing loads. It's much better to break the article into titled pages, especially when Joomla's page-break feature is so easy and painless.

Suppose that in the article editor, you're viewing an article about a picnic that a neighborhood group is throwing. Here's the text of the article:

We're having a picnic!

Where:

Stewart Park

When:

Tomorrow

What to bring:

Potato salads

Sandwiches

Drinks

You can break this article up into pages by clicking the Pagebreak button below the text window in the article editor.

To see how this feature works, follow these steps:

1. **With the article open in the article editor, click the Pagebreak button.**

   A pop-up dialog box asks you for the title of the new page (see Figure 6-15).

2. **Enter a page title, and click the Insert Pagebreak button.**

3. **Repeat Steps 1 and 2 to create as many new pages as you want.**

4. **Click the Save or Apply button in the article-editor page.**

5. **Open the article in the front end.**

   You see the article's table of contents (see Figure 6-16).

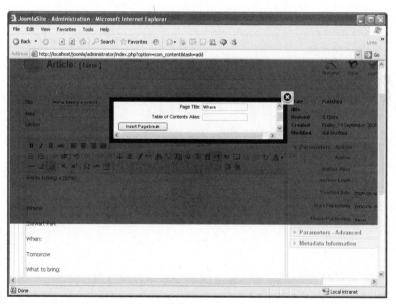

Figure 6-15: Inserting a page break.

Figure 6-16:
Table of
contents.

In Figure 6-16, notice that Joomla uses the article's title as the title of the first page in the article. The text links are the names of page breaks, and Joomla displays << Prev and Next >> links to let users navigate from page to page. The All Pages link in the table of contents displays the whole article without page breaks.

Back (And Forth) to the Future: Publishing at Different Times

You may have articles that need to appear on a certain schedule. Perhaps you're promoting a picnic (and need to take down the notice about it when the picnic is over) or a theatrical production (and need to display the notice only when tickets are available). Joomla helps with this task.

Publishing articles in the future

You can create articles that will be published at some future time. Suppose that your not-for-profit organization is running a raffle from now until

March 2, 2010, and you want to publicize the raffle You create this article by clicking the Add New Article icon in the control panel or by clicking the New button in Article Manager.

Suppose, however, that you don't want this article to appear until December. To make sure of that, set the publication details in the Parameters - Article section on the right side of the article editor. To start publishing on December 1, 2009, at midnight, for example, enter **2009-12-01** in the Start Publishing text box (see Figure 6-17).

Be sure to use *yyyy-mm-dd* format when you enter the date.

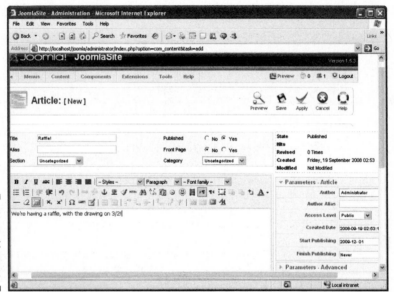

Figure 6-17: Setting a date to start publishing an article.

Stopping publishing in the future

You can also end the publication of an article on a date in the future. To continue the example in the preceding section, perhaps the raffle ends March 2, 2010, so you'd want to stop publication on that date.

That's easy enough to do. To make Joomla end the publication of an article (or *unpublish* the article, taking it off the site), enter the stop date in the Finish Publishing text box of the Parameters - Article section (see Figure 6-18).

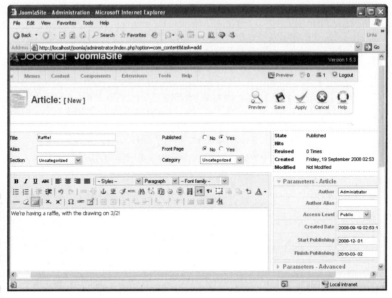

Figure 6-18:
Automatically ending publication of an article.

Unpublishing now

Finally, you can unpublish an article in the present — right now or an hour from now, for example.

To unpublish an article in Joomla, follow these steps:

1. **Click the Article Manager icon in the control panel or choose Content⇨Article Manager in any back-end page to open Article Manager.**

2. **In the article's Published column, click its green check mark to change it to a red X.**

   Figure 6-19 shows the Privacy Policy article being unpublished.

   Unpublishing an article doesn't remove the menu item that points to it, however. The menu item is still listed in its original menu, and if users click that item, they get an error page. So you have to unpublish the menu item as well.

3. **To unpublish the menu item, click the Menu Manager icon in the control panel or choose Menus⇨Menu Manager in any back-end page to open Menu Manager.**

4. **In the Published column of the appropriate menu item, click the green check mark to change it to a red X.**

   You've unpublished both the article and its menu item.

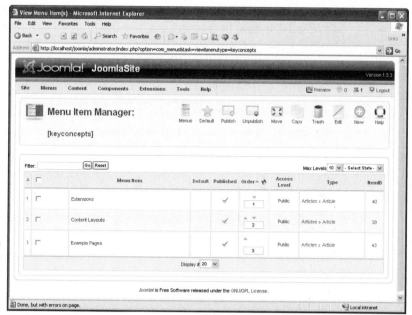

Figure 6-23:
Menu Item
Manager.

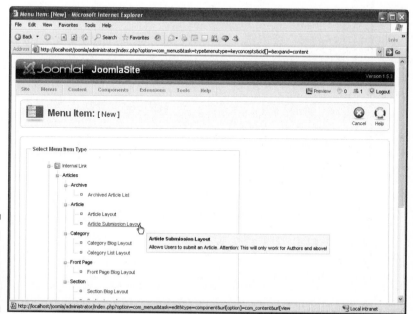

Figure 6-24:
Creating
an article
submission
page.

5. **In the Menu Item Details section, enter a title in the Title text box, and select a setting in the Access Level list (bottom-left corner of Figure 6-25).**

Here are your access-level choices:

- **Public:** Everybody
- **Registered:** Logged-in users
- **Special:** Authors, editors, publishers, and administrators

6. **Click the Apply or Save button to create your new menu item.**

Congratulations — you've also created a new article submission page.

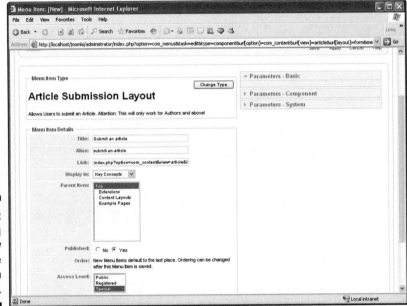

Figure 6-25: Configuring a new article submission page.

Viewing the link to the article submission page

How do you access the new article submission page? If a casual user (without site privileges) looks at the menu, he won't see anything special. For this example, he'd see just the same Key Concepts menu shown in Figure 6-22, earlier in this chapter.

But if the user named author used the login form on the front page to log in, she'd find the new menu item in the Key Concepts menu (see Figure 6-26). Cool!

Figure 6-26:
The new
menu item,
visible after
login.

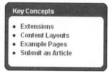

Authors and Editors and Publishers, Oh My!

In this section, we take a look at the capabilities enjoyed by the special users: authors, editors, and publishers. Different levels of users have different levels of options available to them.

Authors can write articles

Assuming that you're logged in as an author, and you click the appropriate menu item, the article submission page appears. Then you can enter and edit text, as shown in Figure 6-27.

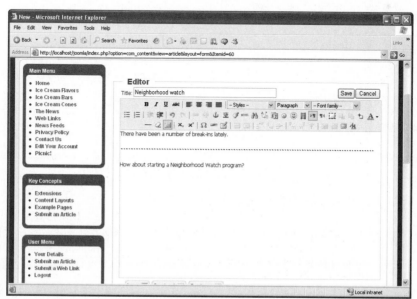

Figure 6-27:
Creating a
new article.

In the figure, the author is submitting a new article named Neighborhood watch, with the dotted line indicating a Read More link. (For details on Read More links, see Chapter 4.)

Submitting an article (author)

Farther down the page, you can select the proposed article's section and category. (In Figure 6-28, the author has selected the News section and the Latest category.) You can enter metadata for the article as well.

When you're done with the new article, click the Save button. Joomla takes you back to the front page and displays a thank-you message (see Figure 6-29).

To log out as author, click the Logout button that appears on the front page after you log in.

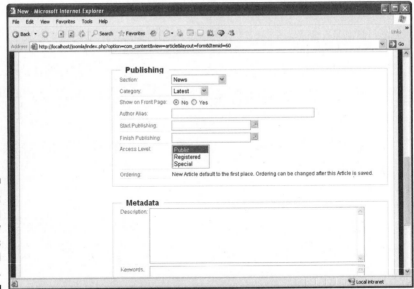

Figure 6-28: Selecting a new article's section and category.

Approving an article (administrator)

So how do administrators learn about new article submissions? Log in to the back end as an administrator and check the mail icon in the top-right corner of the page. If you see a number next to this icon, you have mail waiting (see Figure 6-30).

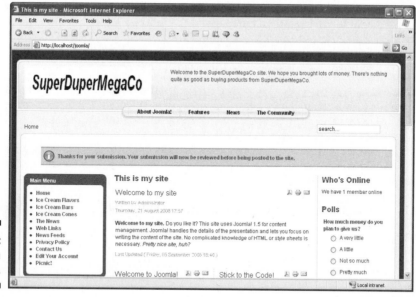

Figure 6-29:
Submitting a
new article.

Mail icon

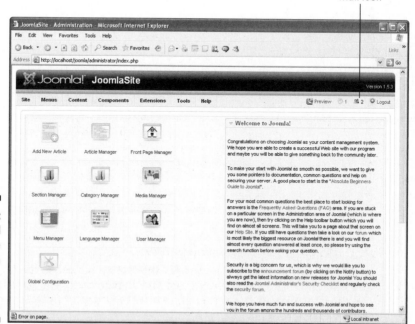

Figure 6-30:
A new mail
message
for an
admini-
strator of a
Joomla site.

The number next to the people icon in the top-right corner tells you how many people are logged on currently.

Click the mail icon to open the page you see in Figure 6-31, and select the title to open the message — in this case, a new article.

You can read the submitted article in Article Manager as well by clicking the article's title in that page.

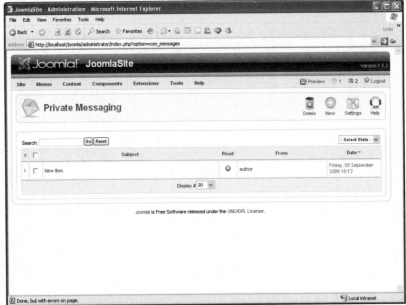

Figure 6-31:
A new
message.

Editors can make changes

Unlike authors, when editors log in, they see a page like the one shown in Figure 6-32. Notice the difference? An Edit icon at the top of all articles allows editors to revise articles.

If you've logged in as an editor, click an article's Edit icon to open its editing page. (Figure 6-33 shows an example.) Make any changes to the article that you want; then click the Save button. The changes are saved and appear on the site immediately.

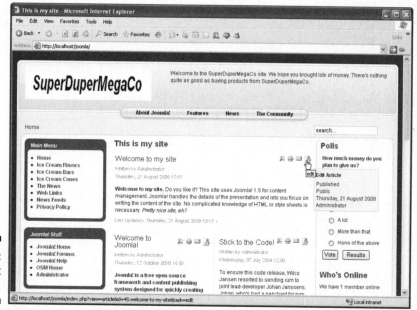

Figure 6-32:
The Edit
icon.

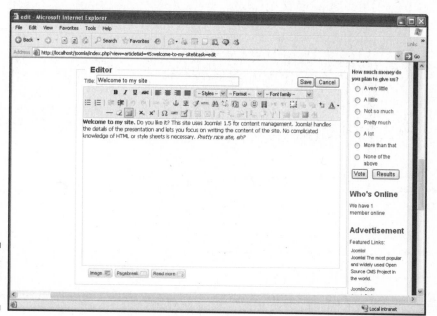

Figure 6-33:
Editing an
article.

Sometimes when an editor tries to edit an article, he gets a message from Joomla saying that the article can't be edited because someone else is already editing it — even if nobody is. This situation can happen when editors don't click the Save or Apply button to save their changes to an article before leaving the editor window. To check in all checked-out articles — and make them accessible to editors — choose Tools⇨Global Checkin in any back-end page.

Publishers can post articles

The last of the front-end-content manipulators are publishers. In practical terms, publishers are the same as editors, except that they can also publish articles to the site.

If you log in as a publisher and then create or edit an article, you see the two options that set publishers apart from editors: the Published and Show on Front Page radio buttons (see Figure 6-34). (Start Publishing and Finish Publishing options are also available to publishers, as you see in the figure.)

Those two options, which don't appear for authors or editors, allow publishers to publish articles to the site — even on the front page.

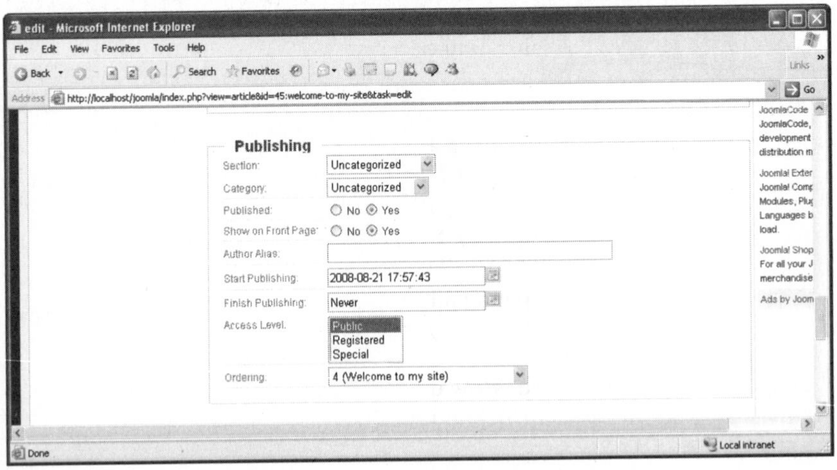

Figure 6-34: Publishing options.

Stand Up and Be Counted: Tracking Page Hits

You can track the number of hits a page on your site has received. Just check the Hits column in Article Manager (see Figure 6-35).

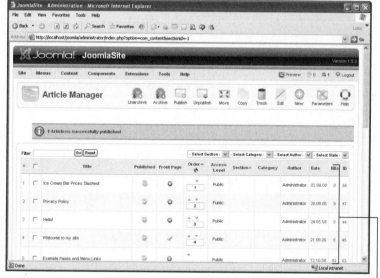

Figure 6-35:
Checking the number of hits each page has received.

Hits

How can you reset the number of hits an article has to zero? Open the article in the article editor, and click the Reset button on the right side, next to the hit counter (the third item down on the right side).

See You Later, Alligator: Taking the Site Offline

One day, you may get a call from a client, who screams into the phone, "We're not ready! Take the site offline!"

Take the site offline? How do you do that? You can use the Global Configuration feature. Follow these steps:

1. **Choose Site⇨Control Panel in any back-end page to open the control panel; then double-click the Global Configuration icon.**

   or

   Choose Site⇨Global Configuration in any back-end page.

   Either way, the Global Configuration page appears, open to the Site tab.

   Notice the first option in the Site Settings pane: Site Offline. That setting is the one you want.

2. **Select the Yes radio button in the Site Offline section.**

3. **Click Apply.**

4. **Click the Save button.**

Your site is down, and surfers see the message shown in Figure 6-36.

Joomla!™

JoomlaSite

This site is down for maintenance. Please check back again soon.

Username

Password

Remember Me ☐

Login

Figure 6-36:
The site is
down.

Want to bring the site back up? Follow these steps:

1. **Reopen the Global Configuration page.**

2. **In the Site Offline section of the Site tab, select the No radio button.**

3. **Click Apply; then click Save.**

Your site is back in business.

Part III
Working with Joomla Modules and Templates

In this part . . .

This part has fun with Joomla modules and templates. *Modules* are those items that appear around the periphery of your page: menus, polls, newsflashes, banners, search boxes, custom HTML, and more. Joomla comes with dozens of built-in modules, and this part of the book is where you master them.

We also cover working with Joomla templates in this part. *Templates* determine every aspect of the layout of your pages, from where the modules go to the images and colors they use. Although Joomla comes with limited template choices, you can download thousands of additional templates from the Internet.

Chapter 7

Fun with Modules: Advertisements, Archives, Banners, Custom HTML, and More

*J*oomla *modules* are those great embedded applications that appear around the edges of your pages. The newsflash (see Chapter 3), which rotates news stories on the front page, is a module. So is the poll that appears on the front page. So are the very advertisements that can appear on Joomla pages.

In fact, even *menus* are modules in Joomla.

The chapters in Parts I and II of this book provide a tour of content handling in Joomla. This chapter and the next one, however, cover modules.

All about Modules

You handle modules in Joomla with Module Manager, which you open by choosing Extensions⇨Module Manager in any back-end page. Figure 7-1 shows Module Manager in the default Joomla installation.

This tool is the main one we use in this chapter and Chapter 8.

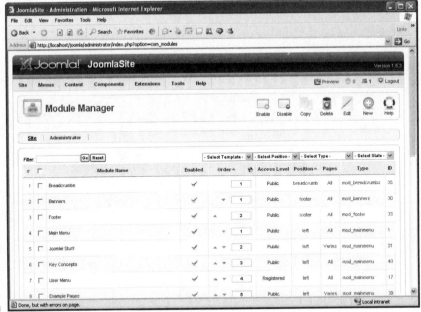

Figure 7-1:
The default
Joomla
Module
Manager.

To work with an individual module, click its name in Module Manager; a customization page for that module opens.

Here are the modules in the default Joomla installation, arranged alphabetically:

Advertisement	Polls
Archive	Popular
Banners	Random Image
Breadcrumbs	Related Items
Example Pages	Search
Feed Display	Sections
Footer	Statistics
Joomla! Stuff	Syndication
Key Concepts	Top Menu
Latest News	User Menu
Login Form	Who's Online
Main Menu	Wrapper
Newsflash	

Module Manager has ten columns for each module:

- ✔ **#:** The number of the module in Module Manager
- ✔ **[Selection Box]:** Option enabling you to work with modules en masse
- ✔ **Module Name:** The name of the module
- ✔ **Enabled:** Option indicating whether the module is enabled
- ✔ **Order:** The order of the module in its subgroup; sets the order of the menu modules on a page
- ✔ **Access Level:** The access levels for various users: Public (everyone), Registered (logged-in users), or Special (authors and above)
- ✔ **Position:** The position on the page where the module should appear
- ✔ **Pages:** The pages on which the module is visible
- ✔ **Type:** The type of the module; sets the module's subgroup and then allows to set the position of the module in its subgroup via the Order column.
- ✔ **ID:** The Joomla ID of the module

In the rest of this chapter, you jump into some modules to see what they offer and what makes them tick.

The Advertisement Module: For Sale; Buy Now!

The Advertisement module shows . . . well, advertisements. You can see it at work on the right side of Figure 7-2. (You can't miss it; it's the module titled Advertisement.)

You open the Advertisement module's administration page by choosing Extensions➪Module Manager to open Module Manager and then clicking the module's name.

Touring the module

Figure 7-3 shows the Advertisement module's administration page. We take a few pages here to describe it because it's typical of Joomla modules.

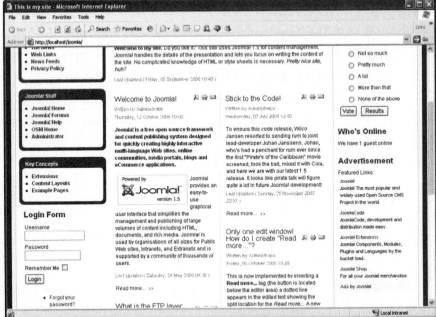

Figure 7-2:
The Adver-
tisement
module.

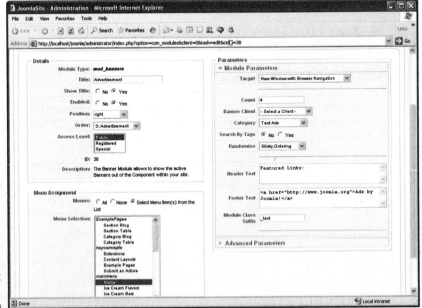

Figure 7-3:
Admin-
istration
page for
the Adver-
tisement
module.

The most important options are in the Details pane:

- ✔ **Title:** Sets the title you want to display above the module.
- ✔ **Show Title:** Specifies whether to display the title.
- ✔ **Enabled:** Allows you to enable or disable the module.
- ✔ **Position:** Sets the position of the module on the page:
  - **breadcrumb:** The breadcrumb position (see "The Breadcrumbs Module: Like Hansel and Gretel," later in this chapter)
  - **debug:** The debug module's location
  - **footer:** The footer of the page
  - **left:** The left side of the page
  - **right:** The right side of the page
  - **syndicate:** The syndicate position
  - **top:** The top of the page
  - **user1:** At user-defined position user1 (depends on template)
  - **user2:** At user-defined position user2 (depends on template)
  - **user3:** At user-defined position user3 (depends on template)
  - **user4:** At user-defined position user4 (depends on template)
- ✔ **Order:** Specifies the order of multiple modules on a page.

  Joomla lists the modules that are already in the position you specified and allows you to select the order of the current module. For the Advertisement module, you can set the order of the module in this list:
  - 0::Polls
  - 2::Who's Online
  - 3::Advertisement
  - 4::Random Image
- ✔ **Access Level:** Sets the access level of the module (Public, Registered, or Special)

The Position and Order options allow you to place your module on the page consistent with where the template you're using places modules when you select right, left, and so on. For details on using templates, see Chapter 9.

Putting ads on certain pages

So far, so good — but how do you set what pages the module appears on?
You assign them in the Menu Assignment pane of the administration page
(see Figure 7-4).

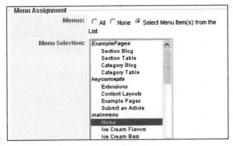

Figure 7-4:
Menu
Assignment
options.

You may be puzzled for a moment: You set what *pages* the module appears in
with a *menu* assignment? But in Joomla, pages are created only when a menu
item is accessed. So you specify what pages a module appears in by specifying
the menu items that point to those pages.

If you want a module to appear on all pages, select the All radio button. If you
want to specify what pages the module appears on, select the radio button
marked Select Menu Item(s) from the List; then select multiple items in the
Menu Selection list. Selecting just the Home item corresponds to the front
page, so if you select that item, the Advertisement module appears only on
the front page.

Configuring the module

Now check out the Parameters section in Figure 7-5, which allows you to set
the specific parameters of a module.

In the case of the Advertisement module, you see options specific to advertising. The setting in the Target drop-down menu, for example, specifies where
the new page opens when the user clicks an ad.

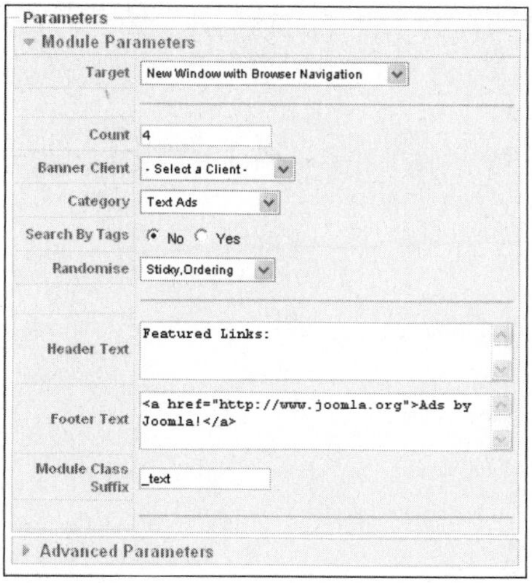

Figure 7-5:
Parameters
of the
Adver-
tisement
module.

Substituting your own ads

Where do the default ads come from, and how can you replace them with your own?

The ads are managed by Banner Manager (figures, doesn't it?). If you check the Parameters section of the module's administration page, the Category drop-down menu shows the type of ads that the Advertisement module is set up to extract from Banner Manager. In Figure 7-5, earlier in this chapter, that menu is set to Text Ads.

To manage the category and substitute your own ad, follow these steps:

1. **Choose Components➪Banner➪Banners in any back-end page.**

   Banner Manager opens (see Figure 7-6).

2. **Disable each ad you no longer want by clicking the green check mark in its Published column, turning the check mark to a red X.**

3. **Click one of the remaining items to open it.**

   If you select the Joomla! item, for example, you see the page shown in Figure 7-7.

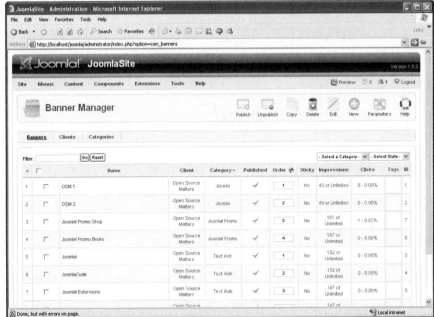

Figure 7-6:
Banner
Manager.

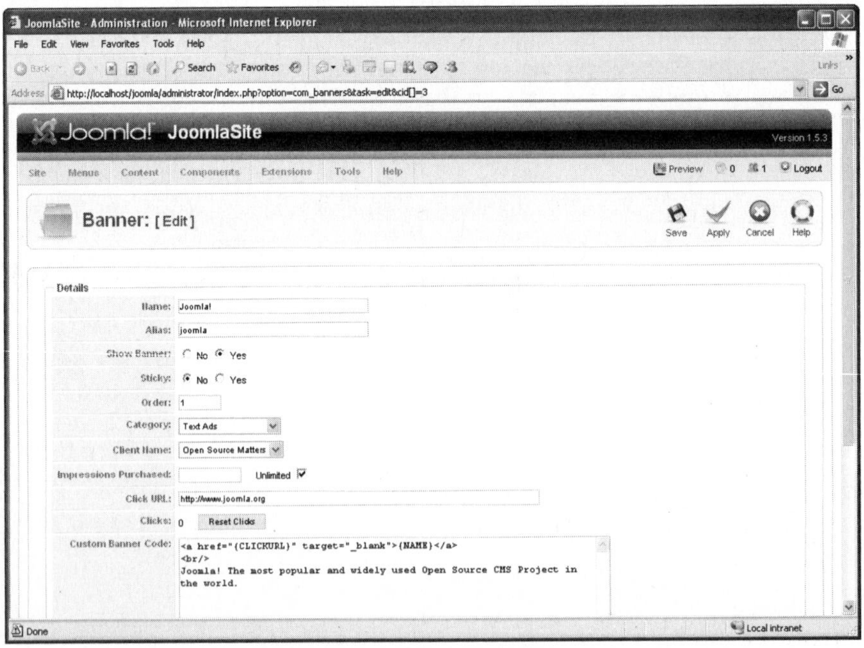

Figure 7-7:
Editing
an ad.

4. **In the Name text box, enter the name of the replacement ad.**

5. **In the Click URL text box, enter the URL of the replacement ad.**

To create a new ad, just click the New button in Banner Manager.

The Archive Module: A Sense of History

Archiving articles stores them on your site but gives them less of a presence. You can archive articles easily in Article Manager. (To open Article Manager, click the Article Manager icon in the control panel or choose Content⇨Article Manager.)

Archiving articles

To archive articles, follow these steps:

1. **Select the articles you want to archive by checking the check boxes at the beginning of their rows.**

2. **Click the Archive button.**

   The articles appear in Article Manager with the keyword [Archived] after their names. Figure 7-8 shows an example of an archived article.

Figure 7-8: Archived article in Article Manager.

Displaying lists of archived articles

You can configure the Archive module to display a list of links to archived articles, arranged by month. Follow these steps:

1. **Choose Extensions⇨Module Manager in any back-end page to open Module Manager.**

2. **Click Archive to open that module's administration page.**

3. **In the Enabled section of the Details pane, select the Yes radio button.**

4. **Make a choice from the Position drop-down menu to specify where on the page the Archive module should appear.**

   You have these choices:

0::Main Menu	7::Login Form
2::Joomla! Stuff	8::Archive
3::Key Concepts	9::Sections
4::User Menu	10::Related Items
5::Example Pages	11::Wrapper
6::Statistics	12::Feed Display

5. **In the Menu Assignment pane, set the menu(s) you want to link the Archive module to.**

   To link the module to the Main menu, for example, select the radio button marked Select Menu Item(s) from the List, and select Home in the Menu Assignment list (see Figure 7-9).

6. **Click the Save button.**

7. **View the front page to see your changes.**

   Figure 7-10 shows an example. Clicking the link would take you to the archived articles for that month and year.

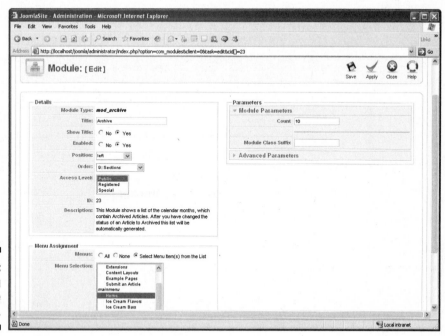

Figure 7-9:
Configuring
the Archive
module.

Figure 7-10:
The Archive
module on
the front
page.

Archive

- September, 2008

The Banners Module: A Picture's Worth a Thousand Words

Banners are advertisements with banner images, like the one you see at the bottom of the default front page (see Figure 7-11).

Figure 7-11:
A banner ad.

When you click a banner, the browser navigates to the ad's URL, just like the banner ads you see all over the Internet.

Viewing the Banner module

To view the Banner module's administration page, choose Extensions⇨ Module Manager in any back-end page to open Module Manager; then click Banners to open the module's administration page.

In the example shown in Figure 7-12, the All radio button is selected, meaning that this module appears on every page, and the Position drop-down menu is set to Footer, so the ads appear at the bottom of every page.

Want to get rid of the banner ads at the bottom of the pages on your site? Just select the None radio button in the Menus section of the Menu Assignment pane, and click the Apply or Save button.

To view all the ads on your site in Banner Manager, choose Components⇨ Banner⇨Banners (refer to Figure 7-6).

Changing banner ads

The available banner images are stored in the Joomla `images/banners` directory, and each image (usually in `.jpg` or `.png` format) is 468 pixels wide by 60 pixels tall. To choose among the available banners when you're editing a banner ad, click the ad's name in Banner Manager (refer to Figure 7-6) and then make a choice from the Banner Image Selector drop-down menu (see Figure 7-13).

You can also click the New button in Banner Manager to create a new ad.

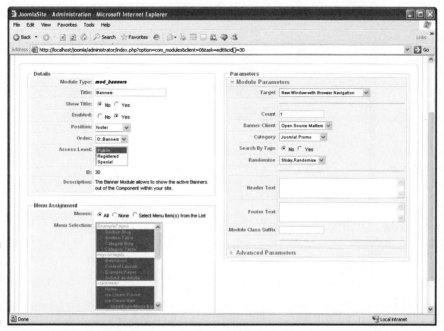

Figure 7-12:
Editing the Banner module.

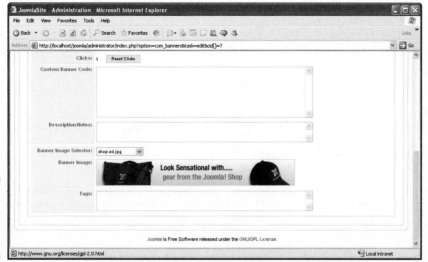

Figure 7-13:
Selecting a banner image.

The Breadcrumbs Module: Like Hansel and Gretel

Breadcrumbs are those link trails you see at the top of articles, such as the trail you see in the top-left corner of Figure 7-14.

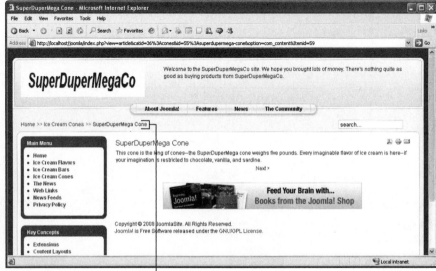

Figure 7-14: Bread-crumbs at work.

Breadcrumbs

Breadcrumbs are innocuous parts of a Joomla site, and you have little reason to fool with them, but you can change them if you like. To edit the module's settings, click its name in Module Manager to open the module's administration page.

The Custom HTML Module: Doing It Yourself

Sometimes, you want to add your own HTML to your site, but the TinyMCE editor (see Chapter 6) usually gets in the way. Suppose that you have HTML generated by eBay, Amazon.com, or PayPal, and you want to paste that code into your site. The TinyMCE editor doesn't allow you to use HTML tags that it doesn't understand, however.

The solution is to create a Custom HTML module, which you do in the following sections.

Changing the default editor

The first phase of creating a Custom HTML module is changing the default editor. To do so, follow these steps:

1. **Choose Site⇨Global Configuration in any back-end page.**

   The Global Configuration page opens.

2. **From the Default WYSIWYG Editor drop-down menu, choose Editor - No Editor (see Figure 7-15).**

3. **Click the Save or Apply button.**

   You've removed TinyMCE as the default editor.

Creating the Custom HTML module

Next, you create the Custom HTML module. Follow these steps:

1. **Choose Extensions⇨Module Manager in any back-end page to open Module Manager.**

   You can look for a Custom HTML module in Module Manager, but you'll search in vain; you have to create it yourself.

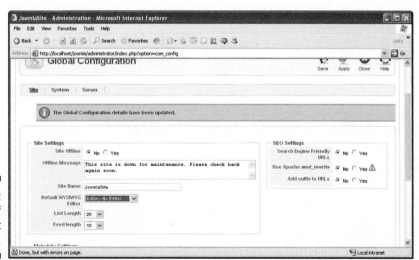

Figure 7-15:
Turning off
the default
editor.

2. **Click the New button.**

   The New Module page opens.

3. **Select the Custom HTML radio button, and click the Next button.**

   The module administration page opens (see Figure 7-16).

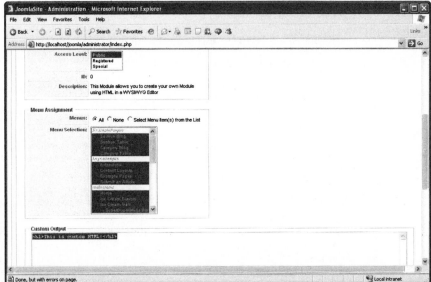

Figure 7-16:
Adding
Custom
HTML.

4. **In the Title text box, type** Custom HTML.

5. **In the Custom Output window at the bottom of the page, enter some sample custom HTML.**

   You can enter anything you want, including JavaScript.

6. **Click the Save button.**

   Joomla saves the new module and returns you to Module Manager.

7. **View your site in a browser.**

   The new Custom HTML module now appears (see Figure 7-17).

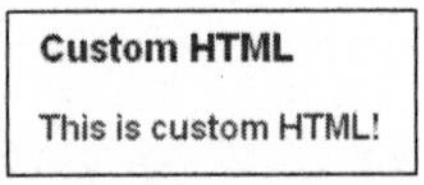

Figure 7-17:
The Custom
HTML mod-
ule at work.

Custom HTML

This is custom HTML!

Don't forget to restore the TinyMCE editor as your default when you're done adding custom HTML. To do that, choose Site⇨Global Configuration to open the Global Configuration page; choose TinyMCE from the Default WYSIWYG Editor drop-down menu; and click the Save button.

The Feed Display Module: Getting RSS Your Way

RSS (which stands for, among other things, Really Simple Syndication) is a great way to spread news through newsfeeds. RSS feeds are supported by thousands of sites, and they allow you to stream their articles into RSS readers — or your Joomla site.

The Feed Display module allows you to display other sites' RSS feeds on your site, which is a great way to add value. Suppose that you have a site about hamsters. If you can find another site that has an RSS feed about hamsters, displaying that feed on your site will keep your content from being static (assuming that you can't find the time to keep adding new articles).

You can find RSS feeds in hundreds of thousands of places on the Internet; just click the XML or RSS button that you see on various sites.

RSS feeds are always XML files.

To add an RSS feed to your Joomla site, follow these steps:

1. **Choose Extensions⇨Module Manager in any back-end page to open Module Manager.**

2. **Click Feed Module to open the module's administration page.**

3. **In the Enabled section of the Details pane, select the Yes radio button.**

4. **In the Feed URL text box, located in the Module Parameters pane, enter the URL of the feed you want to add to your site.**

   If you want to add the RSS feed for *USA Today*'s Money section, for example, enter this URL:

   ```
   http://rssfeeds.usatoday.com/UsatodaycomMoney-TopStories
   ```

   At this point, your settings should resemble Figure 7-18.

5. **Click the Save or Apply button.**

6. **View your site in a browser.**

   You find the RSS feed added to your site (see Figure 7-19).

Figure 7-18:
Configuring
the Feed
Display
module.

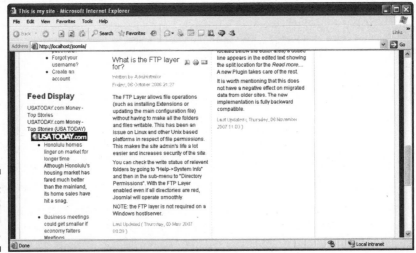

Figure 7-19:
An RSS
feed on a
Joomla site.

Chapter 8

More Fun with Modules: Footers, Search Boxes, Who's Online, Wrappers, and More

In This Chapter

▶ Setting login options

▶ Displaying random images

▶ Setting up search

▶ Showing statistics

▶ Displaying other sites on yours

Chapter 7 reviews the built-in Joomla modules, and this chapter covers the remaining modules, from Footer to Wrapper. In this chapter, you see how to use footers to place text at the bottom of all your pages, how to place search boxes anywhere so your users can search your site, how to place Who's Online boxes to display your site's current users, how to show current site statistics, and how to use wrappers to embed pages from other Web sites in your own site.

The Footer Module: Joomla's Copyright Notice

The Joomla Footer module appears at the bottom of every page by default, as you see in Figure 8-1.

Although you'd think that this module would allow you to set your own copyright text at the bottom of every page, that's not the case. Footer is designed only to display the Joomla copyright notice.

Figure 8-1:
The Joomla
Footer
module.

If you open the Footer module for editing (choose Extensions➪Module Manager in any back-end page and then click Footer), you see that you have no option to enter your own footer text. Your only option is to turn the Joomla copyright notice at the bottom of every page on or off.

But if you're willing to be a little sneaky, you can set your own footer text by replacing the Joomla copyright notice. Joomla stores most text messages in its `language` directory, and the messages for an English-language installation are stored in the `language\en-GB` directory. The footer text is in the file `language\en-GB\en-GB.mod_footer.ini`, which looks like this by default:

```
# $Id: en-GB.mod_footer.ini 9765 2007-12-30 08:21:02Z ircmaxell $
# Joomla! Project
# Copyright (C) 2005 - 2008 Open Source Matters. All rights reserved.
# License http://www.gnu.org/licenses/gpl-2.0.html GNU/GPL, see LICENSE.php
# Note : All ini files need to be saved as UTF-8 - No BOM
# Note : %date% will be auto replaced by current year !Don't translate

FOOTER=Footer
FOOTER_LINE1=Copyright &#169; %date% %sitename%. All Rights Reserved.
FOOTER_LINE2=<a href="http://www.joomla.org">Joomla!</a> is Free Software
            released under the <a href="http://www.gnu.org/licenses/gpl-
            2.0.html">GNU/GPL License.</a>
MOD_FOOTER=<em>mod_footer</em>
THIS MODULE SHOWS THE JOOMLA! COPYRIGHT INFORMATION=This Module shows the
            Joomla! Copyright information
```

You can change the footer text to whatever you want by changing FOOTER_
LINE1 and FOOTER_LINE2. Not bad!

 The Joomla `language` directory is a gold mine if you want to customize Joomla's modules, components, and templates. If you're into customization, get to know the `.ini` files in this directory; you can change the messages Joomla displays.

The Login Form Module: Getting Users on Board

The Joomla Login Form module (see Figure 8-2) allows a user to enter his username and password to log in to the site. By default, the login form appears only on the front page, but you can make it appear anywhere you want.

Login Form

Username

Password

Remember Me ☐

Login

- Forgot your password?
- Forgot your username?
- Create an account

Figure 8-2: The Login Form module.

The login form also shows these links:

- ✔ Forgot Your Password?
- ✔ Forgot Your Username?
- ✔ Create an Account

Clicking the Create an Account link opens the Registration page (see Figure 8-3). Users can create new usernames and passwords on this page. For more on this topic, see Chapter 10.

To make the login form appear on every page, choose Extensions⇨Module Manager to open Module Manager and click Login Form to open the module's administration page.

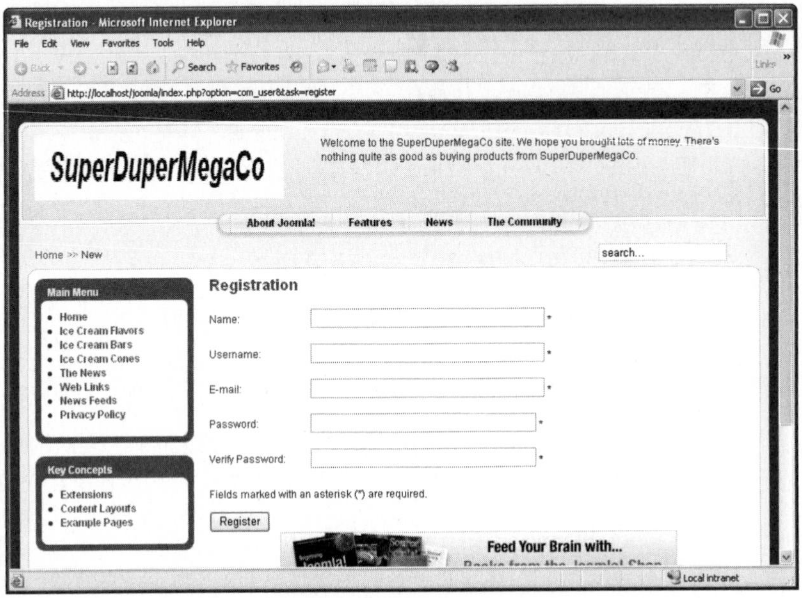

Figure 8-3:
Registering
new users.

The Popular Module: Only the Best and Brightest Articles

The Popular module (nice name for a module) publishes a list of links to the five articles with the most hits. By default, this module isn't enabled. To enable it, choose Extensions➪Module Manager in any back-end page to open Module Manager, and click the red X in the Popular item's Enabled column to turn the red X to a green check mark.

By default, the Popular module appears at top of the page (see Figure 8-4).

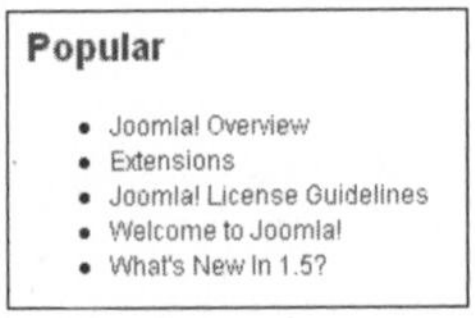

Figure 8-4:
The Popular
module.

Popular

- Joomla! Overview
- Extensions
- Joomla! License Guidelines
- Welcome to Joomla!
- What's New In 1.5?

The Random Image Module: Adding a Little Art

The Random Image module, as its name implies, shows a random image every time the page it appears on is refreshed.

This module is great to use if you want to display some kind of product (such as ice cream cones) on your site. A new image appears each time a visitor comes to the site.

To set the Random Image module, follow these steps:

1. **Choose Extensions⇨Module Manager to open Module Manager.**

2. **Click Random Image to open the module's administration page.**

   Because the Random Image module doesn't appear on any pages by default, you may think that it isn't enabled by default. But that's not true: It *is* enabled. It has no menu assignment, however, so the module never appears by default.

3. **In the Menu Assignment pane, select the radio button labeled Select Menu Item(s) from the List.**

4. **In the Menu Selection list, select the pages on which you want the Random Image module to appear.**

   At this point, your choices in the Details and Menu Assignment panes should resemble Figure 8-5.

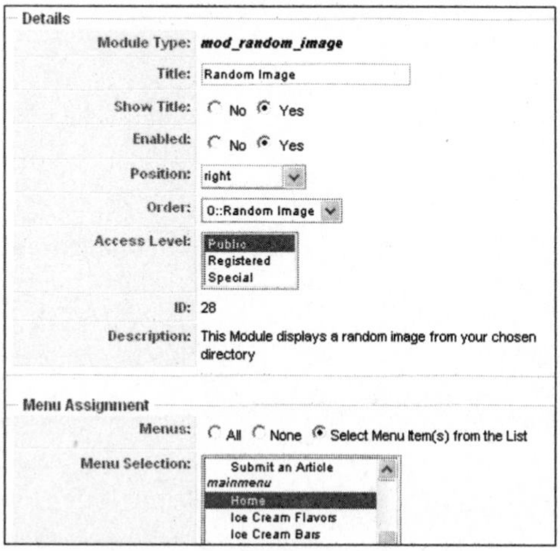

Figure 8-5: Editing the Random Image module.

The settings you make in the Module Parameters section of the administration page specify where the module gets the random images.

5. **In the Image Type and Image Folder text boxes, enter the file extension and location of the images you want to use.**

If you want to use the `.png` images that are already in the Joomla `images` directory, for example, enter **.png** in the Image Type text box and **/images** in the Image Folder text box. Your settings should look like Figure 8-6.

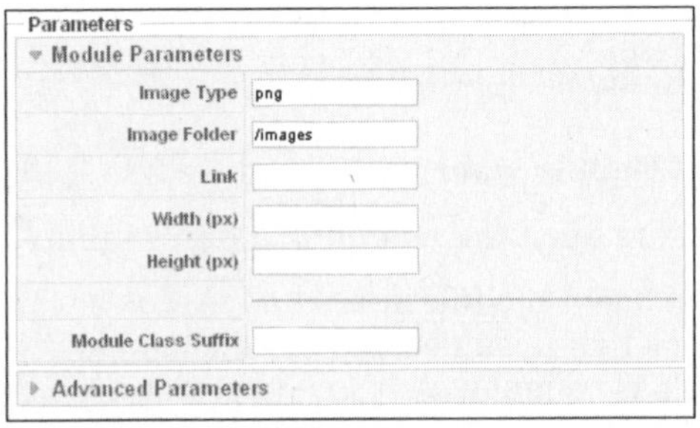

Figure 8-6:
Setting the module's parameters.

6. **Click Apply or Save.**

7. **View your site.**

The module displays a random image from the `images` directory (see Figure 8-7).

Figure 8-7:
The Random Image module at work.

Random Image

Be sure to change the title of this module from Random Image to something more appropriate to the images you're displaying.

The Related Items Module: Unlocking the Keywords

Another nifty module is Related Items, which displays articles related to the current one. How does this module know what articles are related to the current article? It uses the keywords you entered in the metadata settings for each article.

To set up and use this module, follow these steps:

1. **Choose Content⇨Article Manager to open Article Manager.**

2. **Click the name of an article you want to include in the Related Items module.**

   An article-editor page opens for that article.

3. **In the Metadata Information pane on the right side of the page, enter a keyword in the Keywords text box (see Figure 8-8).**

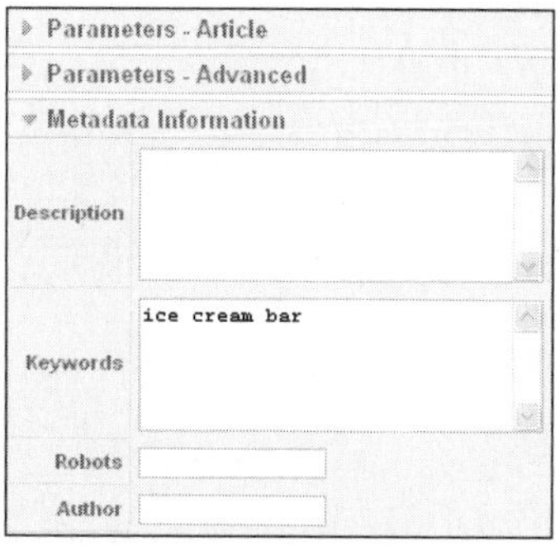

Figure 8-8: Adding metadata keywords.

4. **Repeat Steps 2 and 3 for each article you want to include, using the same keyword each time.**

5. **Choose Extensions⇨Module Manager to open Module Manager.**

6. **Click Related Items to open that module's administration page.**

7. **In the Enabled section of the Details pane, select the Yes radio button.**

8. **In the Menu Assignment pane, select the radio button labeled Select Menu Item(s) from the List; then, in the Menu Selection list, select the pages where you want the Related Items module to appear.**

   At this point, your choices in the Details and Menu Assignment panes should resemble Figure 8-9.

9. **Click Apply or Save.**

10. **View your site.**

    Joomla displays the Related Items module (see Figure 8-10).

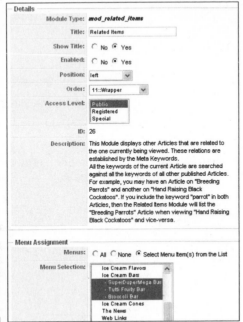

The Search Module: Finding a Needle in a Haystack

One of the big attractions of Joomla is the Search module, which lets users perform a search of all your articles. That's often very hard to implement on a site that you build yourself from the HTML up, but in Joomla, which stores articles in a MySQL database, searching is a snap.

Figure 8-11 shows the Search module: the small text box with the word *search* in it.

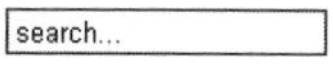

Figure 8-11:
The Search
module.

search...

The Search module isn't the most inviting module, displaying just the terse word *search* — not even capitalized — and not showing a cheery button marked Go! or Find It! But the module does its job, as you see in the example results page shown in Figure 8-12. You enter your search term and press the Enter or Return key on your keyboard to search for that term.

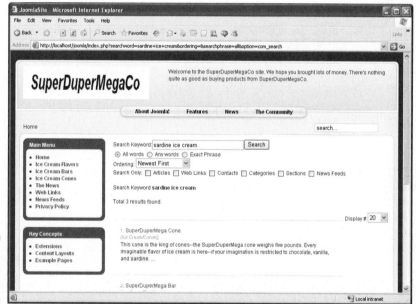

Figure 8-12:
Search
results.

Using the search controls

Joomla offers a full set of search controls in its results page (refer to Figure 8-12), including a Search Keyword text box and a Search button. When users enter a phrase to search for, they can set one of these search options: All Words, Any Words, or Exact Phrase.

Users can also set the order in which the search results are displayed by making a choice from the Ordering drop-down menu: Newest First, Oldest First, Most Popular, Alphabetical, or Section/Category.

Finally, users can restrict the scope of the search to Articles, Web Links, Contacts, Categories, Sections, or News Feeds.

Making search more user-friendly

You can do quite a bit to make the Search module more friendly in Joomla. To do so, follow these steps:

1. **Choose Extensions⇨Module Manager to open Module Manager.**

2. **Click Search to open that module's administration page.**

3. **If you don't want the Search module to appear on all pages (the default setting), change the settings in the Menu Assignment pane.**

4. **Adjust the appearance of the search box by changing the settings in the Module Parameters pane (see Figure 8-13).**

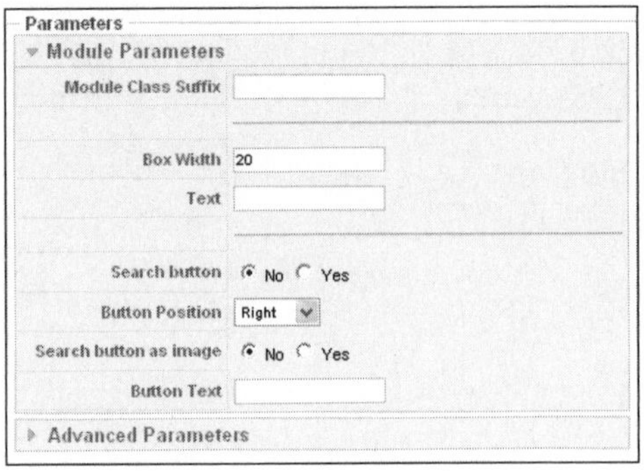

Figure 8-13: Setting search-box parameters.

Here are the parameters you can set to customize the Search module:

• **Box Width:** Width (in characters) of the search text box

• **Text:** The default text that appears in the search text box

• **Search Button:** Whether a search button appears next to the search text box (the default is No)

• **Button Position:** The position of the search button relative to the search text box (Right, Left, Top, or Bottom)

• **Search Button As Image:** Whether to use an image as the search button

• **Button Text:** The search button's caption

> We recommend adding a search button to your Joomla site. Many users don't know that they should press Enter or Return after entering their search term and expect to click a search button.

5. **Click Save or Apply to save your settings.**

The Sections Module: Great for Overviews

Joomla uses categories and sections to help you organize larger sites. "Divide and conquer" is the operative phrase here. When a site gets very large, with a dozen or so active sections, a Main menu showing links to all the articles on the site can become unwieldy, so Joomla introduced the Sections module.

The module displays a bulleted list of the sections on your site; users can click a link to go to the appropriate section page. That's great for maintaining site overview on complex sites.

The Sections module doesn't offer many options to set because it's a very simple module. By default, it isn't enabled and is set to appear on no pages — sort of a double whammy against it.

To see the Sections module at work, check the bottom-left corner of the front page of your Joomla site (see Figure 8-14).

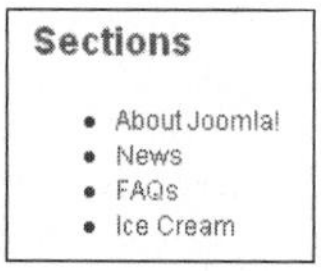

Figure 8-14:
The
Sections
module
at work.

Sections
- About Joomla!
- News
- FAQs
- Ice Cream

The Statistics Module: Stand Up and Be Counted

Want to display what operating system your Joomla site is hosted on? It's hard to know why you'd want to do that, but you can with the Statistics module.

The module also shows useful information such as the total number of registered users your site has (something to boast about) and the total number of hits the site has received.

By default, the Statistics module is disabled and doesn't appear in any menus, but you can set the appropriate options in its administration page (refer to the procedures for other modules earlier in this chapter).

You can also configure what information the Statistics module shows. To see all that the module is capable of doing, select all these radio buttons in the Module Parameters pane of the administration page:

✔ Server Info

✔ Site Info

✔ Hit Counter

Figure 8-15 shows an expanded Statistics module in action.

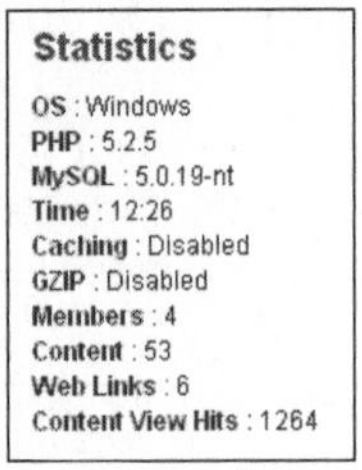

Figure 8-15:
The Statistics module at work.

Statistics

OS : Windows
PHP : 5.2.5
MySQL : 5.0.19-nt
Time : 12:26
Caching : Disabled
GZIP : Disabled
Members : 4
Content : 53
Web Links : 6
Content View Hits : 1264

It's hard to see how operating-system information would be of use to general users, but the number of members, the number of articles (Content), and the total number of hits can be interesting, especially if you have some good numbers to display here.

The module's administration page features a sneaky option: the Increase Counter text box, located in the Module Parameters pane. You can increase the number of hits by the number you enter in that text box, giving your site the appearance of being more popular than it really is — not the most honest of options but an option just the same.

The Syndication Module: Creating RSS Feeds

Want to let users read RSS feeds from your site? You can do that with the Syndication module. Enabling and displaying that module puts an RSS button on the pages in which you've enabled the module (see Figure 8-16).

That button actually is a link to a file named `index.rss` that you can pass to RSS readers, and this file contains an RSS feed for the page. Here's an example from our front page:

```xml
<?xml version="1.0" encoding="utf-8"?>
<!-- generator="Joomla! 1.5 - Open Source Content Management" -->
<rss version="2.0">
    <channel>
        <title>This is my site</title>
        <description>Joomla! - the dynamic portal engine and content management
            system</description>
        <link>http://localhost/joomla/index.php?option=com_
            content&amp;view=frontpage</link>
        <lastBuildDate>Thu, 11 Sep 2008 17:12:44 -0400</lastBuildDate>
        <generator>Joomla! 1.5 - Open Source Content Management</generator>
        <language>en-gb</language>
        <item>
            <title>Welcome to my site</title>          <link>http://localhost/
                joomla/index.php?option=com_content&amp;view=article&amp;id=45:wel
                come-to-my-site</link>
            <description><![CDATA[<strong>Welcome to my site.</strong> Do you
                like it? This site uses Joomla! 1.5 for content management.
                Joomla! handles the details of the presentation and lets you focus
                on writing the content of the site. No complicated knowledge of
                HTML or style sheets is necessary. <em>Pretty nice site, huh? </
                em>]]></description>
            <category>frontpage</category>
            <pubDate>Thu, 21 Aug 2008 21:57:43 -0400</pubDate>
        </item>
```

RSS button

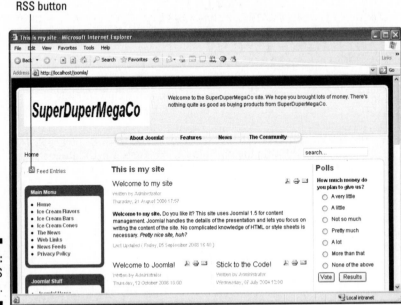

Figure 8-16:
An RSS
button.

The Who's Online Module: Anyone There?

The Who's Online module is a simple one that's enabled by default. It indicates how many guest users and registered users (that is, logged-in users) are on your site at any time.

Figure 8-17 shows the Who's Online module at work.

Figure 8-17:
The Who's
Online
module.

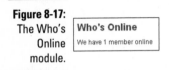

Who's Online

We have 1 member online

You can configure the module to show the names of the current members logged on, if you want. Just select one of these options in the Module Parameters pane of the module's administration page:

- ✔ # of Guests / Members
- ✔ Member Names
- ✔ Both

Figure 8-18 shows the Who's Online module configured to display the names of logged-in users.

Figure 8-18:
The Who's Online module showing logged-in users.

Who's Online

- author

The Wrapper Module: Displaying Other Sites

Here's a cool one: The Wrapper module lets you display external sites in *wrappers* (square frames) on your Joomla site. This feature can be great if you have an allied site that you want people to know about or if you want to show your site visitors the latest news.

You enable the Wrapper module by selecting the Yes radio button in the Enabled section of the module's administration page. In the Module Parameters pane, you also supply the URL of the site you want to wrap by typing it in the URL text box (see Figure 8-19).

That creates a new wrapper for the Joomla site, which you can see in Figure 8-20.

The Wrapper module works by using an HTML IFrame element to wrap and display the external site.

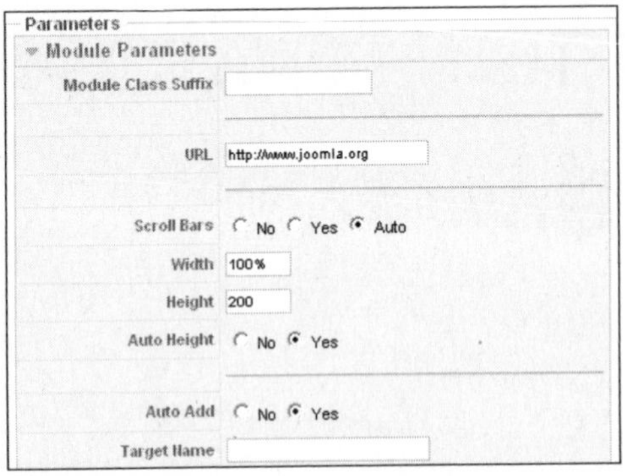

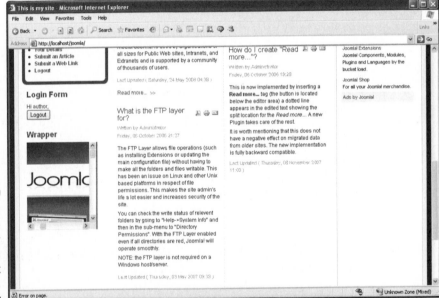

Figure 8-19: Setting wrapper parameters.

Figure 8-20: The Wrapper module on a Joomla front page.

Chapter 9

Laying Out Your Web Pages
with Joomla Templates

In This Chapter

▶ Understanding templates

▶ Using Template Manager

▶ Setting a new default template

▶ Customizing the built-in templates

▶ Getting new Joomla templates

*T*his chapter is all about the layout of your Web site. You can set the layout with menu items, of course, but even more essential are *templates:* those collections of PHP and CSS (Cascading Style Sheets) files that determine the real layout of your Web pages in Joomla.

Templates determine what goes where in Joomla, so they're exceptionally important. Although Joomla itself comes with only a few built-in templates, you can download your own, as you see in this chapter.

Formatting Joomla Sites with Templates

Joomla has built-in HTML editors that allow you to format articles the way you want them, but it has no officially sanctioned editor that allows you to create your own templates. The way your individual pages are laid out — their very look and feel — is totally dependent on the template you use.

What's more, Joomla doesn't have a built-in template editor that allows you to drag components and modules where you want them in a page and design their appearance. As we show you in this chapter, you can edit some template parameters in Template Manager, but you can't make fundamental changes unless you get into the PHP and the CSS files.

Various third-party template editors are available for Joomla, and they're a good start. But we've found the ones we've worked to be unsatisfactory in one way or another, so we can't recommend any of them. If you're interested, do a Google search for *Joomla template editor* or *Joomla template designer*.

It's a pity that Joomla provides such limited template-editing capabilities, but in this chapter, we show you how to get around that limitation by download-ing and installing new templates. You can find hundreds of Joomla templates on the Internet, and installing them is a breeze.

Template Central: Template Manager

In Joomla, you manage templates with — surprise! — Template Manager. To open Template Manager (see Figure 9-1), choose Extensions⇨ Template Manager in any back-end page.

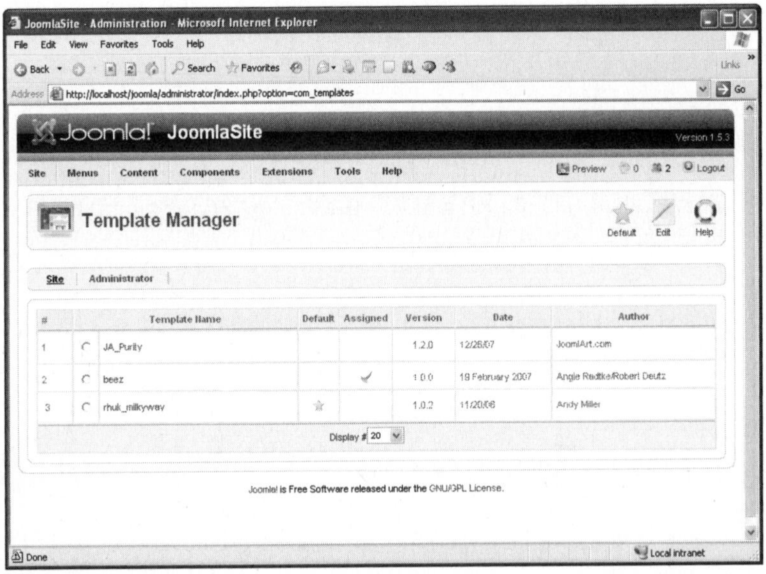

Figure 9-1:
The Joomla Template Manager.

Template Manager gives you as much control of templates as you can get unless you want to get your hands dirty with HTML and CSS.

The three template files shown in Figure 9-1 — JA_Purity, beez, and rhuk_ milkyway — are *site templates,* which is to say front-end templates. (Note that the Site tab is selected in the figure.) Administrator templates are available too, as you see when you click the Administrator tab (shown in Figure 9-2). The default *administrator template* — that is, back-end template — is named Khepri, and if you've taken a look at the Joomla back end, you're already familiar with Khepri.

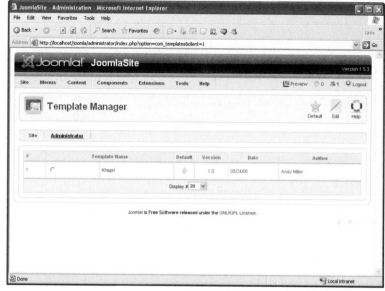

Figure 9-2:
Joomla's
default
administra-
tor template,
Khepri.

Why does Joomla have two sets of templates: site and administrator? The reason is that this arrangement is meant to save you from the problems a dysfunctional template can cause if you install it. If you install a template that has serious problems (and a few like that are out there), your site may be unreadable. How could you change back to the previous template?

That's why the site and administrator templates are different. Even if you mess up your site with an unworkable template, the back end will still be fine, with the Khepri template still purring along. You can use Template Manager to change the site template back to one that works.

Now that you know about this safety net, we show you how to change the default site template.

Changing the Default Template

The default site template in Joomla is Milky Way (`rhuk_milkyway`), which you'll also see spelled *MilkyWay* and *Milkyway*. You can tell that it's the default when you view Template Manager, because a gold star appears in that template's Default column.

To make the Beez template the default instead, select the radio button in the `beez` row in Template Manager and then click the Default button. Template Manager now shows Beez as the default site template (see Figure 9-3).

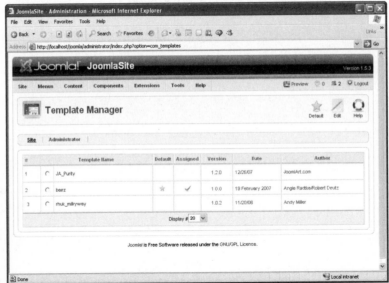

Figure 9-3:
Making
Beez the
default site
template.

To switch back to the Milky Way template, select the radio button in the `rhuk_milkyway` row in Template Manager; then click the Default button.

Editing a Built-In Template

If you're restricted in terms of the number of templates that come with Joomla, can you at least customize the built-in templates? You can, and we show you how in the following sections.

Customizing a template is not something to be undertaken lightly; it demands knowledge of CSS and sometimes of PHP. You can really mess up your site's templates if you don't know what you're doing!

Customizing a template

You can customize a built-in Joomla template, at least to a limited extent. To do so, click the template's filename in Template Manager to open its Edit Template page (see Figure 9-4).

Figure 9-4:
The Edit Template page for `rhuk_milkyway`.

Changing colors, backgrounds, and widths

The Edit Template page allows you to edit some settings, but your options are pretty limited. You can set the main color of elements such as menu borders, for example, with the Color Variation drop-down menu, which contains these options:

- ✔ Blue
- ✔ Red
- ✔ Green

- ✔ Orange
- ✔ Black
- ✔ White

You can also set background colors with the Background Variation drop-down menu. Here are the possibilities:

- ✔ Blue
- ✔ Red
- ✔ Green
- ✔ Orange
- ✔ Black
- ✔ White

Finally, you can set the Template Width drop-down menu to one of these options:

- ✔ Fluid with Maximum (*fluid* means that it resizes with window width)
- ✔ Medium
- ✔ Small
- ✔ Fluid

Assigning templates by page

The Menu Assignment setting is a great feature that lets you assign templates on a page-by-page basis. If you install the Beez template for only one article, for example, while using the Milky Way template on the rest of the site, the result is a page like Figure 9-5. Just select the menu items whose pages you want the template to be used for.

Using different templates on your site can be a good idea if your site is broken up into sections on discrete topics — sports and fashion, for example.

Although the ability to use different templates for different pages is a very powerful feature, you should use it with care to keep your site from looking chaotic.

Editing a template's code

If you want to make more significant changes to a template, you have to change its underlying code.

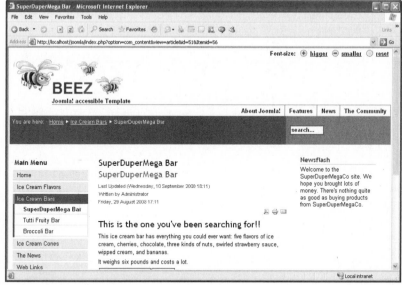

Figure 9-5:
The Beez
template
used for
only one
article.

You can get into a template's actual HTML and CSS code via its Edit Template page (refer to Figure 9-4), which contains Edit HTML and Edit CSS buttons. Click the appropriate button to view the template's HTML or CSS code.

When you customize a template in Joomla, you typically make changes to its CSS code. For that reason, we discuss the CSS file in this section.

Viewing the CSS file

To open a template's CSS file for editing, follow these steps:

1. **In the template's Edit Template page, click the Edit CSS button.**

   The Template CSS Editor page opens (see Figure 9-6). This page lists the CSS files associated with the template — usually, a lot of them.

2. **In the Writable/Unwritable column, check the status of the template you want to edit.**

   Make sure that the template's Writable/Unwritable status is Writable. If it's not, you probably need to change the associated file's protection setting on your Web server before working with that file. (If you don't know what that means, ask your service provider's tech staff for help.)

3. **Select the radio button for the template you want to edit, and click the Edit button.**

   The template's CSS file (`template.css`) opens for editing in Template Manager (see Figure 9-7).

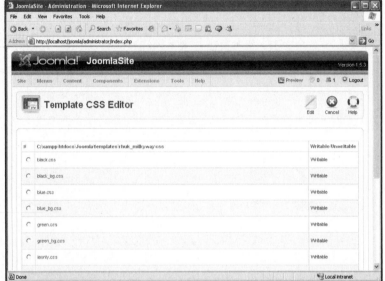

Figure 9-6:
The
Template
CSS Editor
page.

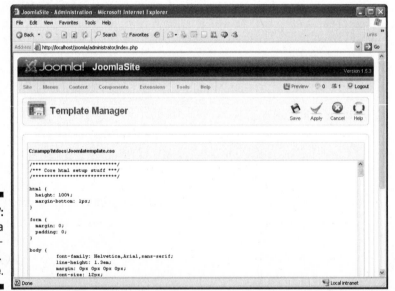

Figure 9-7:
Viewing a
tem-
plate.
css file.

The `template.css` file is a long one — about 16 pages — and that's just one of the files that goes into a Joomla template. It's a bona-fide CSS file, and here's how it starts:

```
/****************************/
/*** Core html setup stuff ***/
/****************************/

html {
   height: 100%;
   margin-bottom: 1px;
}

form {
   margin: 0;
   padding: 0;
}

body {
           font-family: Helvetica,Arial,sans-serif;
           line-height: 1.3em;
           margin: 0px 0px 0px 0px;
           font-size: 12px;
           color: #333;
}

a:link, a:visited {
           text-decoration: none;
           font-weight: normal;
}

a:hover {
           text-decoration: underline;
           font-weight: normal;
}

input.button { cursor: pointer; }

p { margin-top: 0; margin-bottom: 5px; }

img { border: 0 none; }

/*****************************************/
/*** Template specific layout elements ***/
/*****************************************/
#page_bg {
           padding: 10px 0;
           margin-bottom: 1px;
}

div.center {
   text-align: center;
}
```

(continued)

```
div#wrapper {
        margin-left: auto;
        margin-right: auto;
}

body.width_medium div#wrapper {
        width: 950px;
}
        .
        .
        .
```

Unfortunately, to edit this file you really have to know what you're doing — not only in CSS, but also in PHP and HTML — to make your own changes. (A good WYSIWYG code editor built into Joomla would be great for this situation.)

Editing code to this extent is beyond the scope of this book, but see two other titles for help: *HTML, XHTML & CSS For Dummies,* 6th Edition, by Ed Tittel and Jeff Noble, or *PHP & MySQL For Dummies,* 3rd Edition, by Janet Valade (both from Wiley Publishing).

Editing the CSS file

In Chapter 3, we show you how to edit `template.css` to change the logo that you can see at the top of all pages. To do that, you change the `div#logo` item like this:

```
div#logo {
        position: absolute;
        left: 0;
        top: 0;
        float: left;
        width: 298px;
        height: 75px;
        background: url(../images/superdupermegaco.PNG)
        0 0 no-repeat;
        margin-left: 30px;
        margin-top: 25px;
}
```

Templates generate their HTML using a PHP file. and the main PHP file is named `index.php`. Here's the section of that file from the Milky Way template that generates the `<body>` element:

```
<body...>
<a name="up" id="up"></a>
<div class="center" align="center">
```

```
<div id="wrapper">
  <div id="wrapper_r">
    <div id="header">
      <div id="header_l">
        <div id="header_r">
          <div id="logo"></div>
          <jdoc:include type="modules" name="top" />
        </div>
      </div>
    </div>.
          .
          .
          .
    <div id="pathway">
      <jdoc:include type="modules" name="breadcrumb" />
    </div>

    <div class="clr"></div>

    <div id="whitebox">
      <div id="whitebox_t">
        <div id="whitebox_tl">
          <div id="whitebox_tr"></div>
        </div>
      </div>

      <div id="whitebox_m">
        <div id="area">
              <jdoc:include type="message" />

          <div id="leftcolumn">
          <?php if($this->countModules('left')) : ?>
            <jdoc:include type="modules" name="left"
              style="rounded" />
          <?php endif; ?>
          </div>

          <?php if($this->countModules('left')) : ?>
          <div id="maincolumn">
          <?php else: ?>
          <div id="maincolumn_full">
          <?php endif; ?>
            <?php if($this->countModules('user1 or
user2'))
                : ?>
              <table class="nopad user1user2">
                <tr valign="top">
                  <?php if($this->countModules('user1')) :
                    ?>
                    <td>
```

(continued)

```
                         <jdoc:include type="modules"
                            name="user1" style="xhtml" />
                       </td>
                     <?php endif; ?>
                   . <?php if($this->countModules('user1 and
                       user2')) : ?>
                       <td class="greyline"> </td>
                     <?php endif; ?>
                     <?php if($this->countModules('user2')) :
                        ?>
                       <td>
                         <jdoc:include type="modules"
                             name="user2" style="xhtml" />
                       </td>
                     <?php endif; ?>
                   </tr>
                 </table>

                 <div id="maindivider"></div>
               <?php endif; ?>

               <table class="nopad">
                 <tr valign="top">
                   <td>
                     <jdoc:include type="component" />
                     <jdoc:include type="modules"
                      name="footer" style="xhtml"/>
                   </td>
                   <?php if($this->countModules('right') and
                     JRequest::getCmd('layout') != 'form') :
?>
                     <td class="greyline"> </td>
                     <td width="170">
                       <jdoc:include type="modules"
                         name="right" style="xhtml"/>
                     </td>
                   <?php endif; ?>
                 </tr>
               </table>

             </div>
             <div class="clr"></div>
           </div>
           <div class="clr"></div>
         </div>
         .
         .
         .
</body>
```

Note how this works. To include a component (that is, to display article content), you use a `<jdoc:include>` element with the `type` attribute set to `"component"`:

```
<jdoc:include type="component" />
```

To include a module, you use a `<jdoc:include>` element with the `type` attribute set to `"modules"`. Here's how the code includes the footer module:

```
<jdoc:include type="modules" name="footer" style="xhtml"/>
```

If you look at the above code for the `<body>` element, you'll see that the Milky Way template creates Web pages by inserting components and modules into an HTML table, which gives structure to the page and arranges those components and modules on the page.

There's a lot of debate about whether it's better to use HTML tables or CSS to arrange components and modules in Joomla templates; both sides of the argument have strong points. HTML tables, for example, are pretty rigid structures that make it hard for search engines to understand the content of your page. CSS implentations, on the other hand, vary widely from browser to browser, and some older browsers allow you to use only minimal CSS. The Beez template in Joomla is an example of a tableless CSS template.

As you can see, truly customizing a Joomla template is not something to be undertaken lightly. So how do you get the template you want? You can download it.

Working with New Joomla Templates

Want to use a template that's out of the ordinary — one that offers you more color and pizzazz than the built-in templates? You can get fancy templates by the hundreds on the Internet and install them in Joomla, because Joomla is built to be extended.

One of the greatest features of Joomla is extensibility. You can extend the software by installing new plug-ins (tools like CSS editors), components, modules, and templates. Hundreds of such items are available to download from the Internet — some free, some not. The offerings vary widely, from new editors to whole shopping-cart systems to template designers (usually not very good yet) to fancy templates.

In this section, we show you how to find, download, and install new Joomla templates.

Templates you find on the Internet aren't always marked for the version of Joomla they're designed for, so make sure that you install only templates designed for your version. If you try to install a template designed for Joomla 1.5 in Joomla 1.0, for example, Joomla displays a message asking you to install the Legacy plug-in, which helps modules and templates make the transition from 1.0 to 1.5. It's better just to find another template, though.

A word about security: When you download and install new templates, components, modules, or plug-ins, you're asking Joomla to run unknown PHP code on your computer or your host's server. This situation can be a significant security risk. Before you download and install something, make sure that you feel comfortable about it. If you wouldn't feel OK about running an executable program from a given source, think twice.

Finding and downloading a new template

To find templates to install, just search the Internet. At this writing, a Google search for *Joomla templates* turns up a mere 13.9 million matches, whereas a search for *free Joomla templates* yields 823,000 matches, including such sites as Lonex (www.lonex.com), Joomlashack (www.joomlashack.com), and Joomla24 (www.joomla24.com).

For this exercise, you download a free template from Lonex. Follow these steps:

1. **Point your Web browser to** www.lonex.com/content-management-system/joomla/templates.

2. **Scroll down the page to find the template you want.**

   For this exercise, select the Graffiti template (for Joomla 1.5).

3. **Click the Free for Download link.**

   The Graffiti.zip file downloads to your computer.

Most of the items you can install in Joomla come in compressed files, such as .zip files. Usually, all you have to do is to tell Joomla what to install, and it uncompresses and installs the item for you.

Installing a new template

To install your new template, follow these steps:

1. **Log in to Joomla, and choose Extensions⇨Install/Uninstall.**

   You use this command to install or uninstall any extension, including plug-ins, modules, components, and templates.

   Extension Manager opens (see Figure 9-8).

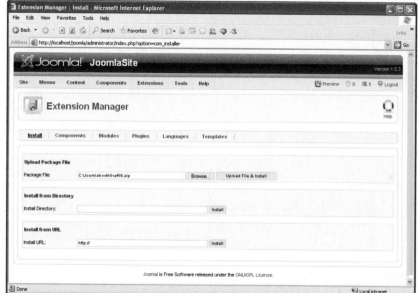

Figure 9-8: Extension Manager.

2. **In the Upload Package file section, click the Browse button to find and select the new template file on your hard drive.**

   For this exercise, select `Graffiti.zip`.

3. **Click the Upload File & Install button.**

   If the installation process (which involves making a new subdirectory named `Graffiti` in the Joomla `templates` directory) went smoothly, you should see a confirmation page.

You can make the new template the default template, if you want, by selecting the Graffiti template's radio button in Template Manager and then clicking the Default button (refer to "Changing the Default Template," earlier in this chapter).

To view the new template (see Figure 9-9), click the Preview link in the top-right corner of any back-end page. Pretty snazzy, eh?

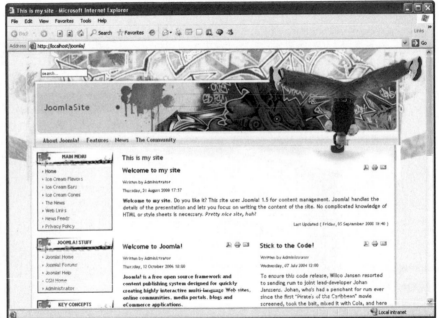

Figure 9-9:
You've
installed
a new
template.

Part IV
Joomla in the Real World

The 5th Wave   By Rich Tennant

"We have no problem funding your Web site, Frank. Of all the chicken farmers operating Web sites, yours has the most impressive cluck-through rates."

In this part . . .

This part takes a look at real-world issues for Joomla sites, starting with managing eight levels of users. With the exception of casual surfers, you create accounts for all these users or allow them to create accounts for themselves. In this part, we show you how to manage your site's users.

We also show you how to drive users to your site through search engine optimization. Finally, we show you how to extend Joomla by downloading and installing new modules, components, and plug-ins.

Chapter 10

Managing Your Web Site's Users

. . . .

In This Chapter

▶ Understanding Joomla's eight user levels

▶ Adding new users to your site

▶ Editing user accounts

▶ Creating a contact page

▶ Managing e-mail on your site

▶ Giving users options that they can manage themselves

. . . .

*T*his chapter is all about giving the users of your site user privileges: author, administrator, registered user, and so on. A Joomla site has eight levels of users; in this chapter, you see all of them and what they can do.

Rest assured that you're still the super administrator — and the super admin can do anything it's possible to do on a Joomla site.

Introducing the Wonderful World of Joomla Users

Joomla sites can have eight levels of users, starting with the front-end users:

   ✔ **Public users** are casual surfers of your site.

   ✔ **Registered users** can log in to see resources that are reserved for them.

The next three levels of front-end users fall into the Special user class, along with all the back-end users:

   ✔ **Authors** can submit articles.

   ✔ **Editors** can submit new articles and edit existing articles.

   ✔ **Publishers** can submit new articles, edit existing articles, and publish articles.

Finally, the back end has three levels of users:

- ✔ **Managers** can manage everything having to do with site content.
- ✔ **Administrators** can perform administrative functions.
- ✔ **Super administrators** can do anything that's possible to do on a Joomla site.

How do you handle these various types of users and give them their privileges in the first place? You use the Joomla User Manager.

Managing Users with User Manager

So how do you manage users? This being Joomla, of course you use a feature called User Manager (see Figure 10-1). To open it, click its icon in the control panel or choose Site⇨User Manager in any back-end page. You can see the User Manager in Figure 10-1.

User Manager is great for adding new users to your team or editing the records of existing users, such as when they change their e-mail addresses. To edit an existing user, check the check box in his row of User Manager and then click the Edit button to open the Edit User page.

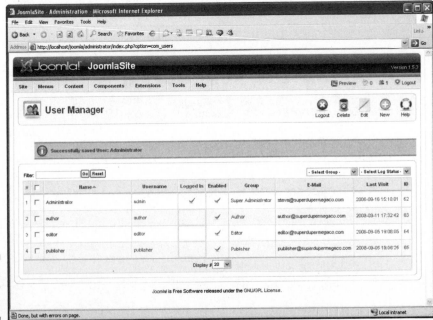

Figure 10-1:
User
Manager.

You can configure several settings in the Edit User page (see Figure 10-2), such as entering a new e-mail address or password, or changing the user's privilege level by resetting the user group (author, publisher, administrator, and so on) to which he belongs. You can also disable the account by selecting the Yes radio button in the Block User section.

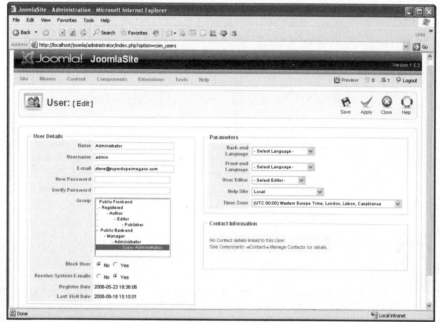

Figure 10-2: Editing a user's records.

If you haven't added any users to the default Joomla installation, only you appear in this page, listed as a super administrator. (Your name is Administrator, even though you're not just an administrator; you're a super administrator.) But your site would be awfully lonely if you were the only user. In the following sections, we show you how to add new users, starting with the most basic type: registered users.

Creating registered users

The most basic users — beyond mere Web surfers who happen by your site — are registered users. They can log in to your site (using the login box that appears on the front page by default) and see resources reserved for registered users.

Joomla provides two ways to create a registered user:

- ✔ The administrator creates the user's account in User Manager.
- ✔ The user herself can click the Create an Account link in the login module on the front page and then fill out a registration page.

We describe both methods in the following sections.

User-created accounts

When a new user registers by creating her own account, however, she can't log in until the account is activated. Joomla sends the new user an e-mail, and she clicks an activation link in the e-mail to register and activate the new account. After the account is activated, the new user can log in to the site.

Joomla activates the account this way because it verifies both the user and her e-mail address, and it allows the user to select her own password. This setup also allows you, as site administrator, to manage new users better. A nonactivated account appears as a blocked account in User Manager, and when you check the record, it will indicate that the user has never signed in. Such an account is easy to delete if necessary.

You don't have to require new users to click a link in an e-mail message to active their accounts, however. Choose Site⇨Global Configuration to open the Global Configuration page; then look at the User New Account Activation option. When you disable user activation, new users will be able to log in immediately after registering. This page also contains an option labeled Require Unique Email, which ensures that the same e-mail account can't be used to create more than one account.

The default user group for newly registered users is Registered, but you can make it Author, Editor, or Publisher by default. To do that, choose Site⇨ Global Configuration to open the Global Configuration page, and select the default user group for newly registered users in the New User Registration Type list.

Administrator-created accounts

Besides allowing users to create their own accounts, you can create accounts for them with User Manager. Follow these steps:

1. **Click the New button in User Manager.**

   The New User page opens.

2. **Enter the account information for the new user.**

   The Public Front-End and Public Back-End items you see in the Groups list box aren't actually groups; they're just placeholders for features that are expected to appear in future versions of Joomla.

   Your settings may resemble Figure 10-3.

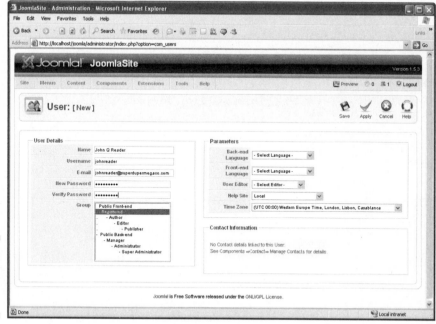

Figure 10-3:
Creating a
new regis-
tered user.

3. **Click the Save button.**

Joomla creates the new account and takes you back to User Manager, where the new registered user appears. The user can log in immediately and view resources that you've marked as needing registered privileges.

Registered users are the lowest level of users that your site keeps track of. We discuss the next level — special users — in the following sections.

Creating authors

Authors can write articles and submit them on your site. To add a new author, click the New button in User Manager to display the New User page; then fill in the user's account information, making sure to add the user to the Author group. When you finish, click the Save button. Your settings may resemble Figure 10-4.

Creating editors

Like authors, editors belong to the Special users group; also like authors, they can submit articles. But they can edit articles, too, and their edits appear on the site as soon as they make them.

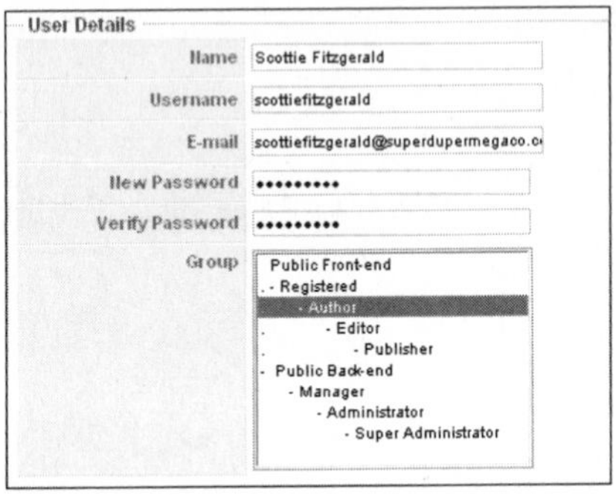

Figure 10-4:
Creating
an author
account.

To add a new editor to your site, enter the appropriate information in the New User page, making sure to add the new user to the Editor group. Your settings may look something like those in Figure 10-5.

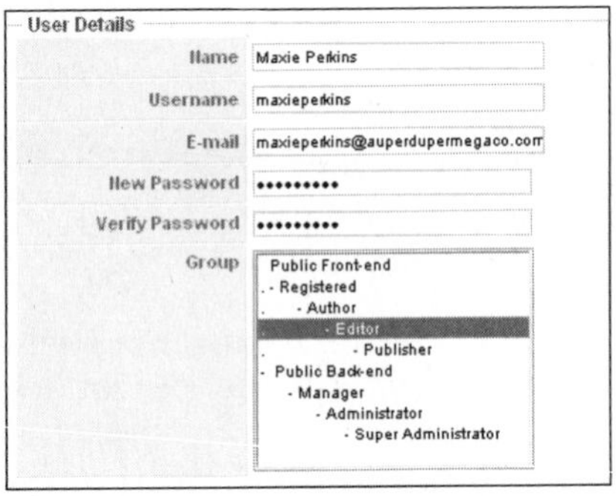

Figure 10-5:
Creating
an editor
account.

Creating publishers

Publishers are the most powerful of the front-end users. Like authors, they can submit articles. Like editors, they can edit articles, and their edits appear online immediately. But they also have the authority to publish articles on your Web site — without back-end approval.

Adding a new publisher is simple enough; just set the appropriate options in the New User page. Your settings may resemble those in Figure 10-6.

Now that you know how to create registered users, authors, editors, and publishers, you're ready to create new back-end users.

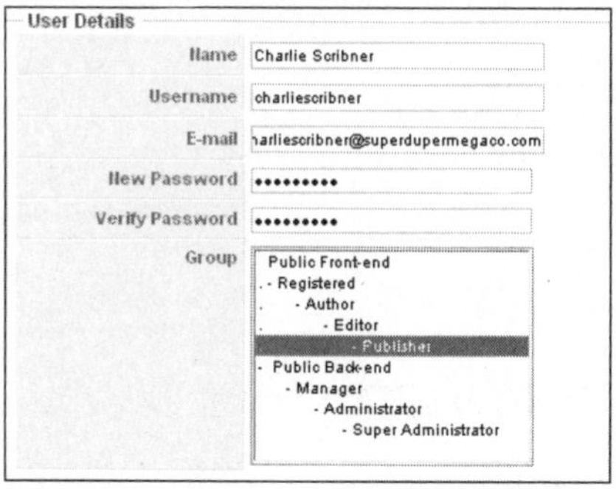

Figure 10-6:
Creating a
publisher
account.

Creating managers

Managers are back-end content managers and can do anything related to the content of your site, such as writing articles, editing them, and publishing them — all from the back end. They can't do the following, however:

✔ Manage users

✔ Install or uninstall modules

✔ Install or uninstall components

✔ Work with some components (as set by the super administrator)

These tasks are reserved for administrators and super administrators.

You create a manager account the same way you create any other user account: in the New User page.

Creating administrators

Administrators are near the top of the Joomla hierarchy. No one is higher than administrators except super administrators.

Administrators can manage other users (except super administrators); they can enable or disable user accounts; they can install or uninstall modules. They can't do the following things, though:

✔ Add to or edit the Super Administrator group

✔ Access the Global Configuration page

✔ Access the Mass Mail function to e-mail multiple users

✔ Manage, install, or uninstall templates

✔ Manage, install, or install language files

Use the New User page to set up an administrator account.

Creating super administrators

Super administrators can do it all: publish and edit articles; set global configurations; install and uninstall modules, components, and templates; disable user accounts; create new accounts — and more. These administrators can do anything that a person can do in Joomla, either from the front end or the back end.

The name *super administrator* fools some people into thinking that you can have only one super administrator per Joomla site, but that's not so. You can have as many super administrators as you like.

You need at least one super administrator for every Joomla site, and when you create a new site, that's you. The default super administrator is given the username admin.

For security reasons, it's a good idea to change the admin username.

Now that you've seen the whole spectrum of Joomla users, from casual Web surfers to super administrators, you're ready to see how to give all these users access to the personnel of a Joomla site.

Building a Contact Page

A contact page is a great addition to any Joomla site. Several big-time corporations' Web sites provide no way to contact anyone, which is very frustrating to users, so think twice before omitting this page.

If you want to list some of your users in a contact page. Joomla can help. In fact, it maintains a Contacts category that makes creating a contact page simple. In the following sections, we show you how to add contacts to your site and then display them in a contact page.

Adding contacts to your site

Joomla maintains — what else? — a Contact Manager to let you add contact information.

To add a contact to your site, follow these steps:

1. **Choose Components➪Contacts➪Contacts in any back-end page.**

   The Contact Manager page opens, listing one default contact (see Figure 10-7).

2. **Click the New button to open the New Contact page.**

   The Information pane has space for a great deal of contact information, including the following:

Contact's Position	Telephone
E-Mail	Mobile Phone Number
Street Address	
Town/Suburb	Fax
State/County	Web URL
Postal Code/ZIP	Miscellaneous Information
Country	

3. **Enter as much contact information as you like in the Information pane.**

4. **In the Details pane, choose Contacts from the Category drop-down menu and the user's name from the Linked to User drop-down menu.**

   Want to create a contact page for someone who's not a user? Just choose No User from the Linked to User drop-down menu.

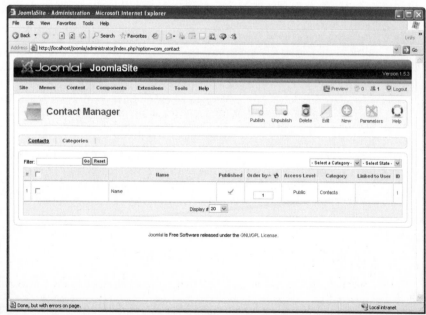

Figure 10-7:
Contact
Manager.

5. **In the Contact Parameters pane, set radio-button options to specify what contact information appears (and doesn't appear) in the user's contact page.**

   Your choices are similar to those in the Information pane.

   At this point, your settings may resemble Figure 10-8.

6. **Click the Save button.**

   You return to Contact Manager, which shows the new contact (see Figure 10-9).

7. **Repeat Steps 2–6 to add as many contacts as you want.**

8. **When you finish adding contacts, delete the default Name entry by selecting that item and clicking the Delete button.**

Creating a contact page

After you add contacts to your site, the next step is creating a contact page and a menu item that links to it.

To create the page and menu item, follow these steps:

1. **Choose Menus⇨Menu Manager menu in any back-end page to open Menu Manager.**

   For more information on using Menu Manager, see Chapter 5.

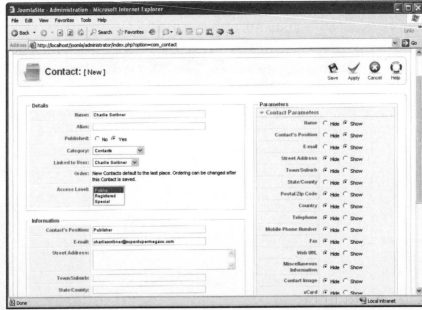

Figure 10-8: Adding a new user to Contact Manager.

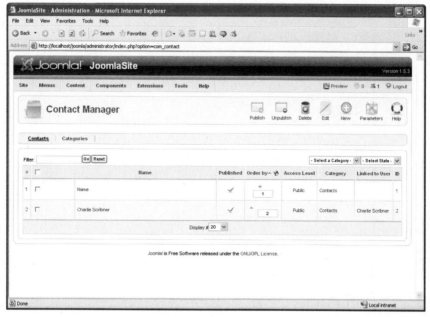

Figure 10-9:
A new user
in Contact
Manager.

2. **In the row of the menu you want to use, click the icon in the Menu Item(s) column to open Menu Item Manager.**

   For this exercise, select Main Menu.

3. **Click the New button to open the New Menu Item page (see Figure 10-10).**

4. **Click Internal Link⇨Category⇨Contact Category Layout to open the Contact Category Layout page.**

   The Contact Category Layout page opens.

5. **In the Title text box, enter the title of the new menu item.**

   For this exercise, type **Contact Us**.

6. **In the Parameters - Basic pane, choose Contacts from the Select Category drop-down menu.**

7. **Click the Save button.**

   You return to Menu Item Manager.

8. **Click the Preview link in the top-right corner.**

   Joomla displays the new menu item on your site.

9. **Click the new menu item to open the contact page (see Figure 10-11).**

Figure 10-10:
The New
Menu Item
page.

Figure 10-11:
A new con-
tact page.

Now, if a user wants to send a message to a particular contact, the user can just click that contact's name to display an e-mail form.

Managing Site E-Mail

What if you want to get in touch with not just one user on your site, but a whole group of users? You can send e-mail en masse with the Mass Mail function. To set up that function, choose Tools⇨Mass Mail in any back-end page to open the Mass Mail page; then set the various options you want to use and enter your message (see Figure 10-12).

You can select the recipient user group(s) in the Group list, or you can select All User Groups to e-mail all the users on your site.

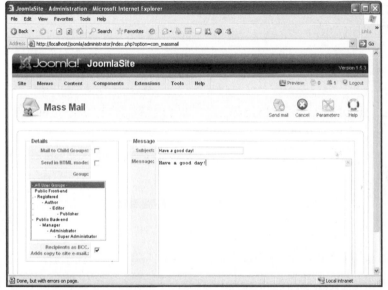

Figure 10-12: Creating a message in the Mass Mail page.

Sending and receiving private messages

You can create and read private messages in Joomla, but for some reason, private messages are available only to members of the Super Administrator group. If you're a super administrator, you can create a new private message to another super administrator by choosing Tools⇨Write Message in any back-end page.

Super administrators see a message icon in the top-right corner of back-end pages (right next

to the logged-in-users icon), and the number of waiting private message is displayed next to that icon. To read your private messages, choose Tools⇨Read Messages in any back-end page.

Joomla itself can also send you private messages — when an article has been submitted by a front-end user and is awaiting approval, for example.

Allowing Users to Manage Themselves

Although you can manage users from the back end, Joomla provides good facilities that permit users to manage themselves as well. You can create pages where users can register, log in, reset their passwords, be reminded of their passwords, and so on.

Creating user-management pages

To create pages that allow users to manage themselves, you use Menu Manager. (For details on using Menu Manager, see Chapter 5.) When you create a menu item, the New Menu Item page displays a entry named User. If you expand that entry, you see the following options:

- ✔ Login⇨Default Login Layout (allows users to log in)
- ✔ Register⇨Default Registration Layout (allows new users to register)
- ✔ Remind⇨Default Remind (allows users to retrieve forgotten passwords)
- ✔ Reset⇨Default Reset Layout (allows users to reset passwords)
- ✔ User⇨Default User Layout (shows a greeting message when a user logs on)
- ✔ User⇨User Form Layout (allows users to edit their account details, set new passwords, and so on)

Allowing users to edit their accounts

You can permit users to edit their own account details in a User Form Layout page. To create such a page and a menu item that links to it, follow these steps:

1. **Open Menu Manager by clicking its icon in the control panel or choosing Menus⇨Menu Manager in any back-end page.**

2. **In the row of the menu you want to use, click the icon in the Menu Item(s) column to open Menu Item Manager.**

   For this exercise, select Main Menu.

3. **Click the New button to open the New Menu Item page.**

4. **Click Internal Link⇨User⇨User⇨User Form Layout (see Figure 10-13).**

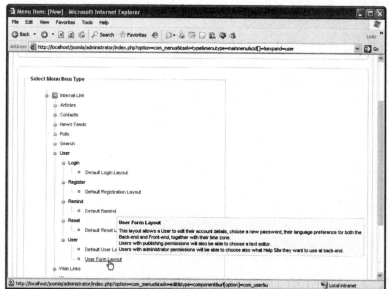

Figure 10-13:
Choosing a
user form
layout.

The User Form Layout page opens.

5. **In the Title text box, enter a title for the menu item.**

For this exercise, type **Edit Your Account**.

6. **Click the Save button.**

You return to Menu Item Manager.

7. **Click the Preview link in the top-right corner.**

Joomla displays the new menu item.

8. **Click the new menu item to open the Edit Your Details page.**

Figure 10-14 shows the page already filled out.

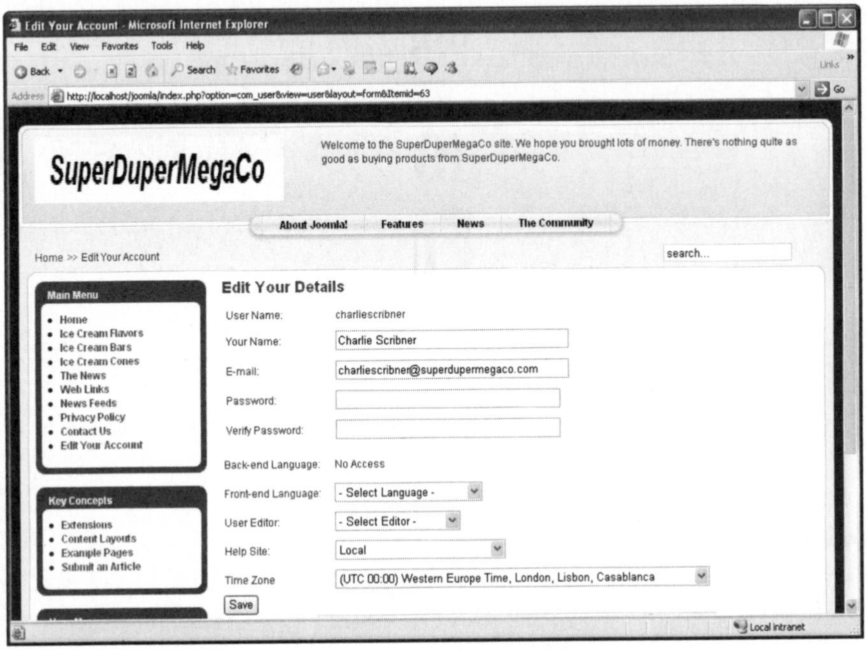

Figure 10-14:
The Edit
Your Details
page.

A user can edit the following items in this page:

User Name	Front-End Language
Your Name	User Editor
E-Mail	Help Site
Password	Time Zone
Verify Password	
Back-End Language (if the user has access to the back end)	

And that's that. Now users can manage much of their own accounts themselves, such as when they move or change their e-mail addresses.

Chapter 11

Driving Traffic to Your Web Site with Search Engine Optimization

You've created your brand-new Joomla site, and you're proud of it. You've got a front page, multiple authors churning out their own articles, menus, modules all over the place, polls, article-rating boxes, search boxes, contact pages, a Who's Online section, even a login form where users can get free access to advanced content.

But you have one problem: Nobody's coming. Your hit counters stay stubbornly at zero.

The reason is that nobody can find your site. You could advertise on Google, but that option is very expensive — so expensive, in fact, that of a dozen people we know who advertised on Google, no one made a profit in the long run.

This chapter is all about *search engine optimization:* making your Joomla site friendly for search engines like Google. By default, Joomla creates sites that are non-search-engine friendly, from using complex URLs (which search engines rank low) for your pages to displaying those pages with templates that rely on HTML tables, making it hard for search engines to follow the content of a page.

This chapter addresses such issues. Here, we show you how to tune your Joomla site to improve its search engine rankings. After all, if you build it and no one can find it, no one will come. We also show you how to submit your site to various search engines.

Understanding Search Engines and Spiders

Search engines like Google and Yahoo! are always looking around the Internet to catalog Web pages and whole sites. The more complete a search engine's database of Web pages is, the better search experience its users have.

The process of automatically searching the Internet is called *spidering*. Search engine spiders "crawl" the Web continuously to get more sites into their database and make them searchable. If your site is on the Internet, chances are that search engine spiders will find it sooner or later.

If you don't like real spiders, take heart: Search engine spiders are also called *robots*.

To optimize your search engine ranking and to make your site appear as early as possible in search results, you want to make your site easy to spider. Unfortunately, Joomla isn't very good at that. To see an example, take a look at Figure 11-1, in which a user is clicking a link titled The News in the default Joomla Main menu.

Figure 11-1: The News menu item.

Now look at this page from a search engine spider's point of view. What's the URL of The News? Why, it's this (fill in your own site's address for www. *yourjoomlasite*.com):

```
www.yourjoomlasite.com/index.php?option=com_content&view=category&layout=blog&id
        =1&Itemid=50
```

That URL is quite a mouthful — and it turns out to be a problem, too. The page is *dynamic* as opposed to static. You can tell because its URL has a question mark (?) in it, indicating that you're passing data to an online script (index.php, in this example). Such data can vary and still display the same page. (You may be passing two numbers to add to an online calculator, for example. Although the numbers to add may change, the page itself stays the same.) Because the contents of dynamic pages change, search engines tend to downgrade their URLs in search results.

In other words, URLs that contain text like index.php?option=com_content&view=category&layout=blog&id=1&Itemid=50 tell search engines that such pages are dynamically created — that is, created on the fly. To avoid pointing to the same page too many times (even though the data you're passing to that page may vary), search engines downgrade dynamic pages.

Ugh. This situation means that the pages Joomla creates by default are downgraded automatically in search engines. Worse, the pages are fetched from Joomla's internal database, so all Joomla pages are created dynamically.

Can you do anything to improve the way search engines treat Joomla pages? Yes. You can instruct Joomla to make its URLs look as though they point to *static* pages — pages whose content doesn't change and whose URLs don't contain question marks or long parameter strings

Making Joomla URLs Search Engine Friendly

Your goal is to make Joomla's dynamic URLs, such as www.yourjoomla site.com/index.php?option=com_content&view=category&layout=blog&id=1&Itemid=50, look like static URLs so that search engines will raise the URLs' rankings — and, therefore, those of the pages they point to.

This issue is such a big one in Joomla that the software allows you to configure it to make static URLs by default instead of dynamic URLs. In Joomla, such URLs are called *search engine friendly* (SEF).

Creating friendly URLs

To turn on SEF URLs, follow these steps:

1. **Log on as a super administrator.**

2. **Choose Site⇨Global Configuration to open the Global Configuration page.**

3. **In the SEO Settings pane, click the Yes radio button in the Search Engine Friendly URLs section (see Figure 11-2).**

Figure 11-2: Turning on SEF URLs.

4. **Click the Apply or Save button.**

5. **View your site in a browser, and click a link.**

   Joomla displays a static URL in the browser's address bar.

If you navigated to the The News page shown in Figure 11-1 earlier in this chapter, this URL would appear in your browser's address bar:

```
www.yourjoomlasite.com/index.php/the-news
```

Wow. That's a far cry from the original:

```
www.yourjoomlasite.com/index.php?option=com_content&view=category&layout=blog&id
     =1&Itemid=50
```

The new static URLs vastly improve your site's search engine rankings.

Simply selecting the Yes radio button in the Global Configuration page doesn't always work on all servers, however. When you tell Joomla to use SEF URLs and then try clicking menu items on your site, you may get 404 errors ("page not found") because the techniques Joomla uses to rename URLs aren't working. In that case, you need to take a few more steps.

Although Joomla-created static URLs are much better than dynamic URLs in search engine terms, they still can be improved. Search engines like to see *keywords* — terms that people can enter in search engines to find your site — listed in the URLs of your various pages. We cover this topic in "Unlocking the Secrets of Keywords," later in this chapter.

Using mod_rewrite to configure URLs

If the SEF URLs setting in Joomla breaks your menu items, creating URLs that can't be found, you still have hope. If you're using the Apache Web server, you can use the `mod_rewrite` module to instruct Joomla to rewrite URLs in SEF versions. (If you have broken URLs and don't use Apache, you might take a look at SEF extensions on the Joomla Extensions Directory site, `http://extensions.joomla.org/`.)

Checking for mod_rewrite

First, find out whether your Apache installation includes `mod_rewrite`. One way is to check with the tech staff of your Internet service provider, but if your ISP's tech staff is anything like ours, they won't have a clue. You can check for the module yourself, however.

To check whether `mod_rewrite` is being loaded, follow these steps:

1. **Create a small test script named `phpinfo.pho` with these contents:**

   ```
   <?php
     phpinfo();
   ?>
   ```

   This script executes the `phpinfo` function, which displays information about your PHP installation.

2. **Upload `phpinfo.php` to your Web server.**

3. **Navigate to the file in your browser.**

   You may have to set the `phpinfo.php` file's protection levels on the host server to executable, just as you would to execute any PHP script. (If you have difficulty with this task, ask your service provider's tech staff.)

4. **Locate the `apache2handler` section in the page that appears (see Figure 11-3).**

   If you don't see `mod_rewrite` in the Loaded Modules section, it isn't being loaded.

To get the `mod_rewrite` module loaded, you can edit the Apache file named `httpd.conf`, which you find in the `apache/conf` directory. In particular, look for the boldface line in the following code:

```
#LoadModule proxy_connect_module modules/mod_proxy_connect.so
#LoadModule proxy_http_module modules/mod_proxy_http.so
#LoadModule proxy_ftp_module modules/mod_proxy_ftp.so
#LoadModule rewrite_module modules/mod_rewrite.so
LoadModule setenvif_module modules/mod_setenvif.so
#LoadModule speling_module modules/mod_speling.so
LoadModule status_module modules/mod_status.so
```

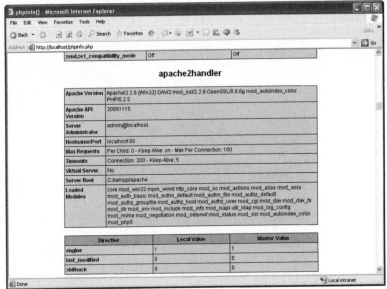

Figure 11-3:
Searching
for mod_
rewrite.

Remove the # at the beginning of this line to uncomment it. Then add this line to httpd.conf:

```
RewriteEngine On
```

Now Apache's mod_rewrite is ready to go.

Configuring Joomla to use mod_rewrite

When mod_rewrite is available, you can configure Joomla to use it by renaming a file in Joomla's root directory. (Remember that you need to do this only if the SEF URL option in the Global Configuration page breaks the URLs on your site.) Follow these steps:

1. **Look in the directory where you installed Joomla for a file named htaccess.txt.**

2. **Rename this file .htaccess.**

3. **Restart Apache.**

   When Apache restarts, your new .htaccess file takes effect.

4. **Choose Site ⇨Global Configuration in any back-end page to open the Global Configuration page.**

5. **In the SEO Settings pane (refer to Figure 11-2, earlier in this chapter), select the Yes radio button in the Use Apache mod_rewrite section.**

   Voilà! SEF URLs should work for you now.

TIP

Getting around a Windows Explorer quirk

If you use Windows, you may have problems changing `htaccess.txt` to `.htaccess` in Windows Explorer, because Windows Explorer won't accept names that aren't in the format *name.ext* (where *name* is the filename and *ext* is the file extension). You can get around this problem in either of two ways:

✔ Choose Start➪Programs➪Accessories➪ Command Prompt to open a command-prompt window, navigate to the Joomla root directory, and execute the command `ren htaccess.txt .htaccess`.

✔ Give the `htaccess.txt` file another name — `ht.acl` is a common substitute — and tell Apache what new filename you're using.

To use the latter method, change `htaccess.txt` to `ht.acl` in Windows Explorer and then locate this line in Apache's `httpd.conf` file:

```
AccessFileName .htaccess
```
Change that line to this:

```
AccessFileName ht.acl
    .htaccess
```
Then save `httpd.conf` and restart Apache.

Working with third-party plug-ins

Although a static URL like `www.yourjoomlasite.com/index.php/the-news` is more search engine friendly than a dynamic URL like `www.yourjoomlasite.com/index.php?option=com_content&view=category&layout=blog&id=1&Itemid=50`, it could be improved.

As we mention earlier in this chapter, search engines like to see a site's URLs contain keywords to help people to find the site. If you have a site about gambling, for example, a URL like `www.yourjoomlasite.com/gambling-news` is better than `www.yourjoomlasite.com/index.php/the-news`.

But Joomla doesn't allow you to write your own URLs, so even if you enable SEF URLs (refer to "Creating friendly URLs," earlier in this chapter), you have no guarantee that people will use the keywords you want them to find your site with — unless you use a third-party plug-in.

You can find SEF plug-ins in the Joomla Extensions Directory (`http://extensions.joomla.org/`). Just search for *SEF.* One popular, highly rated SEF plug-in listed in this directory is sh404SEF (see Figure 11-4).

You install SEF plug-ins as you do any other Joomla extensions. Choose Extensions➪Install/Uninstall in any back-end page; then open the compressed plug-in file that you've downloaded to your computer, or tell Joomla to navigate to the plug-in's URL for it by clicking the Install button.

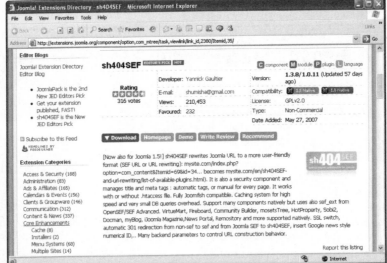

Figure 11-4:
The
sh404SEF
extension
site.

Unlocking the Secrets of Keywords

You help search engine users find your site by telling the search engine spiders what *keywords* to want them to index your site on. Then, when people search for those keywords, the search engine can bring up your page.

Finding keywords to use

How do you determine what keywords to use? All kinds of helpful keyword tools are available online, including these:

✔ Google AdWords (`https://adwords.google.com/select/KeywordToolExternal`)

✔ Wordtracker Keywords (`http://freekeywords.wordtracker.com/`)

✔ SEO Book Keyword Suggestion Tool (`http://tools.seobook.com/keyword-tools/seobook/`)

Just enter a topic, and the keyword tool suggests keywords that you can use to let people search for your topic.

Suppose that you're writing on your Web site about retirement. You could use Google AdWords, for example, to find what keywords Google suggests for the topic and an idea of the search engine traffic you might expect (see Figure 11-5).

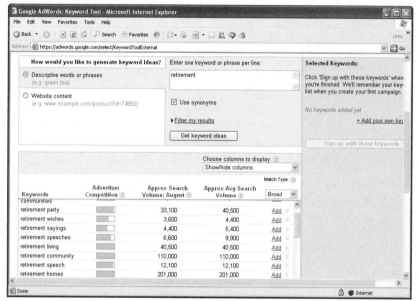

Figure 11-5:
Google's
keywords
tool.

Adding keywords as metadata

After you've settled on your keywords, you can tell Joomla to add them to your pages as metadata. *Metadata* (data about your Web page) is stored on your page in `<meta>` HTML tags, and search engines read those tags. You can place information in the `<meta>` tags that you want search engines to know, such as what keywords you want users to find your page with when they search the Web.

You can use as many keywords on a page as you want, but Google recommends using no more than 20 per page.

To enter keywords for an article, follow these steps:

1. **Click the article in Article Manager to open the article-editor page.**

2. **Click the Metadata Information bar on the right side of the page to open the Metadata Information pane.**

3. **In the Keywords text box, enter the keywords you want to assign to the article, separating them with commas (see Figure 11-6).**

4. **Click the Apply button to save your work, or click the Save button to save your work and close the article-editor page.**

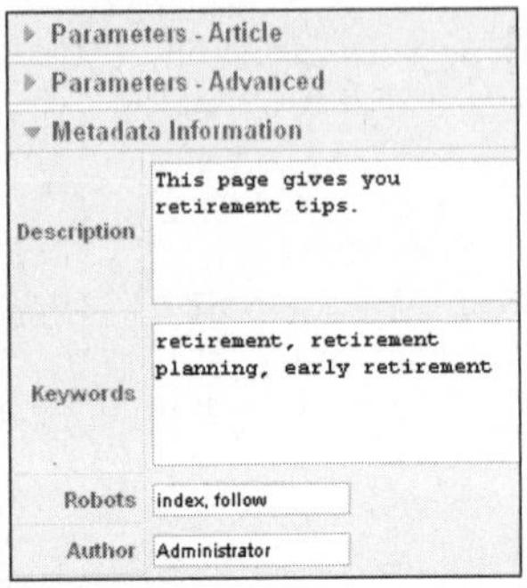

Figure 11-6:
Entering
keywords as
metadata.

Although metadata can be useful, spammers have so abused it that modern search engines sometimes ignore the metadata in a page. That's unfortunate, because it can be difficult to get your keywords into a search engine otherwise; if search engines are discounting that metadata, search engine optimization is tougher for you. We discuss other techniques later in this chapter.

Entering other metadata

Keywords are only one type of metadata you can add to a page. You can also enter the following types of metadata in the Metadata Information pane (refer to Figure 11-6):

- ✔ **Description:** A human-readable description of your page, such as *This page gives you retirement tips.*

- ✔ **Keywords:** A comma-separated list of keywords you want people to use to bring up your page in the search engine, such as *retirement, retirement planning, early retirement.*

- ✔ **Robots:** Instructions to the search engine's spider, or robot, that searches Web pages for metadata. An entry such as *index, follow* (the default setting for all Joomla pages) indicates that the current page should be indexed in the search engine and that the robot should follow any links in the page.

- ✔ **Author:** The name or title of the page's author, such as *Cary Grant.*

Optimizing Pages with Templates

Most Joomla templates are based on HTML tables, which are hard for Web spiders to crawl. CSS-based tableless templates are better, but they still have a problem: The leftmost module (which is the site menu) usually comes first in the Web page's HTML. If a spider has to crawl through the menu first, it may devalue the actual content of the page because that content is so far removed from the start of the page.

To avert that situation, search-engine-friendly Joomla templates are available. These templates float columns to the left and right, depending on the width of the page in a browser, to ensure the correct placement of the Web page's content (as displayed by a Joomla component) and navigation menu (as displayed by a Joomla module). Such templates also have a container element that contains the columns.

Here's what part of such a template might look like in CSS:

```
#container {
    width: 100%;
    display:inline;
}

#column_1 {
    width: 25%;
    display:inline;
    float: left;
}

#column_2 {
    width: 45%;
    display:inline;
    float: right;
}
```

In the template's index.php file, the two columns (column_1 and column_2) would be placed inside the container such that the second column — the one that displays the Web page's content — comes first in the HTML (but actually is positioned to the right in the browser due to the template's CSS). And the second column — the one that displays the menu — would come later in the page's HTML (but actually is positioned to the left in the browser due to the template's CSS).

In other words, the HTML generated by such templates presents the content of the page to a Web spider first, before the main menu. Then the spider bases its analysis on the page's actual content, not on the items in the main menu.

Here's what the column handling might look like in such a template's `index. php` file:

```
<body>
  <div id="container">
     <div id="column_2">
        <jdoc:include type="component">
     </div>
     <div id="column_1">
        <jdoc:include type="modules" name="left">
     </div>
  </div>
</body>
```

Maximizing Your Site for Search Engines

There's more to know about optimizing your Web pages than just metadata and SEF; a lot depends on how you arrange the content of your page as well. Following are some good optimization tips for Joomla sites:

- ✔ **Avoid too much PDF or Flash.** Not all search engines' robots can read PDF (with Google's being notable exceptions).

- ✔ **Use a page headline.** Consider using text from your page title (which is displayed in the search results) in the first text title on your page, which tells the search engine that people who click your listing in its search results will come to the right place.

- ✔ **Vary the site's content.** Don't submit identical pages that use different URLs.

- ✔ **Vary your page titles.** Don't use the same title on different pages. If you do, your pages may look the same to the search engine.

- ✔ **Get everything out in the open.** Don't use hidden or invisible text (text that's the same color as the background) in an effort to cram more keywords into a page. Search engines will penalize your ranking if you do.

✔ **Give clear directions.** Have a site-map page on your site, and use Joomla breadcrumbs (see Chapter 7). Make sure that spiders have an easy link trail to follow to every location on your site.

✔ **Make sure that your pages load quickly.** If a page times out, it won't be indexed.

✔ **Link to home.** Make sure that all pages on your site contain links to the site's home page.

✔ **Add intrasite links.** Sites that have multiple pages linked to one another do better in search engine rankings. Make sure that all your pages are easily accessible via links so robots can find them.

✔ **Link to other sites.** Search engines place great importance on links to other sites. The more sites that link to yours, the more important search engines consider your site to be.

✔ **Include a keyword in your site's domain name.** Select a domain name that includes your most important keyword.

✔ **Use keywords early and often.** The earlier you use keywords in your <body> tags, the better. (Starting at character 1 is best.) You should put some of your keywords in the <body> element in bold with the <b> tag. Coloring them red is also good.

✔ **Switch the order of keywords on the page.** Use a different order for your keywords in the body of a page and your keywords in the <meta> tags.

✔ **Put keywords in comments.** If you're going to use HTML comments, make sure that you use some of your keywords in them.

✔ **Put keywords in alt text.** Include keywords in the alt attribute of images (the text that's displayed when a user hovers a mouse pointer over an image).

✔ **Put keywords up front.** Use the most important keywords in article titles, starting at character 1. But also use the keyword in the title in the body of the article; if you don't, the spider may suspect you of *keyword stuffing* your title.

✔ **Limit keywords.** Use at least five keywords in the body of your page, but don't have too many keywords (known as *keyword spamming*).

If you get into the topic in depth, search engine optimization can be tricky. But dozens of companies will work on your site for you (for a fee!). To find them, search for *SEO* or *SEO companies* in any search engine, and review the ads that pop up.

Automating site optimization

Having trouble with site optimization? Plenty of software is available to check your site and give you a report, complete with recommendations on what to do to get your site in shape.

Following are a few desktop programs, all of which cost money (*note:* Inclusion here doesn't constitute endorsement!):

✔ Web CEO (www.webceo.com)

✔ iBusiness Promoter (www.ibusiness promoter.com/)

✔ WebPosition 4 (www.webposition goldpro.com/)

Following are some online programs, which are free or have free trials:

✔ Web Page Analyzer (www.website optimization.com/services/ analyze/)

✔ SiteSolutions.com (www.sitesolutions.com/analysis.asp)

✔ Search Engine Rankings (http://mikes-marketing-tools.com/ranking-reports/)

Telling Search Engines about Your Site

When your site is tuned up, it's time to submit it to the search engines. (The search engines probably will find your site sooner or later, but you can speed the process by submitting your site to them.)

Submit your site only once to search engines. (Submitting your site more than once in quick succession counts against you with search engines.) Here are submission URLs for three leading search engines:

✔ **Google:** www.google.com/addurl/

✔ **Yahoo!:** https://siteexplorer.search.yahoo.com/submit

✔ **Live Search:** http://search.msn.com.sg/docs/submit.aspx

It can take some time for the search engines to get around to spidering your site after you submit it. MSN can take up to two months to spider your site; Google, up to a month; AltaVista, about a week; AOL, two months; and Excite, six weeks.

You could use third-party search engine submission software to do the job for you, but we don't recommend it. We've found that a lot of this software does a sloppy and incomplete job of submitting sites to any given search engine. Also, sites that are submitted to too many search engines at the same time run the risk of being banned. It's better to do the work yourself, submitting your site to search engines manually.

Chapter 12

Extending Joomla

. . . .

In This Chapter

▶ Knowing how modules, components, and plug-ins differ

▶ Using the Joomla extensions site

▶ Selecting and downloading the right extension

▶ Installing an extension

. . . .

One of the best features of Joomla is the fact that it can be extended. Joomla is very powerful out of the box, of course, but a terrific Joomla community specializes in creating extensions for the software, which is built to be easily extended. Thousands of extensions are available, including new editors, games that can be displayed in Web pages, site-map generators, and shopping carts.

This chapter looks at extensions in depth. We cover many aspects of Joomla extensions in Chapters 7, 8, and 9, but this chapter focuses on them explicitly — especially on the extensions that the Joomla community has created.

Taking a Look at Plug-Ins, Components, and Modules

Joomla extensions fall into three categories: modules, components, and plug-ins.

New Joomla users are considerably confused about the differences, which is understandable; there is considerable overlap among categories of extensions, especially in the Joomla developer community. Complicating matters even further, Joomla extensions can contain any mix of modules, components, and plug-ins.

In the following sections, we help you get the differences down.

Making a splash with modules

The differences between modules and components aren't totally clear-cut. Some developers handle a task such as displaying a site map with a component; others use a module.

Here are the main distinctions between modules and components:

✔ **Modules usually display their content on the periphery of a page.** A Joomla front page usually contains many modules and a single component.

In Figure 12-1, for example, the modules include the top menu, the menus on the left side of the page, and the Who's Online and Polls sections on the right side of the page. Notice that all these modules are on the periphery of the page. The component, by contrast, is in the center of the page, displaying the actual page content.

✔ **Modules accept little or no input.** A typical module is read-only (such as the Who's Online module) or accepts only minimal input (such as the Polls module). A component can accept all kinds of input, from article submissions to user comments in a forum.

Figure 12-1:
Modules and a component in a typical Joomla front page.

✔ **Modules have a simple administrative tool.** You manage a module with Module Manager, which typically offers only a few basic parameters, such as where the module appears on the page. A component, on the other hand, can have a very complex administrative interface complete with many tabs and screens.

✔ **Modules tend to be smaller than components.** The most basic difference is that modules usually are designed to be smaller than components.

Working with components

Components usually do heavier lifting than modules do. Whereas modules perform specific tasks, such as displaying who's online, components usually do general jobs, such as displaying articles.

A component usually takes up the center of a Web page, displaying articles or a site map. Components are like mini-Web pages, in fact; they're designed to present page content. By contrast, typical modules appear on many pages and are more independent of page content.

Components and modules can work together. The Search module is one such example. You enter a search term in the module, and it displays the results in a component.

Grooving with plug-ins

Plug-ins are the most heavy-duty Joomla extensions, giving you the greatest power and control.

Plug-ins often work on both the data that users send to Joomla and the data that Joomla sends to users. An example would be a special type of WYSIWYG editor that accepts data from users as they edit the text and that passes data to Joomla as well.

Plug-ins can focus on either the front end or the back end. Some back-end plug-ins, such as those for online shopping carts, have very complex administrative interfaces.

You can use numerous plug-ins in Joomla, installing them the same way that you do modules and components.

Searching for Joomla Extensions

The main source of free Joomla extensions (although many of the developers would be very pleased if you donated to them) is `http://extensions.joomla.org`.

You can also reach the Joomla extensions site from `www.joomla.org` by clicking the Extensions link in the horizontal navigation bar on the site's front page.

At this writing, no fewer than 3,753 extensions are available for free download from the site. Another thing that makes the site so great is that each extension has user-feedback ratings. If you see an extension with four or more stars and many votes, many people have found it to be a good one. On the other hand, if you find an extension with many votes and zero stars (as you will), don't use it.

Using the search box

How do you find good extensions on the Joomla extensions site? Normally, when you go to the site, you have a particular kind of extension in mind and can enter what you're looking for in the search box. Figure 12-2 shows the result of a search for *games*, which returned four categories. Clicking a category in the search results opens a page that lists all the extensions in that category.

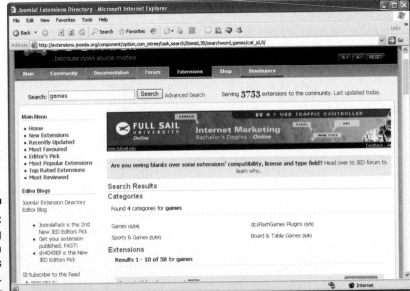

Figure 12-2: Searching the Joomla extensions site.

Browsing by links

Another way to find good extensions is to browse the links on the left side of the search results page:

- ✔ New Extensions
- ✔ Recently Updated
- ✔ Most Favored
- ✔ Editor's Pick
- ✔ Most Popular Extensions
- ✔ Top Rated Extensions
- ✔ Most Reviewed

In practice, the Editor's Pick, Most Popular Extensions, and Top Rated Extensions pages list almost all the same extensions — that is, the ones that are most popular currently. Another drawback is that Most Popular and Top Rated list only the top ten extensions in each category, which doesn't seem like many when more than 3,700 extensions are available. The New Extensions category lists more extensions — typically, 60.

Browsing by categories

You can also browse by category, which is very useful if you know what kind of extension you're looking for. Here are the extension categories:

- ✔ Access & Security
- ✔ Administration
- ✔ Ads & Affiliates
- ✔ Calendars & Events
- ✔ Clients & Groupware
- ✔ Communication
- ✔ Content & News
- ✔ Core Enhancements
- ✔ Directory & Documentation
- ✔ e-Commerce
- ✔ Edition

- ✔ Extension Specific
- ✔ Financial & Statistics
- ✔ Images & Multimedia
- ✔ Languages
- ✔ Miscellaneous
- ✔ Search & Indexing
- ✔ Site Information
- ✔ Sports & Games
- ✔ Style & Design
- ✔ Vertical Markets

If you've got a specific type of extension you want in mind, it's often easiest to browse by category.

After you find several extensions that match your search criteria, how do you decide on the right one? We show you how in the following section.

Choosing an Extension

Figure 12-3 shows an example extension listing — this one, for PUArcade. On the right side of the listing is a Download button; below that button are some icons that give you important information about the extension.

Figure 12-3:
An extension listing.

Pick the right platform

Notice the two icons below the Download button in Figure 12-3: 1.5 Legacy and 1.0 Native. These icons indicate that the extension is *native* — that is, fully supported — for Joomla 1.0 and also works in *legacy* mode in Joomla 1.5. Legacy mode in Joomla 1.5 is for extensions written for Joomla 1.0; this mode allows those extensions to run in version 1.5. (Even though Joomla 1.5 is the current version, a huge number of extensions were written for Joomla 1.0 and are available for Joomla 1.5 only in legacy mode.)

Here are the three platform possibilities for Joomla extensions:

- **1.5 Native:** Supports Joomla 1.5
- **1.5 Legacy** (Joomla 1.0 extension): Runs under Joomla 1.5 in legacy mode
- **1.0 Native:** Supports Joomla 1.0

If you're using Joomla 1.5, your first choice should be 1.5 native extensions; extensions described only as 1.0 native won't work for you. Extensions listed as 1.5 legacy *may* work for you in legacy mode.

To enable legacy mode in Joomla 1.5, choose Extensions⇨Plugin Manager in any back-end page to open Plugin Manager; then find the System - Legacy plug-in, which is disabled by default. Click the icon in that plug-in's Enabled column, changing it from a red X to a green check mark, and then click the Save button.

Know what you're getting

Below the Joomla platform icons are more icons that tell you what items the extension includes. The listing for the PUArcade extension (refer to Figure 12-3) features several of these icons: C (component), M (at least one module), P (at least one plug-in), L (different languages), and S (special, extension-specific code).

If you're looking for an extension that's only a module, look for entries that have only the M icon. If you're looking for a component, look for the C icon, and so on.

Check the ratings

Above an extension's description are star ratings, the number of votes, and the number of reviews. The reviews text is a link; click it to see user reviews for that extension.

User reviews are among the most useful features of the Joomla extensions site. Plenty of times, we've been saved from problems when other users mention something that's germane to our situation (such as "great extension, but your PHP installation needs the GD2 module loaded").

When you find an extension that looks right, click the Download button in its listing to download it to your computer. First, though, read the following section for some pointers.

Downloading a Joomla Extension

Suppose that you want to add a little pizzazz to your site, and you find out that your users have a passion for the game Sudoku. Perhaps you've found an extension that allows your users to indulge that passion. Now all you have to do is download it.

To download an extension from the Joomla extensions site, follow these steps:

1. **On the extension's listing page, click the Download button.**

   You go to a page on the extension developer's site that lists the files available for download for this extension. Figure 12-4 shows an example Sudoku page.

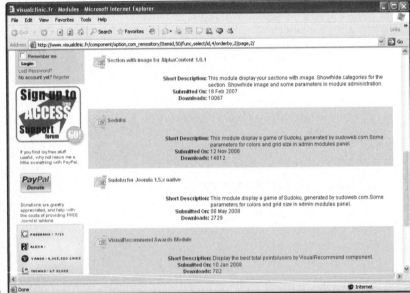

Figure 12-4:
Extension files on a developer's Web site.

2. **Click the link for the package you want to download.**

   You go to the download page.

3. **Click the download link or button in this page.**

   Your browser opens a download dialog box.

4. **Save the compressed extension file to your hard drive.**

   If you're downloading a module file, the filename starts with mod_.

 If you're using Internet Explorer, a yellow security bar may appear at the top of the browser window, blocking the download for security reasons. Right-click the security bar, and choose Download File from the shortcut menu.

Now that you have the extension file, you're ready to expand and install it. In the following sections, we show you how to install the three types of extensions: modules, components, and plug-ins. We start with two types of modules: game and utility.

Installing a Game Module

To install a game module in Joomla, follow these steps:

1. **Choose Extensions⇨Install/Uninstall in any back-end page.**

   Extension Manager opens.

2. **In the Upload Package File section, click the Browse button to browse to and select the module file on your hard drive.**

   The filename appears in the Package File text box (see Figure 12-5).

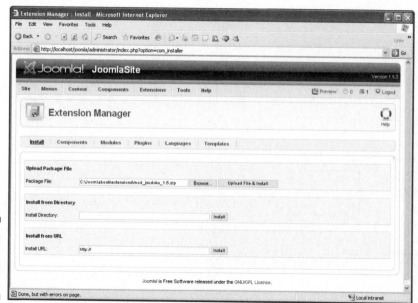

Figure 12-5: Selecting a downloaded extension.

3. **Click the Upload File & Install button.**

   Joomla uploads and installs the file. When it finishes, it displays a message telling you that installation was successful.

4. **Choose Extensions⇨Module Manager to open Module Manager.**

5. **Click the red X in the module's Enabled column, changing it to a green check mark.**

6. **Click the module's name.**

   The Edit Module page opens.

7. **In the Module Parameters pane, make a choice from the Grid Size drop-down menu.**

In this case, grid size refers to the size of the Sudoku board.

Figure 12-6 shows an example selection for a Sudoku module.

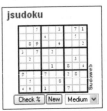

Figure 12-6:
Choosing a
grid size.

8. **Click the Apply button.**

9. **To see the module at work, click the Preview link in any back-end page to view your site.**

   Figure 12-7 shows a Sudoku module at work. Users play by clicking a square and typing a number; they start a new game by clicking the New button.

Figure 12-7:
A Sudoku
module on
a Joomla
page.

The installation process for extensions is the same as the one for templates, which we discuss in Chapter 9. Simply choose Extensions⇨Install/Uninstall in any back-end page to install templates, modules, components, and plug-ins.

Installing a Utility Module

Search engines like Google are using Ajax-enabled (Asynchronous JavaScript and XML) search boxes to help users. As the user enters a search term, Google makes the browser contact Google behind the scenes and display possible clickable matches, as you see in Figure 12-8, saving the user the trouble of typing the whole search term.

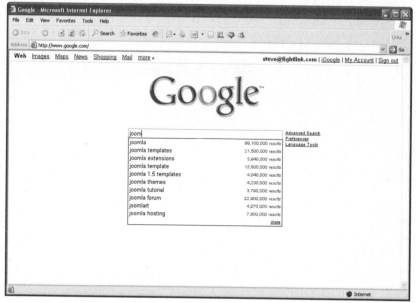

A cool Ajax-enabled search box, PixSearch, is available as a module for Joomla sites. In this section, we show you how to install it.

To get PixSearch, go to the Joomla extensions site at `http://extensions.joomla.org`; type **PixSearch** in the Search box; and click the Search button. Download the PixSearch 1.5 native module — currently named `mod_pix search_J_1.5_v.0.4.0.zip` — and store that file on your hard disk. Then follow these steps to install the module:

1. **Choose Extensions⇨Install/Uninstall.**

   The Joomla Extension Manager page opens.

2. **Click the Browse button to find and select the `mod_pixsearch_J_1.5_v.0.4.0.zip` file on your hard disk.**

   The `mod_pixsearch_J_1.5_v.0.4.0.zip` filename appears in the text box (see Figure 12-9).

3. **Click the Upload File & Install button.**

   The success page you see in Figure 12-10 appears.

4. **Choose Extensions⇨Module Manager to open Module Manager.**

5. **Click the red cross in the PixSearch module's Enabled column, turning it to a green check mark, as shown (in black and white) in Figure 12-11.**

   That's it. No further customization is required.

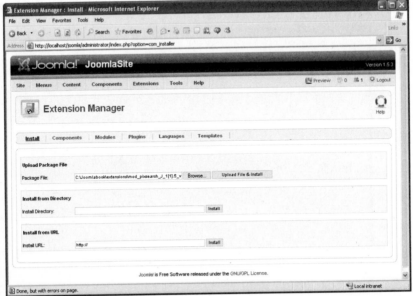

Figure 12-9:
The Joomla
install/unin-
stall page.

Figure 12-9:
The Joomla
install/unin-
stall page.

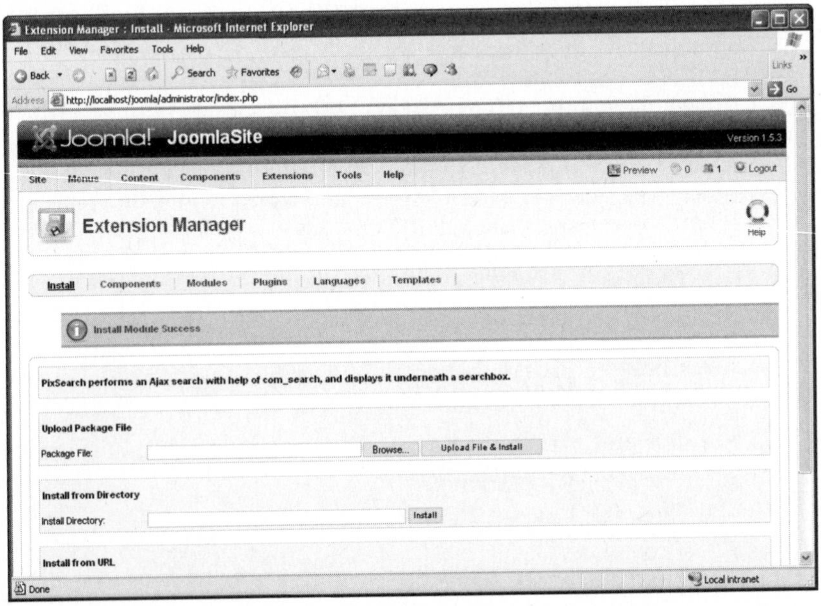

Figure 12-10:
The module
installation
success
page.

Now you've installed the PixSearch module. You can see it at work in
Figure 12-12, contacting the Joomla installation to find matches for the
partial search term *joo* and displaying matching articles — a nice result
for a useful module.

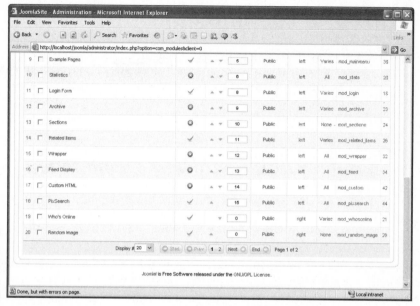

Figure 12-11:
Enabling the
module.

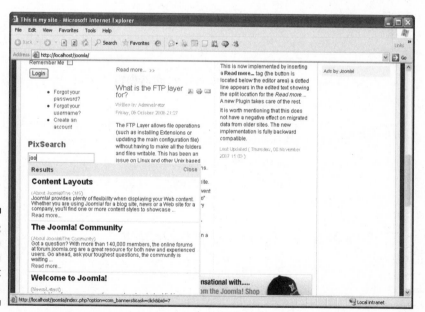

Figure 12-12:
The
PixSearch
module at
work.

As you can see, installing modules isn't difficult, and the results can be well
worth the time you spend to install them. In the next section, we discuss
installing components.

Installing a Component

Although modules fit into existing pages, Joomla components of the kind that you can download at the Joomla extensions site can display whole pages. A good example is the Xmap component, which displays a site map on its own page. Site maps are very useful, especially for search engine spiders, so in this section, we show you how to get one.

Finding and installing a component

To find and install a component, follow these steps:

1. **Navigate to the Joomla extensions site (`http://extensions.joomla.org`).**

2. **Use any of the methods in "Searching for Joomla Extensions," earlier in this chapter, to locate the component you want to use.**

   For this exercise, type **Xmap** in the search text box and then click the Search button.

3. **Download the component to your hard disk.**

   For this exercise, download the Xmap component, currently named `com_xmap-1.2.zip`. (Component filenames start with `com_`.)

4. **Choose Extensions⇨Install/Uninstall.**

   Extension Manager opens.

5. **In the Upload Package File section, click the Browse button to find and select the component file on your hard disk.**

6. **Click the Upload File & Install button.**

   Joomla installs the component and adds it to the Components menu.

Configuring a component

To configure a new component, follow these steps:

1. **Choose Components⇨*name*, where *name* is the component, to open a configuration page (see Figure 12-13).**

   For this exercise, choose Components⇨Xmap.

2. **Change any settings you want.**

   For this exercise, the Xmap component needs no configuration.

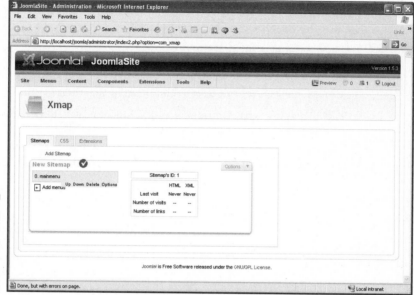

Figure 12-13:
A com-
ponent's
configura-
tion page.

Adding a menu item for the component

To access a component, you simply link a menu item to it. To do that, follow
these steps:

1. **Choose Menus⇨Menu Manager in any back-end page to open Menu
   Manager.**

2. **In the row of the menu you want to use, click the icon in the Menu
   Item(s) column.**

   For this exercise, select Main Menu.

   Menu Item Manager opens.

3. **Click the New button.**

   The New Menu Item page opens, displaying a node tree. You should
   find the component listed in the tree — for this exercise, Xmap (see
   Figure 12-14).

4. **Click the component's name.**

   The Edit Menu Item page opens.

5. **Enter a title for the new menu item in the Title text box.**

   For this exercise, type **Site Map**.

6. **Click the Save or Apply button.**

7. **Click the Preview link to view your site.**

   You see the new menu item.

8. **Click the component's menu item to open the component.**

   For this exercise, click the Site Map item in the Main menu.

   Joomla displays the component — for this exercise, a dynamically generated site map — on your site (see Figure 12-15).

Figure 12-14: The New Menu Item page.

Figure 12-15: A new component on the front page.

Installing a Plug-In

As you may expect, installing plug-ins works just the same way as installing modules and components. Follow these steps:

1. **Find and download the plug-in file from the Joomla extensions site, using any of the techniques we provide earlier in this chapter.**

2. **Choose Extensions⇨Install/Uninstall in any back-end page to open Extensions Manager.**

3. **In the Upload Package File section, click the Browse button to browse to and select the plug-in file on your hard disk.**

4. **Click the Upload File & Install button.**

   Joomla installs the plug-in.

The procedures for configuring the plug-in after installation and putting it to work depend on the plug-in you've installed; see the plug-in's documentation for details. (If you installed a new editor, for example, you need to install it via Joomla's Global Configuration page instead of Extensions Manager.)

As you can see, Joomla extensions can give you a great deal of utility, and thousands of them are available for free. We urge you to support extension developers by donating to them if you find their extensions useful. Doing that is a sure way to ensure a steady flow of new extensions!

Part V
The Part of Tens

The 5th Wave   By Rich Tennant

"See? I created a little felon figure that runs around our Web site hiding behind banner ads. On the last page, our logo puts him in a non lethal choke hold and brings him back to the home page."

In this part . . .

This part of the book is the Part of Tens, which you find in all *For Dummies* books. Here, we look at ten top extensions for Joomla and where to get them. We also provide ten ways to get help on Joomla — from the official Joomla help site to user groups — and introduce ten great sources of Joomla templates. Finally, we point you to ten places to find Joomla tutorials.

Chapter 13

Ten Top Joomla Extensions

In This Chapter

▶ Opening shop online

▶ Permitting blog users to comment

▶ Adding Flash to your site

▶ Posting an events calendar

*O*ne of the most powerful and attractive aspects of Joomla is that you can extend it easily via downloadable templates, modules, components, and plug-ins. In this chapter, we present ten of the top Joomla extensions, all of which are written to be native to Joomla 1.5. All are available from the official Joomla extensions site, `http://extensions.joomla.org`, and most are free. If an extension isn't free, it offers a free trial — typically, for 30 days.

Joomla is a powerful content management system out of the box, but it can use a few additional elements. Take a look at the extensions listed in this chapter; you may find something that would go well on your site. (For more information about installing extensions, see Chapter 12.)

Think twice before downloading and installing an extension rated with fewer than four stars. If it has fewer than four stars, read the reviews to find out what the issue is and to see whether it applies to you.

As we discuss in Chapter 12, you should use extensions native to Joomla 1.5 (assuming that you're using Joomla 1.5). The listings for those extensions — including all the extensions in this chapter — have a "1.5 native" icon.

VirtueMart

```
http://extensions.joomla.org/component/option,com_mtree/
task,viewlink/link_id,129/Itemid,35/
```

VirtueMart is a complete, if complex, online store system that displays your store and catalog, and includes a shopping cart. You can use it to manage an unlimited number of categories, products, orders, discounts, and shopper groups, as well as individual customers.

VirtueMart is famous in the Joomla community because it allows you to integrate an online store with a Joomla site. It has plenty of fans — and also plenty of detractors.

At this writing, VirtueMart has a 4-star rating with 123 user reviews. Some people find it great; others think it's complex and buggy. Read the reviews for more information. You can see a demo of VirtueMart in Figure 13-1.

Xmap

```
http://extensions.joomla.org/component/option,com_mtree/
task,viewlink/link_id,3066/Itemid,35/
```

Xmap provides missing functionality in Joomla, in our opinion, by allowing you to create a site map. The site map is displayed as a hierarchical list of links so that users (and search engine spiders) can navigate your site easily.

This extension is a component, so you can make a menu item point to it; when a user clicks the menu item, the site map appears.

In our experience, this extension is both great and easy to use. For an introduction to Xmap, refer to "Installing a Component" in Chapter 12.

Figure 13-2 shows a demo of Xmap.

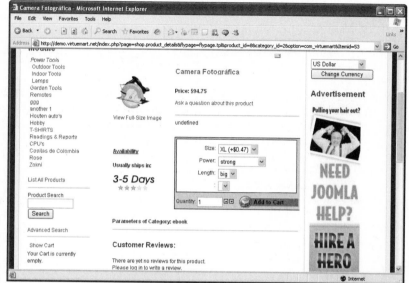

Figure 13-1:
A
VirtueMart
demo.

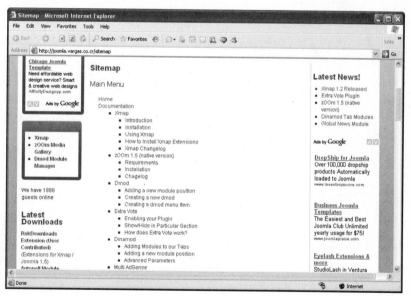

Figure 13-2:
An Xmap
demo.

My Blog

```
http://extensions.joomla.org/component/option,com_mtree/
task,viewlink/link_id,1698/Itemid,35/
```

My Blog currently has a rating of only 3½ stars, and it's not free (it's available as a 30-day free trial). But we think it's important to list a blogging extension in this chapter, because the default Joomla installation lacks one important feature of true blogs: user comments. The extension comes with a built-in dashboard that allows users to write, edit, and manage their own blog posts.

My Blog is a component that comes with five modules: Latest Entries, Latest Comments, Tag Clouds, Most Popular Blogs, and Archive. You can see a demo in Figure 13-3.

JCE Editor

```
http://extensions.joomla.org/component/option,com_mtree/
task,viewlink/link_id,88/Itemid,35/
```

JCE is a popular WYSIWYG editor for Joomla based on Moxiecode's TinyMCE. It includes advanced image and media handling, as well as file handling. It also provides plug-in support and an administration interface for setting its configuration.

JCE's features include an advanced code editor and spell checker. The editor itself is free, but some of the popular add-ons cost money.

Joom!Fish

```
http://extensions.joomla.org/component/option,com_mtree/
task,viewlink/link_id,460/Itemid,35/
```

Joom!Fish is such a popular extension that it has a "hot" icon on its listing page, indicating that it's being downloaded like hotcakes. The reason for its popularity is that it converts Joomla to a true multilingual content management system.

Usually, Joomla sites are written in a single language, but Joom!Fish allows you to set up (and manage) sites with content in multiple languages. Use it to manage translations of your various articles and then present those articles to a user in the correct language.

Figure 13-4 shows a Joom!Fish-enabled site.

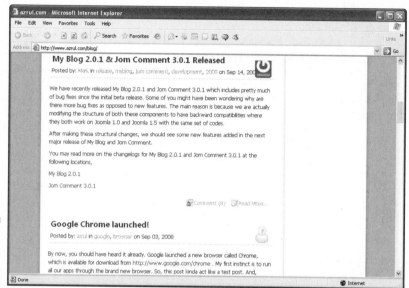

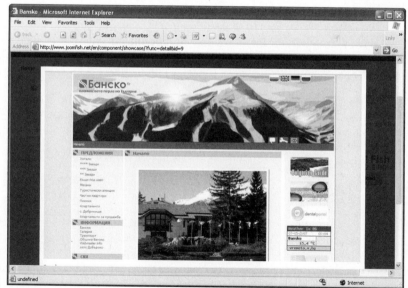

JoomlaPack

http://extensions.joomla.org/component/option,com_mtree/
task,viewlink/link_id,1606/Itemid,35/

JoomlaPack is so useful, you may feel that it should come with the default Joomla installation. This extension allows you to back up and restore your entire site easily.

JoomlaPack is particularly useful for large, complex sites. (If your database became corrupted, what would you do?) It archives all the files on your site and takes a database snapshot. Its installer is based on the standard Joomla installer.

MetaMod

http://extensions.joomla.org/component/option,com_mtree/
task,viewlink/link_id,3391/Itemid,35/

MetaMod allows you to manage your modules in ways that aren't possible with out-of-the-box Joomla. You can make modules appear on certain dates, appear only in certain sections or categories, display different modules depending on what browser the user has, and more.

With MetaMod, you can control the content displayed by modules based on where (geographically) the user is; make a module disappear after a user has logged in; and show different menus based on the language the user has specified.

sh404SEF

http://extensions.joomla.org/component/option,com_mtree/
task,viewlink/link_id,2380/Itemid,35/

sh404SEF is another popular (listed with a "hot" icon) extension that creates search engine friendly (SEF) URLs. It improves on Joomla's SEF support by allowing you to write your own URLs that include keywords for search engine spiders to pick up.

You can see a demo of sh404SEF in Figure 13-5. (Note the URL, which ends in Demo-shop/Hand-tools/View-all-products.html.)

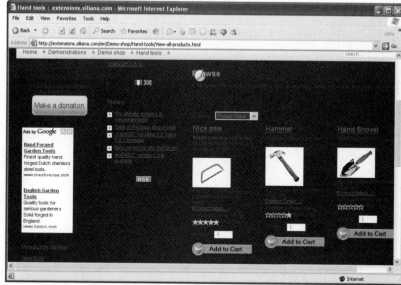

Figure 13-5:
An
sh404SEF
demo.

Exposé Flash Gallery

```
http://extensions.joomla.org/component/option,com_mtree/
task,viewlink/link_id,254/Itemid,35/
```

Exposé Flash Gallery creates smooth-looking slideshows — a useful feature for displaying products on e-commerce sites, for example.

Exposé, which uses Adobe Flash for visual effects, is one of the most popular extensions offered on the Joomla extension site. Figure 13-6 shows a demo.

JEvents Events Calendar

```
http://extensions.joomla.org/component/option,com_mtree/
task,viewlink/link_id,95/Itemid,35/
```

JEvents is another extension that Joomla could have used out of the box. JEvents allows you to post a calendar of events on your site. This powerful extension can display repeating patterns of events as well as one-off events in several formats. You can also categorize events and customize calendar views to show some or all of those categories. You can see a JEvents calendar demo in Figure 13-7.

Figure 13-6:
An Exposé
Flash gallery
demo.

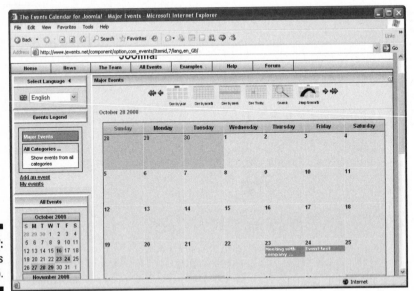

Figure 13-7:
A JEvents
demo.

Chapter 14

Ten Ways to Get Help on Joomla

There's no getting around it: Joomla can be a pretty complex beastie. Luckily, you have all kinds of ways of getting help for Joomla. This chapter gives you the details on those resources.

Take a look at these sites and online documents. Even if you don't need help, they're great for getting you into the Joomla community.

You can also check a search engine for any specific Joomla topic you're interested in. Want help finding an online host that supports Joomla, for example? At this writing, a Google search for *Joomla hosting* returns a mere 8.2 million results.

Joomla Help Site

```
http://help.joomla.org/
```

The official Joomla help site is a searchable site providing help on most Joomla topics, starting with installation requirements and an installation guide. It's a good site with tons of material but a little hard to navigate.

Joomla Official Documentation Wiki

http://docs.joomla.org

This Wikipedia site, which is still a work in progress, is the official Joomla documentation site. It's searchable and a great resource. If you're a beginner, check the Absolute Beginners Guide to Joomla at http://docs.joomla.org/Beginners.

Joomla Forums

http://forum.joomla.org/

Need an answer that you can't find in this book or on the Joomla help site? You can ask your question at the Joomla forums, which are chock full of other Joomla users. All types of forums are available, addressing topics such as extensions, security, and installation.

You can get good answers and search the archives, but the forums do have some downsides: They seem to be a little paranoid about spammers (you'll be warned repeatedly not to spam), and registration is a long process that doesn't always work right. Nonetheless, the forums are the place to ask tough-to-answer questions.

Joomla Community Portal

http://community.joomla.org

The Joomla Community Portal gives Joomla people — especially developers — a place to congregate. Here, you can find lists of Joomla events, find out how to contribute to Joomla, and more.

You can read the Joomla Community Magazine on this site and check JoomlaConnect, which collects Joomla news from around the world. In addition, you can find blogs by members of the Joomla team that tell you where Joomla is headed.

Joomla User Groups

> `http://community.joomla.org/joomla-user-groups.html`

Dozens of Joomla user groups operate worldwide. To find a group near you, check this site, which provides links to user groups everywhere.

Joomla Translation Teams

> `http://community.joomla.org/translation-teams-list.html`

Joomla is installed in many countries — and in many languages. This site provides links to the various teams around the world that are responsible for versions of Joomla ranging from Catalan to Turkish.

Joomla Quick Start Guide

> `http://help.joomla.org/ghop/feb2008/task048/joomla_15_quickstart.pdf`

You can find a nice quick-start guide for Joomla at this URL. (Notice that the URL points to a PDF file, not a Web page.) This guide is a good resource for beginners. It includes material on installation, including installation with XAMPP, and discusses topics such as menus, templates, and modules.

Joomla Quick Start Videos

> `http://help.joomla.org/ghop/feb2008/task167/index.html`

This site provides a video version of the quick-start guide. It's fun to watch many Joomla tasks performed before your eyes, with helpful narration.

Joomla Installation Manuals

```
http://help.joomla.org/content/category/48/268/302/
```

```
http://downloads.joomlacode.org/docmanfileversion/1/7/4/17471/1.5_Installation_
             Manual_version_0.5.pdf
```

Many Joomla installation guides are floating around the Internet; these two are among the best. (The second guide is a PDF, not a Web page.)

Joomla Core Features

```
http://help.joomla.org/ghop/feb2008/task020/Joomla!%20Core%20Features%20V1.2.pdf
```

This URL takes you to a 45-page PDF guide to Joomla's components, modules, plug-ins, and templates. The guide is a good one but a little lightweight, providing more overview than in-depth answers.

Chapter 15

Ten Top Joomla Template Sites

. . . .

Templates are very important in Joomla. Joomla comes with a few built-in templates, but people rarely stick with those; instead, they download and install templates from the Internet. There may be a time when Joomla actually ships with a good assortment of templates, but until then, you're stuck with getting your templates from the Internet.

Chapter 9 covers templates and how to install them in Joomla, and this chapter takes a look at ten top template sites.

Not all the template sites are free. The free sites are the most popular, as you'd expect, but don't neglect the for-pay sites, which often have the most exciting and professional-looking templates.

If you're using Joomla 1.5, make sure that the template you're downloading is targeted to Joomla 1.5.

SiteGround

www.siteground.com/joomla-hosting/joomla-templates.htm

SiteGround (see Figure 15-1) offers many free Joomla templates and claims to be the largest Joomla templates site around. The site offers new releases every week, so check back often.

Joomla-Templates.com

www.joomla-templates.com/

This site is for-pay for the most part (it offers a few free templates), but the templates it has are affordable — usually, about $50 for nonexclusive use. If you want a template that only you can use, the price can run about $850.

Joomla-Templates.com (see Figure 15-2) also offers customization services and a free clip-art gallery.

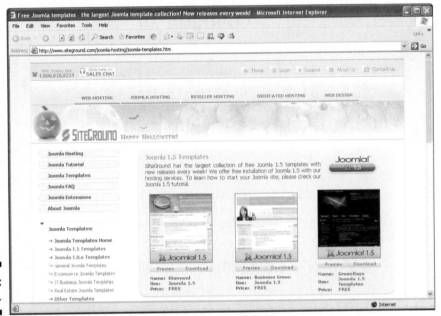

Figure 15-1:
SiteGround.

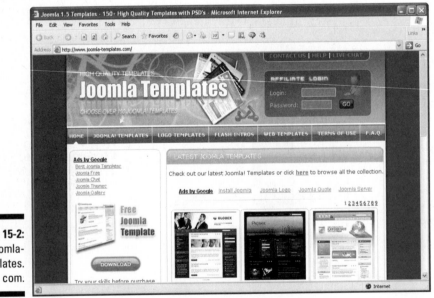

Figure 15-2:
Joomla-
Templates.
com.

Joomlashack

www.joomlashack.com/

Joomlashack is a well-known purveyor of third-party Joomla extensions, and it usually has good stuff, both for-pay and free.

Two things make Joomlashack templates special:

✔ They're XHTML compliant and validate as valid XHTML (which isn't true of most Joomla templates).

✔ They use a lot of XSS instead of HTML tables to arrange elements.

You can see some of the site's free templates in Figure 15-3.

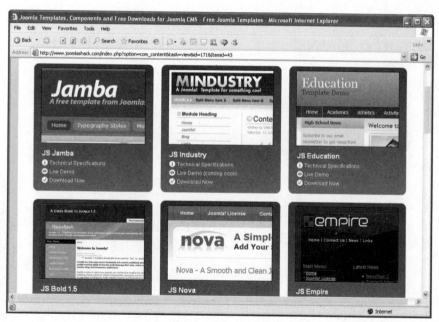

Figure 15-3:
Some free Joomla templates from the Joomla-shack Web site.

Joomla24.com

www.joomla24.com

Joomla24.com is a jumbo site, claiming to have more than 1,500 free templates. That claim may be true; the site accepts template submissions and posts those submitted templates. Although this practice means the site has many templates to offer, it also means that the quality and reliability of those templates varies greatly.

Figure 15-4 shows thumbnails of some of Joomla24.com's templates.

Because the thumbnail images don't do justice to the templates, you can see a preview of any template by clicking its Live Preview link, as shown in Figure 15-5.

JoomlaShine

www.joomlashine.com/

JoomlaShine specializes in high-quality Joomla templates. Its main offering at this writing, JSN Epic 2.0, appears in Figure 15-6. This template is fully customizable, allowing you to configure colors, fonts, styles, and more as template parameters from the back end.

The site is also known for its Adobe Flash–friendly Joomla templates.

JoomlaTP.com

http://joomlatp.com/joomla-1.5-templates/

JoomlaTP.com is another template aggregator site that releases free and for-pay templates. Figure 15-7 shows its free Joomla 1.5 templates page.

The site says that it also offers 3,000 premium (that is, for-pay) templates. If you've been having a hard time finding just the right template, take a look here.

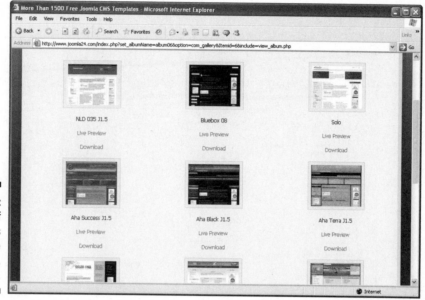

Figure 15-4:
Overview of templates on the Joomla24. com site.

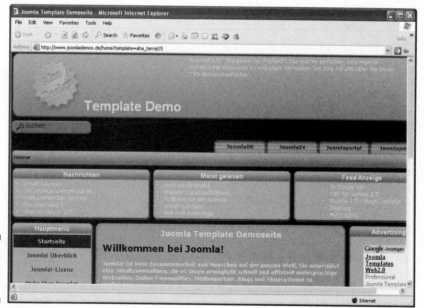

Figure 15-5:
A template demo.

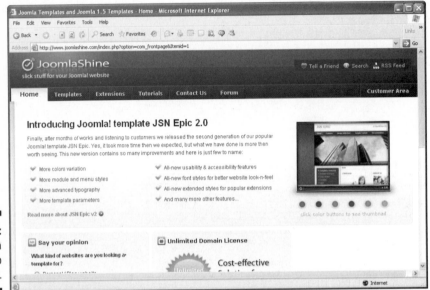

Figure 15-6:
The Joomla Shine Web site.

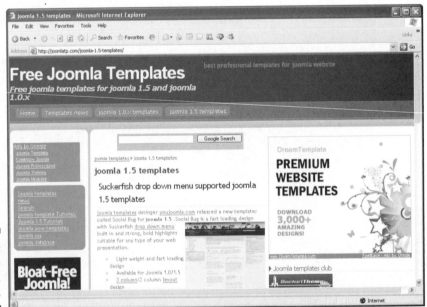

Figure 15-7:
The free JoomlaTP. com site.

Template Monster

www.templatemonster.com/joomla-templates.php

Template Monster sells templates for all kinds of software packages, from WordPress to Drupal. You can see some of its Joomla templates in Figure 15-8. These templates usually cost around $55 each.

Best of Joomla

www.bestofjoomla.com/component/option,com_bestoftemplate/ Itemid,46/

The Best of Joomla site is a very active one that offers discussions and Joomla resources. It ranks its templates — which are professional-quality and for-pay — by downloads, popularity, and so on.

You can get a better idea of what a particular template looks like when you hover your mouse pointer over its thumbnail; a larger pop-up window appears, as shown in Figure 15-9.

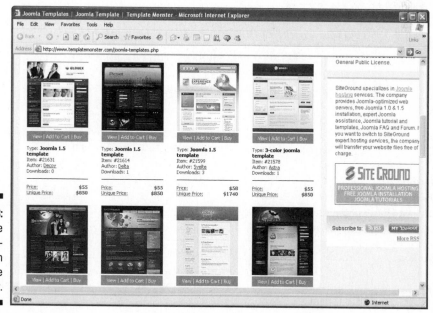

Figure 15-8:
Some Joomla templates on Template Monster.

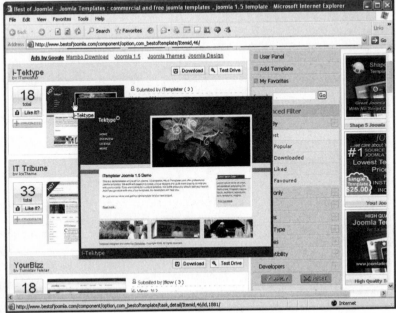

Figure 15-9:
A template
pop-up
window.

JoomlArt.com

www.joomlart.com/blogcategory/club_portfolio.html

JoomlArt.com is a template club that allows members to download and use its templates. (You can still use the templates you've downloaded after your membership expires.) Figure 15-10 shows some of the templates it has to offer.

The site has two primary levels of membership: free and paid. As you might expect, the paid level gives you access to more features.

Compass Designs

www.compassdesigns.net/templates.html

Compass Designs hosts a Joomla blog, Joomla news, and professionally designed Joomla templates (see Figure 15-11). The site also has some free templates available to registered users.

Figure 15-10:
JoomlArt.
com
template
offerings.

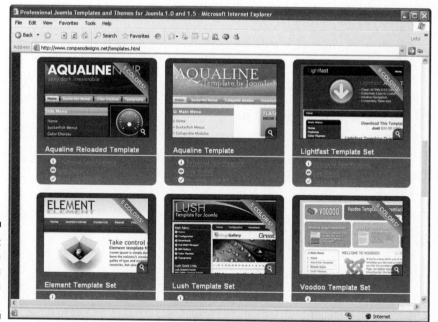

Figure 15-11:
Some
Compass
Designs
templates.

Chapter 16

Ten Joomla Tutorials

. . . .

All kinds of Joomla tutorials are online, and this chapter takes a look at ten of the best. Some are general Joomla tutorials, showing you how to install Joomla and get it up and running; others cover specific topics, such as creating Joomla templates or modules.

Take a look and see what you think. Most of these tutorials are a lot of fun!

SiteGround's General Tutorial

www.siteground.com/tutorials/joomla15/index.htm

SiteGround offers an extensive Joomla 1.5 tutorial (see Figure 16-1), including installation and a good introduction to creating your own Joomla site in a few steps. This tutorial is well illustrated and worth taking a look at.

Joomla Template Tutorial

http://dev.joomla.org/content/view/1136/79/

This page on the Joomla.org Web site is primarily for Joomla developers, and it has a good tutorial on developing Joomla templates, which takes you though the various stages of creating the CSS (Cascading Style Sheets) and PHP for a template. The tutorial also includes a discussion of what makes a template good.

Figure 16-2 shows a page of the tutorial.

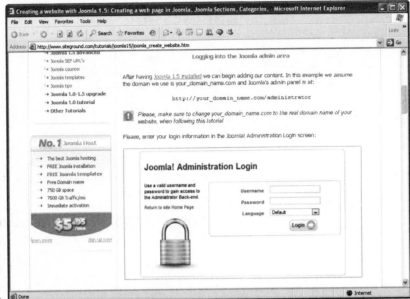

Figure 16-1:
The
SiteGround
tutorial.

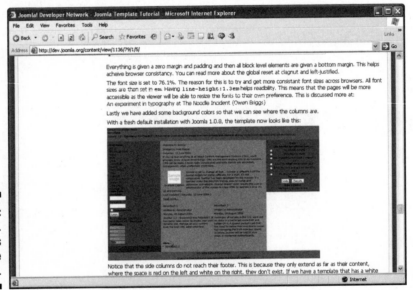

Figure 16-2:
Joomla.
org's
template
tutorial.

Joomlatutorials.com

www.joomlatutorials.com/joomla_tutorials/joomla_1.5_
tutorials.html

Joomlatutorials.com is all about what its name indicates: Joomla tutorials. The site recently added tutorials for Joomla 1.5, as well as template design, and the new tutorials are animated (that is, you play them like videos).

You can see one of the site's animated tutorials at work in Figure 16-3.

Compass Designs' Joomla Template Tutorial

www.compassdesigns.net/tutorials/17-joomla-tutorials/
48-joomla-template-tutorial.html

Compass Design specializes in creating Joomla templates, so it makes sense that the site has a template tutorial. This tutorial is a particularly good one (except for some missing graphics) if you want to learn all the ins and outs of template design, and it includes lots of advanced material.

Figure 16-4 shows the template tutorial.

Joomlaport's Tutorials

www.joomlaport.com/free-joomla-video-tutorials-and-tips.html

Joomlaport.com offers several tutorials — some with video — that cover the basics of installing and using Joomla, as well as creating templates.

Figure 16-5 shows a Joomlaport tutorial.

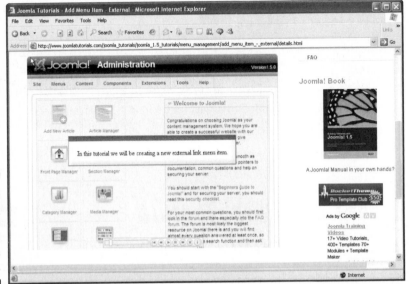

Figure 16-3:
An animated
tutorial from
the Joomla
tutorials.
com site.

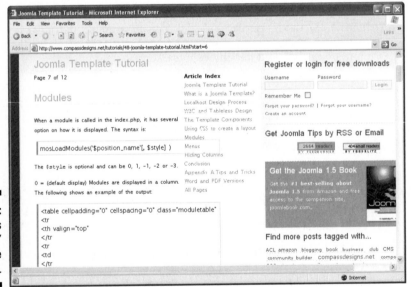

Figure 16-4:
Compass
Designs'
template
tutorial.

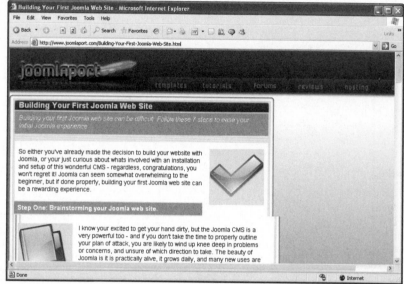

Figure 16-5:
A
Joomlaport
tutorial.

docs.joomla.org's Template Tutorial

```
http://docs.joomla.org/Tutorial:Creating_a_basic_Joomla!_
template
```

The docs.joomla.org site has a good tutorial on creating basic Joomla templates. Although short, the tutorial (see Figure 16-6) contains good material on how the PHP section of a template works.

help.joomla.org's Installation Tutorial

```
http://help.joomla.org/content/category/48/268/302/
```

The help.joomla.org site provides an in-depth installation tutorial, with special sections on manual installation. It's particularly good on troubleshooting, so if you're having problems installing Joomla, take a look.

You can see the installation tutorial at work in Figure 16-7.

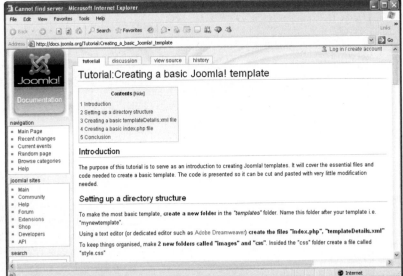

Figure 16-6:
The template tutorial at the docs. joomla.org Web site.

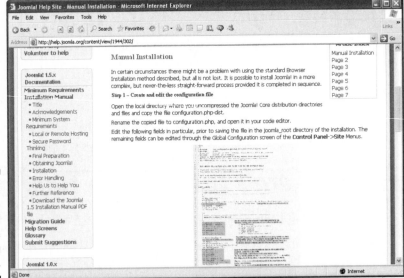

Figure 16-7:
The installation tutorial at the help. joomla.org site.

Robb Luther's YouTube Tutorial

`www.youtube.com/watch?v=hja-GRIX3CA&feature=related`

Robb Luther has a nice 5:38-minute YouTube video on how to add content to a Joomla site by adding new menu items and articles. The tutorial goes through the whole process of creating an uncategorized article step by step. If you're unclear about the process, it can be very useful to see someone actually adding articles and menu items to a Joomla site.

Figure 16-8 shows this YouTube tutorial.

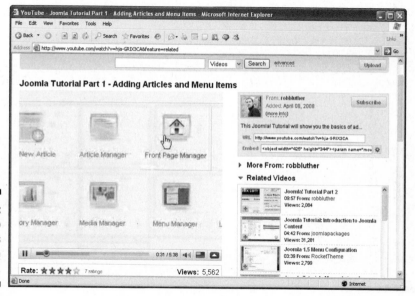

Figure 16-8:
Robb
Luther's
YouTube
tutorial.

CMS Tutorials and Reviews

```
http://needforcontent.com/category/tutorials/joomla-
tutorials/
```

The CMS Tutorials and Reviews section of Needforcontent.com has several Joomla tutorials on a variety of topics, such as "How to Install Joomla," "How to Create a Simple Joomla Site," and "How to Install Joomla Templates and Extensions." These tutorials are well illustrated and helpful.

Figure 16-9 shows the site's tutorials page.

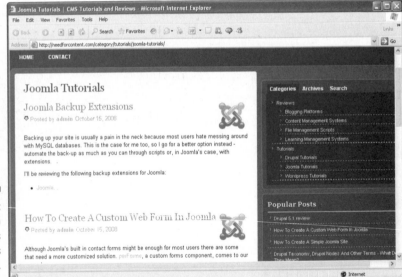

Figure 16-9: Needforcontent.com's tutorials page.

CopesFlavio.com's Module Tutorial

www.copesflavio.com/en/blog/cms/joomla/tutorial-howto-
write-a-joomla-module

CopesFlavio.com has a nice tutorial on creating Joomla modules that takes
you through the steps of creating the XML and PHP files to create a sample
module that fetches some text from the database and displays it — a cool
way to get started creating modules.

You can see the module-creation tutorial in Figure 16-10.

Figure 16-10:
CopesFlavio.
com's "How
to Write
a Joomla
Module"
tutorial.

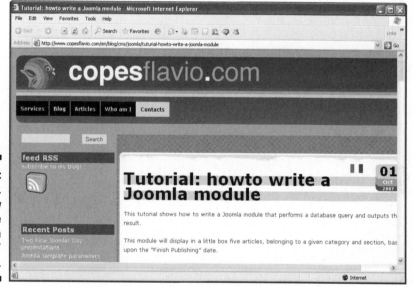

Glossary

Administrator: A user level on a Joomla site just below super administrator. Administrators have access to all front- and back-end capabilities.

Administrator back end: The control panel that administrators use to control and configure Joomla. Access to the back end is restricted.

Admin template: The template used to specify the layout of the administrator back end of a Joomla site.

Alias: An alternative name used throughout Joomla for menu items.

Article: A stand-alone item of content on a Joomla site that may be stored in a particular section and category. Articles usually are text/media items that display the content items on a site.

Author: A user level on a Joomla site that can access functions from the front end, write articles, and submit articles.

Back end: The control panel that administrators use to control and configure Joomla. Access to the back end is restricted.

Banner: A core component that allows you to display banner advertisements on your Joomla site.

Blog: The standard style of article presentation on a Joomla site. Blog format presents some or all of the articles in a particular section or category. Usually, an article's title is a link, followed by some introductory text and a Read More link.

Category: A set of related articles. Categories are one organizational level below sections.

Category Manager: The main visual tool for managing categories in Joomla.

CMS: Acronym for *content management system*.

Component: A content-displaying element that usually places content in the center of a page.

Content: Anything that Web pages can display.

Content management system: An application such as Joomla that allows you to manage the content of a Web site.

Control panel: The main Joomla back-end page that allows administrators to manage the Joomla site.

Editor: A user level on a Joomla site that can access only the front-end, authoring, and editing functions.

Extension: Software that extends Joomla in some way, such as by providing a new module or component.

Front end: The Joomla site that visitors without user privileges see.

Front page: The home page of your Joomla site.

Global Configuration: The settings for a Joomla site and server. You can access the Global Configuration settings through the Site menu in the control panel.

Item: Any piece of content.

Joomla: The popular and capable content management system that this book is about.

Manager: A user level on a Joomla site with access to the back end and some front-end privileges.

Module: A small extension that Joomla can display anywhere on a page, depending on the page's layout.

Open source: Typically refers to software that allows you to view its source code.

Operating system: The software that's in charge of running and managing your computer's functions. Examples include Windows, Linux, and Mac OS X.

Plug-in: A task-oriented extension that intercepts content before it is displayed and works on that content. A typical example is an HTML editor for creating articles.

Poll: A Joomla extension that displays a poll on your site.

Preview: A link in the back end that you click to see what the front end would look like while you're still working in the back end.

Publisher: A user level on a Joomla site with access only to the front end but with privileges to publish content on the site.

Registered user: A user level on a Joomla site with access only to the front end but with functionality that casual users of the site (the lowest user level) don't have.

Search engine friendly (SEF): Refers to URLs that are descriptive in a way that search engines can understand.

Search Engine Optimization (SEO): The process of optimizing your pages to give them higher ranks in the search engines.

Section: A set of categories. Categories may be organized in sections.

Super administrator: The highest user level in Joomla. If anything can be done in a Joomla installation, the super administrator can do it.

Template: The collection of files that defines the layout and styling of the pages on a Joomla site.

Uncategorized article: An article that doesn't belong to any category.

Wrapper: A Joomla component that you can use to "wrap" other Web sites for display on your Joomla site.

WYSIWYG editor: A "what you see is what you get" editor.

Index

• *T* •

• *U* •

Notes

Notes

Notes

Notes

BUSINESS, CAREERS & PERSONAL FINANCE

Accounting For Dummies, 4th Edition*
978-0-470-24600-9

Bookkeeping Workbook For Dummies†
978-0-470-16983-4

Commodities For Dummies
978-0-470-04928-0

Doing Business in China For Dummies
978-0-470-04929-7

E-Mail Marketing For Dummies
978-0-470-19087-6

Job Interviews For Dummies, 3rd Edition*†
978-0-470-17748-8

Personal Finance Workbook For Dummies*†
978-0-470-09933-9

Real Estate License Exams For Dummies
978-0-7645-7623-2

Six Sigma For Dummies
978-0-7645-6798-8

Small Business Kit For Dummies, 2nd Edition*†
978-0-7645-5984-6

Telephone Sales For Dummies
978-0-470-16836-3

BUSINESS PRODUCTIVITY & MICROSOFT OFFICE

Access 2007 For Dummies
978-0-470-03649-5

Excel 2007 For Dummies
978-0-470-03737-9

Office 2007 For Dummies
978-0-470-00923-9

Outlook 2007 For Dummies
978-0-470-03830-7

PowerPoint 2007 For Dummies
978-0-470-04059-1

Project 2007 For Dummies
978-0-470-03651-8

QuickBooks 2008 For Dummies
978-0-470-18470-7

Quicken 2008 For Dummies
978-0-470-17473-9

Salesforce.com For Dummies, 2nd Edition
978-0-470-04893-1

Word 2007 For Dummies
978-0-470-03658-7

EDUCATION, HISTORY, REFERENCE & TEST PREPARATION

African American History For Dummies
978-0-7645-5469-8

Algebra For Dummies
978-0-7645-5325-7

Algebra Workbook For Dummies
978-0-7645-8467-1

Art History For Dummies
978-0-470-09910-0

ASVAB For Dummies, 2nd Edition
978-0-470-10671-6

British Military History For Dummies
978-0-470-03213-8

Calculus For Dummies
978-0-7645-2498-1

Canadian History For Dummies, 2nd Edition
978-0-470-83656-9

Geometry Workbook For Dummies
978-0-471-79940-5

The SAT I For Dummies, 6th Edition
978-0-7645-7193-0

Series 7 Exam For Dummies
978-0-470-09932-2

World History For Dummies
978-0-7645-5242-7

FOOD, GARDEN, HOBBIES & HOME

Bridge For Dummies, 2nd Edition
978-0-471-92426-5

Coin Collecting For Dummies, 2nd Edition
978-0-470-22275-1

Cooking Basics For Dummies, 3rd Edition
978-0-7645-7206-7

Drawing For Dummies
978-0-7645-5476-6

Etiquette For Dummies, 2nd Edition
978-0-470-10672-3

Gardening Basics For Dummies*†
978-0-470-03749-2

Knitting Patterns For Dummies
978-0-470-04556-5

Living Gluten-Free For Dummies†
978-0-471-77383-2

Painting Do-It-Yourself For Dummies
978-0-470-17533-0

HEALTH, SELF HELP, PARENTING & PETS

Anger Management For Dummies
978-0-470-03715-7

Anxiety & Depression Workbook For Dummies
978-0-7645-9793-0

Dieting For Dummies, 2nd Edition
978-0-7645-4149-0

Dog Training For Dummies, 2nd Edition
978-0-7645-8418-3

Horseback Riding For Dummies
978-0-470-09719-9

Infertility For Dummies†
978-0-470-11518-3

Meditation For Dummies with CD-ROM, 2nd Edition
978-0-471-77774-8

Post-Traumatic Stress Disorder For Dummies
978-0-470-04922-8

Puppies For Dummies, 2nd Edition
978-0-470-03717-1

Thyroid For Dummies, 2nd Edition†
978-0-471-78755-6

Type 1 Diabetes For Dummies*†
978-0-470-17811-9

* Separate Canadian edition also available

† Separate U.K. edition also available

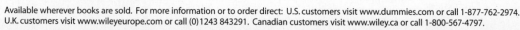
Available wherever books are sold. For more information or to order direct: U.S. customers visit www.dummies.com or call 1-877-762-2974.
U.K. customers visit www.wileyeurope.com or call (0)1243 843291. Canadian customers visit www.wiley.ca or call 1-800-567-4797.

WILEY

INTERNET & DIGITAL MEDIA

AdWords For Dummies
978-0-470-15252-2

Blogging For Dummies, 2nd Edition
978-0-470-23017-6

Digital Photography All-in-One Desk Reference For Dummies, 3rd Edition
978-0-470-03743-0

Digital Photography For Dummies, 5th Edition
978-0-7645-9802-9

Digital SLR Cameras & Photography For Dummies, 2nd Edition
978-0-470-14927-0

eBay Business All-in-One Desk Reference For Dummies
978-0-7645-8438-1

eBay For Dummies, 5th Edition*
978-0-470-04529-9

eBay Listings That Sell For Dummies
978-0-471-78912-3

Facebook For Dummies
978-0-470-26273-3

The Internet For Dummies, 11th Edition
978-0-470-12174-0

Investing Online For Dummies, 5th Edition
978-0-7645-8456-5

iPod & iTunes For Dummies, 5th Edition
978-0-470-17474-6

MySpace For Dummies
978-0-470-09529-4

Podcasting For Dummies
978-0-471-74898-4

Search Engine Optimization For Dummies, 2nd Edition
978-0-471-97998-2

Second Life For Dummies
978-0-470-18025-9

Starting an eBay Business For Dummies, 3rd Edition†
978-0-470-14924-9

GRAPHICS, DESIGN & WEB DEVELOPMENT

Adobe Creative Suite 3 Design Premium All-in-One Desk Reference For Dummies
978-0-470-11724-8

Adobe Web Suite CS3 All-in-One Desk Reference For Dummies
978-0-470-12099-6

AutoCAD 2008 For Dummies
978-0-470-11650-0

Building a Web Site For Dummies, 3rd Edition
978-0-470-14928-7

Creating Web Pages All-in-One Desk Reference For Dummies, 3rd Edition
978-0-470-09629-1

Creating Web Pages For Dummies, 8th Edition
978-0-470-08030-6

Dreamweaver CS3 For Dummies
978-0-470-11490-2

Flash CS3 For Dummies
978-0-470-12100-9

Google SketchUp For Dummies
978-0-470-13744-4

InDesign CS3 For Dummies
978-0-470-11865-8

Photoshop CS3 All-in-One Desk Reference For Dummies
978-0-470-11195-6

Photoshop CS3 For Dummies
978-0-470-11193-2

Photoshop Elements 5 For Dummies
978-0-470-09810-3

SolidWorks For Dummies
978-0-7645-9555-4

Visio 2007 For Dummies
978-0-470-08983-5

Web Design For Dummies, 2nd Edition
978-0-471-78117-2

Web Sites Do-It-Yourself For Dummies
978-0-470-16903-2

Web Stores Do-It-Yourself For Dummies
978-0-470-17443-2

LANGUAGES, RELIGION & SPIRITUALITY

Arabic For Dummies
978-0-471-77270-5

Chinese For Dummies, Audio Set
978-0-470-12766-7

French For Dummies
978-0-7645-5193-2

German For Dummies
978-0-7645-5195-6

Hebrew For Dummies
978-0-7645-5489-6

Ingles Para Dummies
978-0-7645-5427-8

Italian For Dummies, Audio Set
978-0-470-09586-7

Italian Verbs For Dummies
978-0-471-77389-4

Japanese For Dummies
978-0-7645-5429-2

Latin For Dummies
978-0-7645-5431-5

Portuguese For Dummies
978-0-471-78738-9

Russian For Dummies
978-0-471-78001-4

Spanish Phrases For Dummies
978-0-7645-7204-3

Spanish For Dummies
978-0-7645-5194-9

Spanish For Dummies, Audio Set
978-0-470-09585-0

The Bible For Dummies
978-0-7645-5296-0

Catholicism For Dummies
978-0-7645-5391-2

The Historical Jesus For Dummies
978-0-470-16785-4

Islam For Dummies
978-0-7645-5503-9

Spirituality For Dummies, 2nd Edition
978-0-470-19142-2

NETWORKING AND PROGRAMMING

ASP.NET 3.5 For Dummies
978-0-470-19592-5

C# 2008 For Dummies
978-0-470-19109-5

Hacking For Dummies, 2nd Edition
978-0-470-05235-8

Home Networking For Dummies, 4th Edition
978-0-470-11806-1

Java For Dummies, 4th Edition
978-0-470-08716-9

Microsoft® SQL Server™ 2008 All-in-One Desk Reference For Dummies
978-0-470-17954-3

Networking All-in-One Desk Reference For Dummies, 2nd Edition
978-0-7645-9939-2

Networking For Dummies, 8th Edition
978-0-470-05620-2

SharePoint 2007 For Dummies
978-0-470-09941-4

Wireless Home Networking For Dummies, 2nd Edition
978-0-471-74940-0

OPERATING SYSTEMS & COMPUTER BASICS

iMac For Dummies, 5th Edition
978-0-7645-8458-9

Laptops For Dummies, 2nd Edition
978-0-470-05432-1

Linux For Dummies, 8th Edition
978-0-470-11649-4

MacBook For Dummies
978-0-470-04859-7

**Mac OS X Leopard All-in-One
Desk Reference For Dummies**
978-0-470-05434-5

Mac OS X Leopard For Dummies
978-0-470-05433-8

Macs For Dummies, 9th Edition
978-0-470-04849-8

PCs For Dummies, 11th Edition
978-0-470-13728-4

Windows® Home Server For Dummies
978-0-470-18592-6

Windows Server 2008 For Dummies
978-0-470-18043-3

**Windows Vista All-in-One
Desk Reference For Dummies**
978-0-471-74941-7

Windows Vista For Dummies
978-0-471-75421-3

Windows Vista Security For Dummies
978-0-470-11805-4

SPORTS, FITNESS & MUSIC

Coaching Hockey For Dummies
978-0-470-83685-9

Coaching Soccer For Dummies
978-0-471-77381-8

Fitness For Dummies, 3rd Edition
978-0-7645-7851-9

Football For Dummies, 3rd Edition
978-0-470-12536-6

GarageBand For Dummies
978-0-7645-7323-1

Golf For Dummies, 3rd Edition
978-0-471-76871-5

Guitar For Dummies, 2nd Edition
978-0-7645-9904-0

**Home Recording For Musicians
For Dummies, 2nd Edition**
978-0-7645-8884-6

**iPod & iTunes For Dummies,
5th Edition**
978-0-470-17474-6

Music Theory For Dummies
978-0-7645-7838-0

Stretching For Dummies
978-0-470-06741-3

Get smart @ dummies.com®

- **Find a full list of Dummies titles**
- **Look into loads of FREE on-site articles**
- **Sign up for FREE eTips e-mailed to you weekly**
- **See what other products carry the Dummies name**
- **Shop directly from the Dummies bookstore**
- **Enter to win new prizes every month!**

* Separate Canadian edition also available
† Separate U.K. edition also available

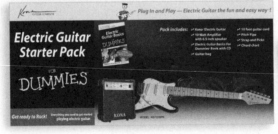